I

24A

D1252770

HARVARD HISTORICAL MONOGRAPHS

XXIX

Published under the direction of the Department of History
from the income of the Robert Louis Stroock Fund

The Founding of the French Socialist Party (1893-1905)

Aaron Noland

Cambridge · HARVARD UNIVERSITY PRESS · 1956

To my brothers
ELI AND MAX

Preface

In April 1905, the French Socialist party (Parti socialiste, section française de l'internationale ouvrière) was founded in Paris. This new party included within its fold the overwhelming majority of the organized French Socialists. During the decade that followed, the Socialist party loomed ever larger on the national political scene, representing as it did a significant and constantly increasing segment of the French electorate. In 1914, the party held one-sixth of the seats in the Chamber of Deputies and could boast of the support of one-sixth of the electorate. After the First World War, however, the Socialist party was torn by internal dissension; and in 1920 it underwent a schism. Out of this split in the ranks came the Socialist and Communist parties which at the present time play such important roles in French national affairs.

The Socialist party created in 1905 was the end product of the *rapprochement* between several Socialist parties and factions which began in the early 1890's. The purpose of this book is to present a clear and comprehensive account of this confluence of the French Socialist forces during the period 1893–1905.

I want to acknowledge my indebtedness to Professor Donald Cope McKay of Amherst College. At Harvard, Professor McKay first stimulated my interest in the history of the French Socialist movement; and in the preparation of this book, his discriminating advice and criticism were of inestimable value. I want to thank Mr. Werner Blumenberg of the Internationaal Instituut voor Sociale Geschiedenis

(International Institute for Social History) in Amsterdam, for placing the Jules Guesde Archives at my disposal. I am also grateful to Miss Ann Louise Coffin for assistance in preparing the manuscript. Finally, I want to express my gratitude to my wife, Dorothy Noland, for her generous assistance and constant encouragement.

New York, N. Y.   AARON NOLAND
April 23, 1956

Contents

The Founding of the
French Socialist Party

Chapter 1

Introduction

The fall of the Paris Commune and the savage repression that followed dealt the French Socialist movement the most staggering blow of its history. Shorn of its leadership, its press silenced, its organization suppressed, in 1871 the Socialist movement had almost ceased to exist. Indeed, so complete was its collapse, that many keen observers of social affairs were certain that France would be free of Socialism for at least half a century.

During the period 1871–1876, frequent attempts were made, particularly by the International Workingmen's Association (the First International), to revive the Socialist movement in France, but met with notable failure. Police and government agents, armed with the Dufaure Law of 1872 which outlawed the International and made affiliation with it a crime, succeeded in rounding up the majority of propagandists and organizers before any significant work could be accomplished. At Paris, Lyons, Toulouse, and elsewhere, tribunals meted out harsh punishment to such representatives of the International. The few Socialist groups that managed to survive this era of repression were able to do so only by functioning as secret societies. In constant fear of discovery, inhibited in their efforts at propaganda and organization, they remained outside of the main stream of the social movement in France and exercised no influence on the national political scene.[1]

In time, however, the fires of repression died down. The fears of

[1] Alexandre Zévaès, *De la Semaine sanglante au congrès de Marseille, 1871–1879*

civil strife engendered by the Commune gradually abated; and by
1876 the French Government felt secure enough to permit a revival
of Socialist agitation, so long suppressed. The Socialist movement
that now began to take shape was not inspired by those doctrines
that had gained currency in France before the tragic events of 1871.
With the collapse of the Commune, Proudhonism and Blanquism,
the most influential Socialist ideologies during the period of the
Second Empire, lost much of their appeal. The principal doctrinal
basis of the revived Socialist movement was Marxian, or "Scientific,"
Socialism.

Before 1871, the writings of Karl Marx were little known in
France. Marx's spirited defense of the Commune, however, brought
his name and his doctrines before the public, and slowly his ideology
won adherents. Yet, it was not principally through the writings of
Marx that his brand of Socialism gained currency in France, for
even after the revival of the Socialist movement in 1876, the classics
of Marxism — the *Communist Manifesto* and *Capital* — were not
very widely read.[2] That Marxism became the most influential ideology in the modern French Socialist movement was due in large
measure to the persistent and indefatigable efforts of a handful of
journalists and propagandists who were imbued with the ideas of
Karl Marx and Friedrich Engels.

The most important of these pioneers of Marxism in France was
Jules Guesde, born in Paris in 1845. During the early years of his
political activity, Guesde was a fervent republican, hating the Second Empire and all that it stood for. While he did not take an active
part in the Commune, his support of it in the press earned Guesde
the condemnation of a Versailles court and a sentence of five years'
imprisonment. To escape his sentence, he fled to Switzerland where,
at Geneva, he came under the influence of Anarchists and quickly
shed republicanism. In the conflict which then raged between the

(Paris, 1911), pp. 3–17; Paul Louis, *Histoire du socialisme en France, 1789–1945*
(Paris, 1946), pp. 214–216.

    [2] Albert Richard, "Les Propagateurs de l'Internationale en France," *Revue socialiste,*
23: 643 (1896); Alexandre Zévaès, "L'Introduction du marxisme en France," *Nouvelle
Revue,* 138: 181–182 (1935).

Marxists and the Anti-Marxists for control of the First International, he sided with the latter, decrying the intolerant and domineering role of Marx in that organization. However, before his exile came to an end, Guesde once more changed his ideological stance, and, when he finally returned to France in 1876, he was a convinced Socialist, prepared to expound the doctrines of revolutionary collectivism. Guesde's arrival in Paris coincided with the revival of Socialist activity. A newspaper of vague Socialist tendencies, the *Droits de l'Homme*, served as the organ of aggressive young radicals and labor militants who inhabited the Latin Quarter. Guesde joined their ranks and became a contributor to their journal. His articles on current political affairs and cogent analysis of existing economic and social conditions soon won him a significant following in left-wing political and labor circles.[3]

Before long, a group of young, enthusiastic collectivists led by Guesde decided that the time had come to found a newspaper of their own; and in November 1877 a signal event in the history of modern French Socialism took place: *Egalité*, the first French newspaper devoted to the exposition of Marxian Socialism made its appearance. In its first issue (November 18, 1877), the newspaper, which was edited by a committee headed by Guesde, made a forthright declaration of policy: "*Egalité* will be not only Republican in politics and atheist in religion; it will be, above all, Socialist . . . We believe, with the collectivist school, to which almost all the serious minds of the proletariat of both continents belong, that the natural and scientific evolution of humanity is inevitably leading it to the collective appropriation of the land and of the instruments of labor." Although the editors of *Egalité* favored the republican as compared with the monarchical form of government, they made it quite clear in the initial issue that they harbored no "illusions" about the French Republic: "We know very well that the Republic does not exclude the exploitation of the many by the few . . . that it does not prevent the worker from being the victim of greedy employers . . . under

[3] Adéodat Compère-Morel, *Jules Guesde* (Paris, 1937), pp. 1–77; Alexandre Zévaès, *Jules Guesde* (Paris, 1929), pp. 22–23, 33–34; Samuel Bernstein, *The Beginnings of Marxian Socialism in France* (New York, 1933), pp. 114–115.

the Republic, as under the Monarchy, one is imprisoned, deported, and shot." Yet the Republic, though it be essentially bourgeois in character, was a better form of government than Monarchy, for it was the last word in "purely political and governmental evolution." Under republican institutions, the class conflict between the proletariat, that is, those who possessed only their labor, and the bourgeoisie, or property-owning class, was at last laid bare; and the way was cleared for the social and economic revolution which would substitute the "real equality of things" for the present "nominal equality of rights."

In subsequent issues of *Egalité*, Guesde emphasized the importance of creating a workers' political party distinct from all bourgeois parties. Guesde cautioned the workers, however, that political action alone would not bring about the end of capitalist exploitation. No matter how many representatives of the working class sat in Parliament, the ruling class of France would never "allow the Fourth Estate to become a majority in the Chamber of Deputies." The bourgeois ruling class would take "extralegal" action to prevent the proletariat from assuming the political control of the state through the use of universal suffrage and the conquest of political office. The final struggle between the proletariat and the bourgeoisie for political and economic power would be fought not with ballots, but with arms. The purpose of a workers' political party was to prepare the ground for this inevitable revolutionary action. The formation of such a party would serve to make the workers class-conscious on the political plane just as the labor *syndicat* (union) made them conscious of their class interests on the economic plane.[4] Guesde's objectives, as he defined them in a letter (1879) to Karl Marx, were to free the French worker from the "dupery of bourgeois radicalism" and to drive home to him the fact that his economic and social emancipation would come only through the overthrow of capitalism and the establishment of a collectivist society.[5]

---

[4] *Egalité*, January 13, March 2, 1878. See also Jules Guesde, *La République et les grèves* (Paris, 1878), p. 8.

[5] See the text in Alexandre Zévaès, *De l'Introduction du marxisme en France* (Paris, 1947), pp. 92–95.

The extent of the influence of *Egalité* in political and labor circles was indicated by two events which occurred shortly after its appearance. For the first time in a municipal election, a candidate ran for office in Paris in January 1878 on a collectivist program. Of greater significance was the evidence presented at a national congress of labor organizations that took place in Lyons in February of that same year, which disclosed that several delegates had been won over to collectivist notions of a Marxist variety. At the congress, an amendment to a resolution on labor unions was introduced which called for the collective ownership of land and of the instruments of labor. Although the amendment was voted down, the fact remained that collectivism was now becoming an ideological factor in the labor movement. Commenting on the Lyons Congress in *Egalité*, Guesde expressed the belief that collectivist doctrines would soon win the allegiance of a majority of the labor militants.[6]

In the interim between the Lyons Congress and the next national labor congress that was scheduled for the following year, the Marxists carried on a concerted campaign to gain control of the labor movement. Although their own newspaper, *Egalité*, was forced by police interference to suspend publication in July 1878, the flow of collectivist propaganda did not cease. At public lectures and in widely distributed manifestoes and pamphlets, the basic tenets of Marx's Socialism were vigorously expounded by Guesde and his associates. No opportunity was lost to press this campaign. When Guesde, together with a number of other Socialists, was arrested in September 1879 for seeking, in defiance of a police prohibition, to hold a meeting in Paris, he took advantage of the occasion presented by his trial to expound at length his collectivist views.[7]

As Guesde had predicted, the national congress of labor organizations which took place in Marseilles in October 1879 did indeed witness the triumph of collectivism over moderate trade-unionism. This was clearly indicated in the resolutions approved by the delegates. Individual ownership of property, for example, was condemned as contrary to the "equal rights" of all men to the fruits of

[6] February 10, 17, 1878.
[7] Bernstein, p. 148; Zévaès, *Jules Guesde*, pp. 41–44.

their labor. It was "unjust and inhuman," the congress declared in a resolution, that "some produce everything, others nothing, and that it is exactly the latter who possess all the wealth, all the pleasures, as well as all the privileges." As this unfair distribution of wealth and privilege would never be voluntarily altered "by the good-will of those whose interest it is to continue its existence," only the "collectivization of the soil, subsoil, and the instruments of production" would bring about a redress of the existing inequities.[8]

The Marseilles Congress, affirming that there was an irreconcilable antagonism between the interests of the proletariat and the bourgeoisie, took steps to organize the former in a class party, distinct from any and all bourgeois political parties. It approved a resolution calling for the creation of a new organization, the Fédération du Parti des travailleurs socialistes de France (Federation of the Socialist Workers' party of France). The party was to be composed of six regional federations, linked by an Executive Committee. Each regional organization was to hold its own annual congress and to administer local affairs, while the Executive Committee was to carry out the decisions of the annual national congress.[9] The approval of this project by the Marseilles Congress was a sweeping victory for the collectivists, particularly for Guesde, who had stressed again and again the need for a proletarian political party.

While the Marseilles Congress had established the basis for a political organization, it had not formulated a party program. What the new party now required, Guesde believed, was a program of minimum economic and social objectives, comprehensible to all workers. With such a program, participation in electoral campaigns would be useful for purposes of propaganda and recruitment. A program of social reforms, specifically aimed at the workers' level of interest, would spell out for them the difference between a proletarian class party and the existing bourgeois political organizations. This program would attract workers to the new Socialist party where they could then be indoctrinated with the entire collectivist

[8] See the text in *Séances du congrès ouvrier socialiste de France, tenu à Marseille du 20 au 31 octobre 1879* (Marseilles, 1880), pp. 813–814.

[9] *Séances*, pp. 817–818.

ideology. After consulting with other leading French Marxists, Guesde went directly to see the masters themselves, Karl Marx and Friedrich Engels, to secure their assistance in formulating such a program.

This program was finally drafted in Marx's study in London in May 1880. The preamble to the program, which cogently set forth the collectivist thesis, was exclusively the work of Marx. It declared that the emancipation of the producing class was in reality the "emancipation of all human beings"; and that this class would be free when it was collectively in possession of the means of production — land, factories, ships, banks, etc. This collectivist form of ownership could come "only through the revolutionary activity of the producing class, or the proletariat, organized in a distinct political party." The political demands of the *programme minimum*, as it came to be known, called, among other things, for the abolition of all laws restricting the press, assembly, and association; the suppression of all articles of the legal code which placed the worker in an inferior position vis-à-vis the employer; the nationalization of the property of religious orders; and the arming of the people as a substitute for the standing army. The important extensive economic demands contained in the *programme minimum* were the following: the abolition of all indirect taxes and the substitution for all direct taxes of a progressive tax on incomes and inheritances; a minimum wage law; a six-day week and an eight-hour day for adults; and the participation of workers in the management of factories and shops.[10]

Guesde submitted the *programme minimum* to a regional congress of the new Socialist party which met at Paris in July 1880. Despite the vociferous protest of an Anti-Marxist minority, it was approved. The congress also affirmed Guesde's conception of political action. Although such action was deemed by the delegates

[10] For the text of the program, see *Egalité*, June 30, 1880. See also Engel's letter to Eduard Bernstein, dated October 25, 1881, in Bernstein, "Lettres inédites de Frédéric Engels sur la politique socialiste," *Mouvement socialiste*, 4: 517 (1900); and Paul Lafargue, "Die Sozialistische Bewegung in Frankreich von 1876–1890," *Neue Zeit*, 8: 345 (1890).

to be useful in the class struggle as a means of propaganda and recruitment, and though political action served to unify the proletariat in the presence of the enemy class — the bourgeois class — the emancipation of the proletariat and the establishment of a Socialist order would not, they agreed, be realized through the use of legal methods alone: "The social revolution remains the only possible, final solution." [11]

Guesde hailed the work of the regional congress as a clear indication that the French workers were at last prepared to translate their desire for a better world into action. "For the first time," he declared, "an assembly of workers has taken a practical decision; for the first time the workers' party, in the very process of formation, has left the domain of theory; it has finally understood that there is more to do than constantly discuss matters. It has felt the necessity to act and it has adopted the means of action . . ." He was certain that the coming national congress of the Fédération du Parti des travailleurs socialistes would adopt the *programme minimum* as the charter for the entire organization. [12]

However, unlike the Marseilles Congress, the national congress of the Fédération which was held at Le Havre in November 1880 proved to be no rubber stamp for the collectivists. The non-collectivist trade-union elements, routed at the Marseilles Congress, had consolidated their position in the new party during the year 1880 and were able to offer strong opposition. The first session of the Le Havre Congress witnessed the separation of these elements from the collectivist minority with the latter leaving the meeting in a body. With the departure of the Marxists, the rump congress voted a sweeping condemnation of collectivism and took steps to set up a new labor organization. [13]

Meanwhile, the collectivists held their own congress. They reaffirmed the *programme minimum* as the "fundamental charter" of

[11] *Egalité*, July 28, 1880.

[12] *Egalité*, July 28, 1880. See also Guesde's articles in *Egalité*, June 30, July 21, 1880.

[13] Léon Blum, *Les Congrès ouvriers et socialistes français* (2 vols., Paris, 1901), I, 61. This organization, the Union des chambres syndicales ouvriers de France, never became an important force in the labor movement.

French Socialism, and voted to retain the name and structure of the party founded at Marseilles in 1879. The congress also prepared the party for participation in the approaching general legislative elections: while the *programme minimum* was to serve as the basis for political action, individual party candidates were granted the right to stand for election on a "more defined program" should they so desire.[14] This provision, which could be construed as allowing for all sorts of alterations and modifications of the fundamental charter, was later to be a source of conflict and schism within the organization.

Despite the separation of the non-collectivist trade-union elements from the newly formed party, Guesde and his followers could well feel satisfied with their achievements. In the relatively brief period of four years, they had popularized the doctrines of revolutionary collectivism and had founded a political party dedicated to the task of realizing a Socialist order. They were now prepared to enter the political arena to contend with other political parties for the support of the masses whose interests they claimed to serve.

Before the general elections of October 1881 took place, a new Socialist organization came into existence. In July of that year, the Comité révolutionnaire central (Central Revolutionary Committee), was constituted in Paris. Composed in the main of the pre-Commune followers of Auguste Blanqui (d. 1881), the Comité, in its newspaper, *Ni Dieu Ni Maître*, expounded an ideology which embodied many of the collectivist tenets of Marxian Socialism and the conspiratorial tactics and methods of Blanquism. Like the Marxists, the members of the Comité, popularly known as "Blanquists," rejected any piecemeal reform of the existing social order and advocated collective ownership of property as the only means of realizing the emancipation of the proletariat. The Blanquists likewise conceived of universal suffrage and political action by the workers simply as means for propaganda and recruitment, and believed that the conquest of the bourgeois state and the subsequent overthrow

[14] *Prolétaire*, November 4, 1880; Blum, I, 62–64.

of capitalism would ultimately be achieved through revolutionary action.[15]

The Blanquists, however, differed from the Marxists on a question of tactics. The former did not adhere to the thesis that the future social revolution would be the task of the proletariat alone. They contended that the proletariat was not sufficiently aware of its own class interests, was too ignorant of revolutionary tactics, to play the leading role assigned to it by the Marxists in the final struggle for power. The Blanquists believed that the overthrow of the existing order would be achieved by a relatively small group of men, the educated but alienated and rootless *déclassés* — principally intellectuals and radicals of the French bourgeois class — who, acting in the interests of the proletariat, would seize state power by a *coup d'état* and institute the communist state.[16]

They differed from the Marxists also in their conception of the function of labor *syndicats*. Unlike the Marxists who looked upon the unions as propaganda centers for collectivism and recruiting agencies for the proletarian political party, indeed, as little more than appendages of the party, the Blanquists considered them as being on the level of economic organization as important an instrument of class struggle as the proletarian party was on the political level; and they respected the autonomy of these labor organizations.[17]

The influence of the Comité was at first limited to Paris and its environs, and only in the early nineties did it begin to play a significant role in the Socialist movement. When it did become a force, however, it abandoned all thought of a *coup d'état*. Taking cognizance of the realities of political life under republican institutions and recognizing the value of democratic political action as a means of social transformation, the Blanquists gave up their conspiratorial

---

[15] *Ni Dieu Ni Maître*, January 16, May 15, 1881. See also Alexandre Zévaès, *Auguste Blanqui* (Paris, 1920), pp. 142–146.

[16] *Ni Dieu Ni Maître*, June 19, 1881. "The *déclassés*, invisible weapon of progress, is the yeast which today sustains the masses and stops them from falling back into the morass. Tomorrow, the *déclassés* will be the reserve of the revolution." Auguste Blanqui, *Critique sociale* (2 vols., Paris, 1885), I, 219–220.

[17] Louis, pp. 229–230.

tactics and entered the political arena to conquer state power by means of the ballot.

In the general legislative elections of October 1881, the Socialists got only a very small fraction of the total vote. Not a candidate of the Fédération du Parti des travailleurs socialistes was victorious, while the party polled some 60,000 votes out of a total of almost 7,000,000. The Blanquist Comité révolutionnaire central received less than 3,000 votes.[18] The poor showing of the Fédération disappointed many of its members and gave rise to dissension within the ranks. An open conflict for control of the party soon developed between the revolutionary collectivists or revolutionary Socialists proper — the "Guesdists" as they came to be known after their leader — and the moderate collectivists or reformist Socialists.

Since the founding of the Fédération there had been a section of the rank and file which did not accept the doctrines of Karl Marx (as expounded by Guesde and his followers) as gospel, even though they considered themselves collectivists. Repudiating the notion of an inevitable proletarian revolution, these party members believed that a communist society could be realized through the peaceful, legal, and piecemeal introduction of social reforms into the existing capitalist order. They criticized the Marxist *programme minimum*, arguing that the needs and aspirations of the French workers were too variegated to be comprised in any single political program. Each constituency of the party, they contended, should be permitted to elaborate its own electoral program in conformity with local conditions and the particular demands of the workers of the region, without reference to any one theoretical statement of Socialist "dogma." The fact that a German, Marx, had formulated the preamble of the *programme minimum* also offended the patriotic sensibilities of many of these members.[19]

At the national congress of the Fédération, which took place at

[18] Ministère du commerce, *Annuaire statistique de la France, 1882* (Paris, 1882), p. 459; Alexander Zévaès, *Les Guesdistes* (Paris, 1911), p. 21; A. Zévaès, *Le Socialisme en France depuis 1871* (Paris, 1908), p. 49.

[19] See the *Prolétaire*, November 12, 19, 1881; Sylvain Humbert, *Les Possibilistes* (Paris, 1911), p. 9.

Rheims shortly after the general elections of October 1881, the reformist elements scored heavily against the Guesdists. The Rheims
Congress replaced the Executive Committee, which the reformists
charged served as a tool for Guesde's domination of the party, with
a new central organ, called the National Committee, so constituted
as to prevent the Guesdists from having more than a minority representation. The reformists also sought to reject the *programme
minimum*, which they declared was responsible for the defeat of
party candidates in the recent elections. In a spirited defense of the
program, Guesde charged that to change the charter of the party at
every national congress would only result in confusing the workers,
and he argued that to leave to each local party organization the task
of formulating its own political program (a proposal brought forth
by two of the reformist leaders, Paul Brousse and Benoît Malon)
would result in a multiplicity of "contradictory programs." [20] The
Rheims Congress attempted to resolve the matter by adopting two
somewhat incompatible resolutions. The first condemned the *programme minimum* for failing to satisfy the "different aspirations"
of the workers and for promoting the defeat of the party candidates
in the recent elections. The second declared that this same program,
for the time being at least, was to remain *"en vigueur"* as the charter
of the party.[21]

After the Rheims Congress, the unity of the party, renamed by the
Congress as the Parti des travailleurs socialistes (Socialist Workers'
party), was indeed tenuous; and the acrimonious conflict which
continued between the Guesdists and the reformist Socialists
grouped around Brousse and Malon was further aggravated by the
"Joffrin Case." In December 1881, Jules Joffrin, a reformist member
of the Parti des travailleurs socialistes was a candidate in a legislative election at Paris. In formulating his electoral program, Joffrin,
in conformity with the resolution on electoral tactics which had been
approved by the Le Havre Congress (1880), not only dropped certain articles from the party *programme minimum*, substituting for

---

[20] *Cinquième Congrès national du Parti ouvrier socialiste français, tenu à Reims
du 30 octobre au 6 novembre 1881* (Paris, 1882), pp. 14, 55.
[21] *Cinquième Congrès*, p. 57.

them reforms embodied in the electoral programs of republican candidates, but he also deleted in its entirety its preamble, elaborated by Marx himself.

Guesde and his followers sharply reproached Joffrin for "mutilating" the party program and abandoning its principles.[22] The *Prolétaire*, a Parisian Socialist newspaper which reflected the views of Brousse and his followers, vigorously defended Joffrin's actions. "We prefer to abandon the 'all-at-once' tactics practiced until now," the newspaper declared, "tactics which generally resulted in achieving 'nothing-at-all.'" The newspaper went on to assert that it was proper to seek piecemeal, immediate social reforms rather than hold out for thoroughgoing socialist measures: "We desire to divide our ideal ends into several gradual stages, to make many of our demands immediate ones and hence *possible* of realization, instead of exhausting our energies marking time on one spot . . ."[23]

Guesde ridiculed this conception of piecemeal reforms. He contended that to alter the party program simply in order to achieve success at the polls would result in the "embourgeoisement" of the party. If, under the pretext of what Guesde called "Possibilisme," the coherence and unity of the *programme minimum* were violated and every candidate permitted to elaborate his own platform, the truly revolutionary character of the party would soon be lost.[24] The reformist Socialists, now labeled "Possibilists," charged Guesde with being a dictator and branded his followers as "Impossibilists" and "Authoritarians." To this Guesde replied: "If it means to be authoritarian to wish to follow the decisions of our congresses where the will of the individual is subordinated to the general will as translated into resolutions and programs, then indeed we are authoritarians."[25]

The conflict between the Guesdists and Possibilists as crystallized

[22] *Egalité*, December 25, 1881; Blum, I, 74–75.

[23] *Prolétaire*, November 19, 1881, quoted in Humbert, p. 6. See also the *Prolétaire*, January 28, February 4, 11, 18, 1882.

[24] See Guesde's articles in *Egalité*, December 25, 1881, January 15, 22, 1882. See also Lafargue's article in the *Citoyen*, September 16, 1882.

[25] *Egalité*, January 1, 1882. See also the *Prolétaire*, September 2, 9, 1882; and Benoît Malon, *Le Nouveau Parti* (2 vols., Paris, 1882), II, 59.

in the Joffrin Case grew increasingly more bitter until the national congress of the Parti des travailleurs socialistes in September 1882 in Saint-Etienne. The Saint-Etienne Congress, far from resolving the controversy, witnessed the formal schism of the party. From the opening session, the Guesdists were marked for condemnation, as the Possibilists comprised a majority of the delegates. The congress refused Guesde the opportunity to present his case against Joffrin before an impartial body, that is, a group of party members not directly involved in the dispute. Believing that a fair judgment of their case was no longer possible, the Guesdists walked out of the congress and, subsequently, out of the party.[26]

The remaining delegates voted to abandon the *programme minimum*. Henceforth, each local constituency of the party was to formulate its own electoral program. The party structure was also changed: the six regional federations comprising it were granted almost complete autonomy, and a new National Committee, charged with the task of executing the decisions of the party congresses, was placed under the supervision of the regional federations. Lastly, the delegates adopted as the name for their organization, the Parti ouvrier socialiste révolutionnaire (Revolutionary Socialist Workers' party), with the subtitle, Fédération des travailleurs socialistes de France.[27] This subtitle was more commonly used to designate the Possibilist party.

In the nearby town of Roanne, Guesde and his little band of followers held their own congress. After denouncing the Possibilists for seeking to emasculate the *programme minimum* and to "parliamentarize" (*parlementariser*) the Socialist movement, the Roanne Congress reaffirmed the Marxist charter and declared that participation in electoral campaigns should be viewed not as a means of winning political offices, but simply as "a means of propaganda, organization, and struggle." [28] The congress wanted to make it clear that

---

[26] *Sixième Congrès national du Parti ouvrier socialiste révolutionnaire français, tenu à St. Etienne du 25 au 30 septembre 1882* (Paris, 1882), pp. 6–27; the *Citoyen*, September 29, 1882.

[27] *Sixième Congrès*, pp. 167–175; the *Prolétaire*, October 7, 21, 1882.

[28] *Egalité*, October 8, 1882. See also Lafargue's article in the *Citoyen*, October 14, 1882.

the Guesdists were prepared to employ extralegal, violent means of action as well as legal, peaceful means in the class struggle for the emancipation of the proletariat. Guesde underscored this view when, reacting sharply to the emphasis placed upon universal suffrage and the conquest of political power by peaceful political action by the Possibilists, he declared (November 5, 1882) in *Egalité*: "It is not on the question of dynamite that we separate ourselves from the Anarchists, since we are ready to employ, like the Anarchists, all the resources that science provides for our task of emancipating humanity . . . we are the successors — and the avengers — of the *pétroleurs* of 1871."

The Roanne Congress founded a new Socialist organization, the Parti ouvrier français (French Workers' party). The new party resembled the old Fédération du Parti des travailleurs socialistes, except that it was more centralized in administration and control. The Parti ouvrier français was composed of six regional federations which were to be under the supervision of the central executive organ, the National Committee. Strict adherence to the *programme minimum* was demanded of all local party units.[29]

The formation of the Parti ouvrier français at Roanne was immediately followed by an intensive and widespread campaign of propaganda and organization by the Guesdists designed to win the adherence of the workers to the banner of Marxism. Guesde himself set the pace for this campaign. As a propagandist and public speaker, he had few rivals. In a voice that was vibrant and sharp edged, Guesde delivered his speeches with all the intensity and sincerity of a prophet. Free of pose and pedantry, rejecting elaborate phraseology, he expounded the party doctrines in simple yet trenchant terms. Other party militants, notably Gabriel Deville and Paul Lafargue in Paris, Gustave Delory in Lille, and Raymond Lavigne in Bordeaux, joined with him in waging this campaign.[30]

One of the most talented of these propagandists, Lafargue, came

[29] For the party regulations, see *Egalité*, October 8, 1882.
[30] Zévaès, *Jules Guesde*, p. 185; Gustave Delory, *Aperçu historique sur la Fédération du Nord du Parti socialiste* (Lille, 1921), pp. 32–58; Samuel Bernstein, "Jules Guesde, Pioneer of Marxism in France," *Science and Society*, 4: 46 (1940).

to play a role in the Parti ouvrier français second in importance only to that of Guesde. Lafargue was born in Santiago, Cuba in 1842. At the age of nine he came to France and began his schooling at *lycées* in Bordeaux and Toulouse. Later, while pursuing his medical studies in Paris, he took an active part in the radical political agitation which became vocal during the last years of the Second Empire. As a consequence of his political activities, Lafargue was barred from all French universities in 1866, and shortly thereafter went to England to complete his studies. In London he came under the influence of Karl Marx, and became an exponent of the latter's ideology. When he finally returned to France on the completion of his medical studies, he brought Marx's daughter, Laura, with him as his wife. Lafargue participated in the Socialist movement until the fall of the Paris Commune. Then, in order to escape the vengeance of the Versailles Government, he fled to Spain and later to England. It was not until 1882, two years after general amnesty had been granted Communards, that he returned to France. Lafargue identified himself with the Guesdist wing of the Parti des travailleurs socialistes after joining the party; following the schism of Saint-Etienne, he participated in the formation of the new Guesdist party. Lafargue's talents as a popularizer of Marxian doctrines soon earned him the respect and confidence of Guesde, and the two leaders collaborated closely in the task of building the young Parti ouvrier français.[31]

In March 1884, the leaders of the Guesdist party took time out from their propaganda and organizational campaign to hold a national congress at Roubaix. Under the direction of Guesde, this congress adopted important resolutions which served to define the doctrine and tactics of the Parti ouvrier français for almost a decade. The *programme minimum*, which had been ratified by the Roanne Congress (1882), was reaffirmed as the fundamental charter of the party. No local group or section of the party was to participate in electoral action without maintaining the program *in toto*. The

---

[31] Alexandre Zévaès, *Sur l'Ecran politique, ombres et silhouettes, notes, mémoires et souvenirs* (Paris, 1928), p. 181; J. Varlet, *Paul Lafargue, théoricien du marxisme* (Paris, 1933), p. 8.

Roubaix Congress also adopted an important resolution on party tactics which defined the character of the future revolution that was to overthrow capitalism, and which set forth the role that the party was to play before, during, and after that revolution. "The revolution," it asserted, "cannot be decreed; it will not be a spontaneous phenomenon, it does not depend on the more or less animated restlessness of those interested in the revolution. The revolution will be the fatal consequence of the universal movements which have created modern society." In other words, the future revolutionary situation would be generated by contradictions within the capitalist economy itself, rather than by the activities of dedicated revolutionists. This, of course, was the orthodox Marxist view. The period before the revolution was to be one of preparation; its essential tasks were "to educate the masses and recruit an army capable of profiting from a revolutionary situation." The organization of the proletariat on the political level as a distinct class party struggling against all bourgeois parties was, of course, a vital part of this preparatory work. Upon the outbreak of the revolution, the party was to act rapidly and energetically, the immediate object being the seizure of political power. To consolidate this assumption of state power, the party was then to establish a dictatorship in the name of the proletariat. It would not be expedient during this period, the resolution contended, "to have recourse to universal suffrage." With the revolution realized, the capitalist order overthrown, and the socialization of the means of production an accomplished fact, the party would no longer have a *raison d'être*, and would be dissolved. "Party of class, it disappears with the classes. Party of struggle, it vanishes when the goal of that struggle — the political and economic expropriation of the bourgeoisie — is achieved." [32]

The Roubaix Congress was the last national conclave of the Parti ouvrier français until 1890. In the interim, the Guesdists devoted themselves to the tasks of increasing the party membership and ex-

[32] *Septième Congrès national du Parti ouvrier, tenu à Roubaix du samedi 29 mars au lundi 7 avril 1884* (Paris, n.d.), pp. 16–20. For a detailed description of the revolution envisioned by the Guesdists, see Lafargue's articles in the *Socialiste*, December 31, 1887, January 7, 14, 21, 1888.

tending the party organization into the industrial and mining regions of the country. The appearance of a party newspaper, the *Socialiste*, in August 1885, greatly aided their efforts; and new sections of the party were soon formed in the departments of the Nord, Pas-de-Calais, Seine, Loire, and the Bouches-du-Rhône. According to one Socialist leader, the strength of the Parti ouvrier français in the departments of the Nord and the Pas-de-Calais in the late 1880's was such as to make Guesde "itch for revolutionary action." [33] As subsequent events were to show, however, the Guesdist party was never to participate in such action in the Nord, the Pas-de-Calais, or anywhere else.

The Fédération des travailleurs socialistes, which, like the Guesdist party, had issued from the schism at the Saint-Etienne Congress (1882), developed in the 1880's along lines that contrasted sharply with those of the Parti ouvrier français. For, while the Guesdists endeavored to build a party, national in scope, highly centralized in administration, and intransigently revolutionary in doctrine and tactics, the Possibilists tended increasingly to restrict their efforts at propaganda and party organization to those regions where they believed electoral triumphs could most readily be obtained, to decentralize the party administration, and to expound the most reformist of Socialist doctrines. Finally, while the Guesdists sought to create a class party, a proletarian party, the Possibilists bent their efforts to build an organization which would include elements of the bourgeoisie as well as workers.

The reformist character of the Possibilist party was clearly indicated in the electoral programs which it adopted in 1885. These programs underscored the fact that the Possibilists believed that a Socialist order could be achieved through the peaceful, gradual socialization of the existing capitalist economy. This process of sociali-

---

[33] Marcel Sembat, *Defeated Victory*, p. 88, quoted in Harold Weinstein, *Jean Jaurès, A Study of Patriotism in the French Socialist Movement* (New York, 1936), p. 14. In this connection, see Guesde's articles in the *Cri du Peuple*, May 19, June 15, 1884, November 15, 1886; and the declaration of the Agglomération parisienne of the Parti ouvrier français in the *Socialiste*, October 17, 1885.

zation, as stated in the party's legislative program, was to be realized by the "resolute" intervention of the state "in the different branches of private work, shops, companies, banks, agricultural, industrial, and commercial enterprises." At first the state would intervene in order to impose on the employers decrees protecting the interests of both the workers and the general public. Subsquently, the state would act "to transform progressively all bourgeois industries into Socialist public services" in which the conditions of labor would be regulated by the workers themselves.[34] According to the Possibilist municipal program, privately owned monopolies, such as transportation, water, and gas, were to be transformed into communal or departmental public services to be provided for all at cost price or free of charge. To hasten the end of the "regime of private property," the communes were to establish municipal industries of every description, which workers themselves would operate in the general interest of the community.[35]

To bring about the socialization of the existing capitalist order, the Possibilists believed that the immediate task of the proletariat was to conquer governmental power in the commune, department, and state. The weapon to be employed to achieve this goal was the ballot. Significantly, the Possibilists at this time considered dropping the word révolutionnaire from their party label.[36]

Armed with attractive reform programs and strengthened by electoral alliances with various non-Socialist political groups, the Possibilists, in the 1880's, had considerably more success at the polls than the Guesdists or Blanquists. By 1886, the party had three representatives on the Municipal Council of Paris — the first Socialists to have seats on that body. And, as a result of the municipal elections of

---

[34] See the legislative program adopted by the Fourth Regional Congress of the Center of the Possibilist party (held in Paris, May 1885), quoted in Léon de Seilhac, *Les Congrès ouvriers en France de 1876 à 1897* (Paris, 1899), p. 131.

[35] For the text of the program, see Fédération des travailleurs socialistes de France, *Compte rendu du Neuvième Congrès national, tenu à Charleville du 2 au 8 octobre 1887* (Paris, 1888), pp. 54–56.

[36] Fédération des travailleurs socialistes de France, *Compte rendu du Huitième Congrès national, tenu à Rennes du 12 au 19 octobre 1884* (Paris, 1885), p. 23; Seilhac, p. 123.

1887, the number of Possibilists on the Council increased threefold. As victories multiplied, however, the leaders of the party came to devote considerably more time and effort to the scramble for votes and political offices than they did to the rather pedestrian tasks of party organization and propaganda in the provinces. And, once in office, many Possibilists, bending to the pressure of electoral consideration, trimmed their doctrinal sails and more or less surreptitiously abandoned many of their Socialist ideas and aims. This development was to create a crisis within the Fédération des travailleurs socialistes.

In July 1889, the date which marked the centenary of the beginning of the great French Revolution, delegates from many of the Socialist parties and labor organizations of Europe and America gathered at Paris for two international congresses. One was organized by the Possibilists, who had acted upon a commission granted to them by the Second International at a meeting in London in 1888; the other by the Guesdists and Blanquists, who had been commissioned for the task by an international congress of German, Swiss, Belgian, and Dutch Socialist parties which had met at The Hague early in 1889. The German and Belgian Socialists made several attempts to bring about a merger of the two congresses, but their efforts proved futile. The Possibilists were adamant in their refusal to meet with the Guesdists in the same hall. Consequently, a "Possibilist" Congress, composed principally of the moderate Socialist and labor delegations, and an "Independent" Congress, which was attended by the Marxist and revolutionary delegations of France, Germany, and other nations, were held in separate halls, purposely chosen, so Henry Hyndman, the English Socialist leader, declared, "at some distance from one another in order to avoid the possible consequences of fraternal greetings." [37]

The two congresses manifested much the same tendencies and voted similar resolutions. It was the Independent Congress, how-

[37] Henry M. Hyndman, *The Record of an Adventurous Life* (New York, 1911), p. 404. See also Humbert, pp. 57–59.

ever, which adopted the famous resolution of the French Marxist, Lavigne, establishing May 1st as an annual day of celebration for the workers of all countries.

In accordance with this decision, popular demonstrations were held throughout France by Socialist and labor organizations on May 1, 1890. The leaders of the Possibilist party, however, refused to sanction the participation of their organization in the demonstrations. This caused widespread dissension within the ranks of the Fédération des travailleurs socialistes and brought into the open a conflict which had long been brewing between sections of the rank and file and the party leadership. For some time, many Possibilists had looked askance at the growing *embourgeoisement* of their party. Specifically, they were perturbed by the failure of the party leadership to carry on the work of propaganda and party organization on a national scale, and they were alarmed at the preoccupation of their leaders with purely political matters — that is, with the conquest and retention of political offices. The opposition of the Possibilist leaders to the participation of their party along with the Guesdist, Blanquist, and other Socialist factions in the May Day demonstrations appeared to confirm the worst fears of these dissident rank-and-filers that the party leadership was neglecting the vital interests of the organization.[38]

The leading spokesman for these dissident Possibilists was Jean Allemane, a compositor by trade. Born in Sauveterre, France in 1843, Allemane went to Paris as a youth, and he actively participated in the labor movement under the Second Empire. For his part in the Paris Commune, he was sentenced to life imprisonment in New Caledonia, but the general amnesty granted Communards in 1880, brought freedom, and he returned to France to resume work in the labor movement. Allemane joined the Possibilist party soon after its formation, and became a leading figure in the important Parisian section of the party.

In the newspaper, the *Parti Ouvrier*, which he edited, Allemane

---

[38] See Jean Allemane's articles in the *Parti Ouvrier*, August 1, 1889, October 6, 12, 1890. See also Maurice Charnay, *Les Allemanistes* (Paris, 1912), pp. 5–6.

and other dissident Possibilists censured their party leadership for its conduct,[39] and demanded that a national congress be summoned for the purpose of reorganizing the party. Specifically, these dissident elements wanted to have those members of the party holding political offices in the commune, department, and the state — the party *élus*, as such members were called — placed under the immediate supervision of the regional federation with which they were affiliated. The *élus* would be directly responsible to the federation for their conduct as political officials.[40]

The national congress of the Fédération des travailleurs socialistes, held at Châtellerault in October 1890, was the occasion for the schism between the moderate Possibilist faction grouped around Brousse and other party leaders, and the dissident elements identified with Allemane. The latter element withdrew from the party at the initial session of the Châtellerault Congress after the committee for the verification of mandates, which was controlled by Brousse and the moderate majority of delegates, declared a number of the mandates held by the dissidents to be invalid.[41] This schism was a severe blow to the Possibilist party, for, though the dissident faction, which came to be known as the "Allemanists," was only a minority of the rank and file, it constituted the most energetic element of the party. From its formation at Saint-Etienne in 1882 to the Châtellerault Congress, the Possibilist had been the largest and most politically significant of the French Socialist parties, but during the following decade, it gradually deteriorated. By the turn of the century, the Possibilists no longer possessed a national organization, and local sections that survived functioned chiefly as electoral committees.

[39] Brousse, for example, had aroused the indignation of many fellow Possibilists when, as Vice-President of the Municipal Council of Paris, in July 1890, he approved a motion which called for the organization of a reception in honor of the men and officers of two battalions of Marine Light Infantry, which, as it happened, had taken part in the suppression of the Paris Commune. See Humbert, p. 66.

[40] See the *Parti Ouvrier*, October 7, 9, 1890. See also Charnay, pp. 10–12.

[41] Fédération des travailleurs socialistes de France. Parti ouvrier socialiste révolutionnaire. *Compte rendu du Dixième Congrès national, tenu à Châtellerault du 9 au 15 octobre 1890* (Poitiers, 1891); Seilhac, pp. 172–180.

In June 1891, a number of Allemanists gathered in Paris to found a new organization, the Parti ouvrier socialiste révolutionnaire (Revolutionary Socialist Workers' party), commonly referred to as the Allemanist party. The party adopted reform programs similar in important respects to those of the Possibilist organization; but on several points of doctrine and method the Allemanists differed from the Possibilists, as well as from the Guesdists and Blanquists. Their stand on the question of tactics was a case in point. Unlike the Possibilists, the Allemanists were not at all convinced that a collectivist society could be realized through the peaceful, piecemeal socialization of the existing capitalist order; nor, on the other hand, were they certain that a revolution would be required. The Allemanists believed that all methods of action should be considered as legitimate and proper and that particular emphasis should not be placed on any one of them. The Allemanists contended that political action was an effective means of propaganda and recruitment, but unlike the Possibilists, they considered it a method of action to be employed with extreme caution. The Allemanists maintained that when a Socialist was elected to political office, he more often than not became so absorbed in his new role as politician as to neglect his duties and obligations as a Socialist. To prevent this from happening to their *élus*, the Allemanists placed each *élu* under the direct supervision of the party unit with which he was affiliated. Thus, upon taking political office a member of the party deposited his resignation, complete except for the date it was to take effect, with the party group that had nominated him. At the first infraction of party discipline, the resignation would be sent to the proper public authorities by the party group. Moreover, as long as they held political office, the *élus* were expected to give a large part (in some cases more than half) of their stipends to the party.[42]

---

[42] See the report on the question of tactics approved by the Tenth Regional Congress of the Federative Union of the Center of the Allemanist party in 1891 in Fédération des travailleurs socialistes de France, *Compte rendu du Dixième Congrès régional de l'Union fédérative du Centre, tenu à Paris les 1ᵉʳ, 2, 3 et 5 octobre 1890 et les 12, 13, 14, 15, 16 et 17 mars 1891* (Paris, 1891), p. 76; and the resolution on tactics adopted by the Ninth National Congress of the party in Parti ouvrier socialiste révolutionnaire, *Compte rendu du Dixième Congrès national, tenu à Paris du 21 au 29*

During the years immediately following the formation of their party, the Allemanists ran candidates in municipal and general elections, and, unlike the Possibilists, generally refused to form electoral coalitions with any other political party; nor would they support a coalition candidate even where the candidate was a Socialist. Eventually, however, the Allemanists abandoned this tactic; and it was more than a little ironic, that Allemane, who had always vigorously opposed political maneuvers, was himself elected (1901) to the Chamber of Deputies as a coalition candidate of several republican and Socialist groups.[43]

Another of the principal Allemanist beliefs at the time of the party's formation was that the emancipation of the proletariat not only *ought* to, but *must*, be the work of the proletariat itself. As Allemane declared: "The people have been victimized every time they entrusted the task of defending its interests to individuals belonging to the bourgeoisie, that is to a class whose education, interests, and propensities, whose spirit of domination and gain, make it inevitably the enemy of the proletariat — the irreconcilable enemy of the moral, intellectual, and material emancipation of the proletariat." [44] The Allemanists maintained that the workers must group themselves in labor unions for concerted action in the economic level as well as in a class party for action on the political level. They contended that the importance of political action in the struggle for emancipation had been exaggerated by other Socialist factions; and more than any other Socialist party, the Allemanists gave attention to those means of action to be employed on the economic level, notably, the general strike (the more or less complete cessation of work by all laborers at the same time). Believing that the success of a general strike would depend upon the mass of workers acting as a disciplined, cohesive force, the Allemanists

---

juin 1891 (Paris, 1892), pp. 100–101. See also the *Parti Ouvrier*, October 11–12, 1892, November 21–22, 1893, September 17–18, 1894.

[43] *Parti Ouvrier*, February 10, 24, 1901.

[44] *Nôtre Programme* (Paris, 1895), p. 6. See also the preamble of the legislative program adopted by the Saint-Quentin Congress of the party in 1892 in Parti ouvrier socialiste révolutionnaire, *Compte rendu du Onzième Congrès national, tenu à Saint-Quentin du 2 au 9 octobre 1892* (Paris, 1893), p. 54.

emphasized the importance of the union as the instrument for creating a strong class consciousness and a capacity for unity of action amongst the workers.[45]

At the same time the Allemanist party was organized (1891), its stronghold was the department of the Seine, where it possessed several militant groups and exercised a real influence in municipal elections. During the years 1892–1896, the party extended its organization and influence into the provinces. 1896, however, marked the apogee of *Allemanisme*. Thereafter, as a consequence of internal dissension and large-scale defections, the party deteriorated rapidly. In 1896, two Allemanists holding seats on the Municipal Council of Paris and two Allemanist *élus* in the Chamber of Deputies, all objecting to the rigorous control which the party exercised over members holding public office, endeavored to show their independence by refusing to give it part of their stipends as required by party statutes. The Paris branch of the party, which held the signed but undated resignations of the four *élus*, immediately dispatched their resignations to the proper authorities.[46] This action aroused considerable dissension within the party ranks; and as a result several local groups that sided with the *élus* withdrew from the national organization. These groups joined forces in 1897 to form yet another Socialist party, the Alliance communiste révolutionnaire (Revolutionary Communist Alliance). Lacking the following and resources to stand alone, the Alliance soon entered into a close working arrangement with the Blanquist party. The former adopted almost *in toto* the doctrine and tactics of the Blanquist organization, and until the Alliance dissolved in 1902, it functioned as a sort of appendage of that organization.[47]

[45] See the resolution on *syndicats* approved by the Tenth National Congress of the party at Paris in 1891 in Parti ouvrier socialiste révolutionnaire, *Compte rendu du Dixième Congrès national*, p. 112. On the attitude of the Allemanists toward the general strike, see Parti ouvrier socialiste révolutionnaire, *Compte rendu du Quatorzième Congrès national, tenu à Paris 24–25 septembre 1896* (Paris, 1897), pp. 19–34, 145; and Allemane's articles in the *Petite République*, September 1, 1893; and the *Parti Ouvrier*, September 17–18, 1894, July 4–5, 1895, September 24–25, 1896.

[46] *Parti Ouvrier*, March 19–20, April 3–4, October 1–2, 1896.

[47] Charnay, p. 80; Léon de Seilhac, *Le Monde socialiste* (Paris, 1904), pp. 87–88.

In the early 1890's, the Guesdist party, in an endeavor to strengthen its position in electoral campaigns, adopted extensive electoral programs which were affixed to the fundamental charter, the *programme minimum*, of the Parti ouvrier français. During the eighties, the Guesdists, in marked contrast to the Possibilists, had failed to achieve any success at the polls. The Guesdist vote in the general and municipal elections had amounted on the average to something like one per cent of all the votes registered. This poor showing at the polls was due in large part to the fact that the Guesdists themselves had not made a concerted effort to win votes. They had participated in electoral campaigns solely for the purposes of propagating the party doctrines and building the party cadres. They had not actively sought to secure political power, that is, political offices in the local and state government. This conduct was in keeping with their belief that political action was only one means of furthering the class struggle and that this struggle would ultimately be resolved through revolutionary action. By 1890, however, it had become apparent that the revolutionary situation the Guesdists had for so long anticipated was even more remote than it appeared to be in 1880, when republican institutions were not at all stable and secure. In terms of practical politics this meant that the Guesdist party had to accept, for the time being at least, republican institutions as the milieu in which it would operate if it were to exercise a real influence on the political and social movements of the country. The Guesdist leadership had come to realize that democratic political institutions such as universal suffrage and elective municipal and national organs must be utilized to a greater extent than heretofore to advance their interests, while awaiting the creation of the anticipated revolutionary situation.[48] The Guesdist party, therefore, decided to emulate the electoral success of the Possibilists, and they, too, adopted attractive, moderate electoral programs designed to win the votes of various sections of the electorate, non-proletarian as well as proletarian. The adoption of these programs had a number of

[48] See Guesde's articles in the *Socialiste*, December 26, 1891, March 13, April 23, 1892. See also Alexandre Zévaès, *Notes et souvenirs d'un militant* (Paris, 1913), p. 135.

unanticipated consequences and affected in a most important way the relations between the several Socialist factions.

In preparation for the approaching municipal elections, the Guesdist party, at its national congress in Lyons in November 1891, adopted a program which, among other things, called for the following reforms: an eight-hour workday and a legal minimum wage for all municipal employees; municipal nurseries and maternity wards; and free medical service.[49] Commenting on this program in the *Socialiste*, Guesde pointed out that his party did not believe that the conquest of power in the communes would mean the emancipation of the proletariat. This could only be realized after the seizure of the political power of the state. Guesde, however, justified the participation of his party in municipal elections by stating that the conquest of municipalities at the polls would weaken the position of the capitalist class, for the municipalities controlled by the Socialists would constitute "bases of operations" for the final struggle for state power.[50]

For the Socialist parties in general and for the Guesdists in particular, the May 1892 municipal elections proved a striking victory. The Guesdists, who participated in the elections in some eighty-two communes, won all or a majority of the seats on twenty-six Municipal Councils. More than 400 members of the Guesdist party were elected Councilors — approximately twice the number victorious in the municipal elections of 1888. The total vote received by party candidates was over 100,000 — almost as many votes as the

[49] See the text in *Neuvième Congrès national du Parti ouvrier, tenu à Lyon du 26 au 28 novembre 1891* (Lille, n.d.), pp. 14–16. See also the *Socialiste*, December 5, 1891.

[50] *Socialiste*, December 26, 1891. See also the *Socialiste*, March 13, 1892, January 12, 1896; and the *Petite République*, April 5, 1896. Writing in the *Citoyen* on May 11, 1882, Lafargue had declared: "The only reforms possible of realization in a capitalist society are those which promote the interests of the ruling classes. Although fully aware of this fact, the Parti ouvrier wages battle on the municipal terrain because municipal elections provide it with occasions to affirm its collectivist doctrines and to oppose them to the monkeyshines (*chinoiseries*) of the Radicals and other bourgeois elements . . . to familiarize the party members with struggles in the public arena, and to accustom the workers to think and act for themselves. Such electoral struggles are 'les écoles de guerre' of the party."

total received by the candidates of all the Socialist parties in the general elections of 1889.[51] Guesde, while hailing the results of the election as a great triumph for Socialism, cautioned his party that if its success at the polls were to be consolidated and extended at the coming general elections, it would have to enlist the support of sections of the rural population. "The party will have to carry our propaganda," he declared, "into a milieu which we have neglected up to now, namely, the countryside, where . . . an ever growing agrarian proletariat is being formed." Numerically, the peasantry of France constituted the most important segment of the population, and it was inconceivable to Guesde that his party could become a dominant political force without first gaining the support of at least the agrarian proletariat.[52]

In July 1892, the Guesdist National Council (which had replaced the National Committee in 1890 as the party's central organ) undertook an inquest into the conditions of the French peasantry. By means of a detailed questionnaire sent to party groups located in or adjacent to rural districts, it sought information concerning such matters as the working conditions of the agrarian day laborer, the kind of land tenure and the size of the holdings of the peasant proprietors, the extent of farm mechanization, etc. On the basis of the information obtained, the Guesdists, at a party congress in Marseilles in September 1892, adopted an extensive program of agrarian reforms. Among the reforms called for were the following: a minimum wage for day laborers as well as for those hired by the year; agricultural pensions for the sick and the aged; the reduction of tax rates for the *métayer* (sharecropper) and the small peasant proprietor; and free courses of instruction in agricultural methods and techniques.[53] The Marseilles Congress declared that this agrarian program, the first to be formulated by any European Socialist party,

---

[51] *Socialiste*, May 15, 22, 1892; Adrien Veber, "Mouvement social en France et à l'étranger," *Revue socialiste*, 16: 105 (1892).

[52] *Socialiste*, July 17, 1892.

[53] The text of the program is given in *Dixième Congrès national du Parti ouvrier, tenu à Marseille du 24 au 28 septembre 1892* (Lille, n.d.), pp. 34–36. There is a collection of these filled-out questionnaires in the Guesde Archives.

would "rally the workers of the fields to Socialism." [54] To this program the next national congress of the Guesdist party, held at Nantes in September 1894, affixed a preamble which included the following statement: "In France at least, it is not true in the domain of agriculture as it is in the domain of industry, that the means of production are so concentrated in the hands of capital that they can only be restored to the producers under a collectivist or Socialist regime, since the means of production, that is, the farm lands, are in many cases owned by the producers themselves . . . [and] considering that if in the case of great properties concentrated in the hands of their idle proprietors (as in the case of the mines, railroads, factories, etc.) the duty of Socialism is to give the agricultural proletariat possession of them under the collective or social form, the duty of Socialism is no less compelling to sustain the peasant proprietor in the possession of his plot of land, against debts, usury, and the encroachments of new landlords . . ." [55]

The Guesdist party's adoption of the agrarian program provoked a storm of protest from orthodox Marxists of other countries. No less an authority than Friedrich Engels, writing in the leading Socialist journal in Europe, the *Neue Zeit*, shortly after the Nantes Congress, subjected the program to a thoroughgoing criticism and chided the French Marxists for their opportunism in adopting it. Engels reiterated the orthodox Marxian view that in agriculture, as in industry, the same general laws of capitalistic production and accumulation asserted themselves. It was impossible, therefore, to consider the peasant proprietor as anything but "a future proletarian." The pledge of the Guesdists to protect the peasant proprietor in his land holdings, Engels declared, "does not serve to protect his liberty, but rather serves to maintain the special form of his bondage: it only prolongs a situation in which he can neither live nor die." Engels attributed the deviations from orthodox Marxism embodied in the agrarian program to the impatient desire of the Guesdists to win, immediately, the votes of the French peasantry. "They could

---

[54] *Dixième Congrès*, p. 34. See also the *Socialiste*, October 4, 10, 1892.

[55] The text is given in *Douzième Congrès national du Parti ouvrier français, tenu à Nantes du 14 au 16 septembre 1894* (Lille, 1894), pp. 18–21.

not hope to attain this end except by making very general and daring promises which they could only justify by means of an even more daring declaration of policy." Engels expressed confidence that the Guesdists would soon amend this opportunistic program, for they were "too intelligent not to know that the property of the peasant is destined to become collective property." [56] Intelligent or not, the Guesdists generally ignored Engels' criticism, and did not revise the agrarian program in any way.

During the period which witnessed the adoption of these reform programs, the Guesdists, now ardently in pursuit of political offices, concomitantly abandoned the intransigent electoral tactic which they had practiced rather consistently during the 1880's; henceforth they frequently entered into electoral alliances with other Socialist factions and even with the electoral committees of republican parties. Lafargue, a member of the Guesdist National Council, won a seat in the Chamber of Deputies in 1891 as the result of a coalition between various Socialist and republican factions. The striking victories of the Guesdist party in the municipal elections of 1892 at Lyons, Marseilles, Montluçon, and Bordeaux were due in part to similar tactics.[57]

The collaboration of the Guesdists with other political organizations was a common practice in the general legislative elections of 1893. That January the Guesdists joined with Blanquist, Possibilist, and Allemanist groups in Paris to form the Ligue d'action révolutionnaire pour la conquête de la république sociale (League of Revolutionary Action for the Conquest of the Social Republic). The principal function of the Ligue was to coordinate the political activities of these groups in the approaching elections in order that the Socialist and labor forces of Paris might present a unified front against reactionary elements. In an electoral manifesto, formulated by a committee headed by Guesde and Allemane, the Ligue called upon the

[56] F. Engels, "Die Bauernfrage in Frankreich und Deutschland," *Neue Zeit*, XIII, 1: 292–306 (1894). See also G. G. Benjamin, "German and French Socialists and the Agrarian Question," *Journal of Political Economy*, 34: 354–355 (1926); and Hubert Lagardelle, "Les Origines du socialisme parlementaire en France," *Mouvement socialiste*, 26: 90–95 (1909).

[57] *Socialiste*, November 14, 1891, September 25, 1892.

proletariat to support Socialists of all schools in their common struggle to end the political regime of the "corrupt bourgeoisie" and institute the "Social Republic." [58] Another significant attempt to achieve a *rapprochement* between the various Socialist factions for electoral purposes was the alliance of Guesdist and so-called "Independent" Socialists (those who did not subscribe to any single, well-defined ideology and were not enrolled in any of the nationally or regionally organized Socialist parties). [59] This took form in January 1893, at the famous mass meeting of Socialist and left-wing republicans at the Tivoli-Vaux Hall in Paris. There Guesdists and Independent Socialists joined with Radicals and Radical-Socialists in formulating a manifesto which called upon the workers to "save" the Republic from the "parasitic ruling class" by voting for "progressive" candidates. [60] Following this meeting, Guesdists and Independent Socialists frequently campaigned together, speaking from the same platforms in Lille, Calais, Bordeaux, and elsewhere. [61]

The legislative elections of August and September 1893 took place under conditions which were extremely propitious for Socialist candidates. The failure of the government to ameliorate the conditions of the workers through a broad program of social reforms, the

[58] See the text in the *Socialiste*, January 1, 22, 1893. See also the *Parti Ouvrier*, January 3–4, 7, 19–20, 1893; the *Parti socialiste*, January 8–14, 1893; and the *Prolétaire*, February 18, 1893; Lagardelle, 84.

[59] The first important organization of Independent Socialists was the Fédération républicaine socialiste de la Seine (Republican Socialist Federation of the Seine), constituted in Paris in February 1893. The founders of the Fédération (René Viviani, Alexandre Millerand, and Gustave Rouanet, among others), declared in a public manifesto that the purpose of the new organization was to bring together those Socialists who did not want "to imprison their doctrinal affirmations in any narrow formulation which could not possibly contain the manifold aspirations of the modern world *en plein essor de développement économique, politique, mental et moral.*" Quoted in Albert Orry, *Les Socialistes indépendants* (Paris, 1911), p. 19. See also Adrien Veber, "Mouvement social en France et à l'étranger," *Revue socialiste*, 17: 365–366 (1893). The daily newspaper, the *Petite République*, which adopted a Socialist stance when Millerand became editor in 1893, and the monthly, the *Revue socialiste*, founded by Malon in 1885 and edited by him until 1894, were the principal organs of the Independent Socialists.

[60] See the text in Veber, "Mouvement social en France et à l'étranger," *Revue socialiste*, 17: 239–240.

[61] *Socialiste*, March 12, 19, 1893.

tragic shooting of a number of men, women, and children by government troops during the May Day celebration at Fourmies (Nord) in 1891, and the political and financial scandals of the Panama Affair — all served to create discontent among the working class. Many lost confidence in the government and were prepared to accept the Socialist view that the capitalist order was synonymous with tyranny and corruption.[62]

Strengthened by numerous alliances with Radicals and Radical–Socialists, the Socialists were able to capitalize on this popular discontent; they registered an impressive victory in the legislative elections. Thirty-seven Socialists were elected to the Chamber of Deputies — twenty Independents, six Guesdists, five Allemanists, four Blanquists, and two Possibilists; while the combined votes obtained by all the Socialist candidates was in excess of a half-million, roughly four times the Socialist vote in the legislative elections of 1889.[63]

Guesde, who for the first time had won a seat in the Chamber, declared to the workers of Roubaix, where he had scored his success, that the victory of the Socialist forces constituted "a veritable revolution — the beginning of the revolution which will make free men of you." [64]

[62] Lagardelle, pp. 81–83.

[63] The figures given above were compiled from the following sources: the *Petite République*, August 22, 23, September 5, 6, 1893; the *Socialiste*, August 26, 28, 1893; the *Parti Socialiste*, August 27–September 3, 1893; and the *Parti Ouvrier*, September 5–6, 1893. The following Socialists were elected to the Chamber of Deputies: Alexandre Avez, Emile Basly, Eugène Baudin, Antide Boyer, Louis Calvinhac, Edmond Charpentier, Jacques Chassaing, Emmanuel Chauvière, René Chauvin, Jules Coutant, Valentin Couturier, Victor Dejeante, Prudent Dervillers, Eugène Fabérot, Paul Franconie, Emile Girodet, Paschal Grousset, Arthur Groussier, Guesde, Abel Hovelacque, Clovis Hugues, Jaurès, Antoine Jourde, Emile Labussière, Arthur Lamendin, Aimé Lavy, François Masson, Millerand, Rouanet, Charles Sauvanet, Marcel Sembat, Léon Thivrier, Edmond Toussaint, Edouard Vaillant, Pierre Vaux, Viviani, and Albert Walter. There is no consensus on the number of Socialists elected in 1893. Louis (*Histoire du socialisme en France*, p. 236) and Zévaès (*Le Socialisme en France depuis 1871*, p. 148) both set the number at fifty, and André Daniel (*L'Année politique, 1893* [Paris, 1894], p. 281) gives the figure of forty-nine; but all three include in their totals Radical-Socialists and former Boulangists who ran on Independent Socialist and Guesdist platforms. The problem here is the difficult one of separating Socialists from "Socialist" Radicals, that is, *les Socialistes conscients* from *les demi-adhérents*.

[64] *Socialiste*, August 26, 1893.

The Socialist victory in 1893 did not prove to be "a veritable revolution" as Guesde had so enthusiastically proclaimed. Nevertheless, the 1893 elections were a milestone in the history of the French Socialist movement, for in a sense, the elections marked its coming of age. Socialism had at last become a factor of real political significance; henceforth Socialist forces were to be an important influence on the national political scene. Socialist Deputies of the various factions, by forming a bloc in the Chamber, for the first time were to play a significant part in its activities; thus they were in a position to determine to some extent the course of French political life. As the following chapter will show, the *rapprochement* among Socialist Deputies in the Chamber during the years 1893–1898 — the period of "Parliamentary Socialism" as it came to be known — constituted a long step towards eventual unification of the Socialist forces in a single party.

Chapter 2

Parliamentary Socialism

Before undertaking an examination of the parliamentary activity of the Socialist Deputies from 1893–1898, its seems appropriate to consider the man who provided it with vigorous and resourceful leadership. This was Jean Jaurès — unquestionably the most prominent Socialist of the Third French Republic.

Jean Jaurès was born in 1859 at Castres, a small mercantile and industrial center in the south of France. His family belonged to the provincial bourgeoisie. Jaurès began his formal education at the modest Collège de Castres and later attended the renowned Lycée Louis-le-Grand in Paris. In 1878, he entered the Ecole Normale Supérieure, perhaps the most distinguished school in the country. Endowed with a brilliant, penetrating mind and the concentration of a medieval monk, Jaurès devoted himself to the study of philosophy and history. In 1881, he was graduated from the Ecole Normale, third in his class. (The philosopher, Henri Bergson, was second.) Shortly after, he became professor of philosophy in a lycée in Albi.

Like so many vigorous and energetic men, Jaurès found the passive, relatively cloistered life of the academician rather dull and unchallenging; after less than four years of teaching, he abandoned the classroom for the political arena. In 1885, he made his political debut when he stood as a candidate for Albi and was elected to the Chamber of Deputies. He was then only twenty-six years of age, the youngest member of the Chamber. After being defeated in the general elections of 1889, he returned for a time to academic life.[1]

During the years 1889–1893, as a consequence of his research into the social and economic problems raised by the growth of modern capitalism, his study of the writings of Marx, Proudhon, Malon, and other Socialists (he wrote a doctoral thesis on the origins of German Socialism during this period), and his intimate relationship with Lucien Herr, the Marxist librarian of the Ecole Normale, Jaurès gravitated toward Socialism. Reflection on his experience with the realities of politics and the social forces that determined the course of events led Jaurès to abandon one of the basic assumptions of his early social philosophy, namely, that the bourgeoisie, proud of its struggle for political freedom against the feudal aristocracy and sincerely interested in the welfare of the nation as a whole, would take the lead in bringing about the amelioration of the conditions of the underprivileged. From experience he had learned that a great many members of the bourgeoisie were indifferent, if not hostile, to social reform. Indeed, he came to believe that the big industrialists and financiers constituted a new feudal aristocracy within the capitalist order. To the wealthy bourgeoisie, "the Republic was only the substitution of the financial oligarchy for the landed oligarchy, of the large manufacturer for the country squire, of the capitalist hierarchy for the clerical hierarchy, of the banker for the priest, and of money for dogma." Jaurès arrived at the conclusion that the proletariat was the only class vitally interested in social justice, and that this goal could only be realized through the evolution of the "entire Republic toward Socialism."[2]

In the Socialist doctrine that he now began to develop, Jaurès sought to reconcile and synthesize many of the conflicting tenets of liberal idealism and orthodox Marxism. His conception of history was a case in point. He believed that the contradiction between the

---

[1] For biographical details on Jaurès, see J. Hampden Jackson, *Jean Jaurès, His Life and Work* (London, 1943); and Marcelle Auclair, *La Vie de Jean Jaurès, ou la France d'avant 1914* (Paris, 1954).

[2] Jaurès, "Réponses et questions," in *Oeuvres de Jean Jaurès*, ed. Max Bonnafous (9 vols., Paris, 1931–1939), III, 131, 133. See also Weinstein, *Jean Jaurès*, pp. 48–58.

idealistic and materialistic interpretations of historical change was more apparent than real; idealism and materialism were not mutually exclusive. Jaurès readily accepted the notion that economic forces were the "mainspring of human history" and that the operation of these forces in contemporary society made the evolution of a collectivist order inevitable. On the other hand he insisted that moral, intellectual, and aesthetic ideas, operating independently of economic forces, were likewise of the utmost importance in determining the movement of history. "In the great crises in the life of the world," he wrote, "the economic forces are not the only ones in play: moral forces, concord, disinterestedness, wisdom are sometimes decisive." Indeed, the social transformation that was to usher in the future order of social justice would be brought about not only by the operation of economic forces, but by the "force of men, by the energy of consciences and of wills" as well.[3] Moreover, if historical materialism as formulated by Marx suggested that Socialism was inevitable, to Jaurès idealism proved that Socialism was also just, humane, and the fulfillment of mankind's destiny. According to Jaurès, from the beginning of its existence, long before the appearance of what could be called an economic system, humanity bore "within its soul" the idea of justice. Throughout history it has struggled against oppression and exploitation to realize this immanent idea at the core of human nature. The moral and spiritual force of this aspiration for justice in human society gave "intelligible direction" to the evolution of history. This, to a great extent, determined the progressive transformation of economic forms from primitive cannibalism to slavery, from slavery to serfdom, from serfdom to the wage system of capitalism, and from the wage system to the future Socialist order. "Since the whole process of history springs from the essential contradiction between the nature of man and the use that is made of man, this process must tend towards an economic order in which the use that is made of man will be in conformity with his nature." It was through a series of economic forms, each of which embodied to a greater extent than the last

---

[3] Jaurès, *La Convention, 1792* (Paris, 1904[?]), p. 208. See also Jaurès, *La Constituante, 1789–1791* (Paris, 1901[?]), pp. 6–7.

the human ideal, that humanity was "realizing itself." It was not necessary, therefore, to view the materialist and idealist conceptions
of history as being in opposition to one another. "They merge in a
unique and indissoluble development, because, though one cannot
consider man apart from his economic relationships, neither can
one consider economic relationships apart from man; and while
history is from one aspect a phenomenon evolving in accordance
with mechanical laws, it is at the same time an aspiration working
itself out within the framework of an ideal." [4] It was Socialism
alone that constituted the economic order in which both the material needs and spiritual aspirations of humanity would find fulfillment: a Socialist society would realize "the whole idea of human
justice" and thus all the rich, variegated potentialities of "the human
personality." [5]

Another element in Jaurès's Socialism was his conception of, and
his veneration for, the French Republic. The establishment of the
Third Republic, he believed, was the "supreme expression" of the
egalitarian and "Socialist" tendencies of the French Revolution. The
Republic, which to him was synonymous with La Patrie, was not
only the definitive form of political democracy; it was also the indispensable instrument for the attainment of economic and social
democracy. Since the Republic recognized the political sovereignty
of the people, it was logical and inevitable that the economic sovereignty of the people, which was implicit in the legislation of the
French Revolution, would follow in due course. Jaurès contended
that just as the Republic, with its "progressive" conception of the
political sovereignty of the people, had grown out of the French
Revolution, so Socialism, with its "progressive" conception of the
economic sovereignty of the people, would grow out of the Republic. To Jaurès, the Socialist movement was in essence the extension
and development of the democratic movement of the Republic. And,
since the Third Republic was the most propitious milieu for the
growth of the Socialist movement, he concluded that it was the

[4] Jaurès, "Idéalisme et matérialisme dans la conception de l'histoire," in *Oeuvres*,
VI, 7–18.
[5] Jaurès, "Le Socialisme et la vie," in *Oeuvres*, VI, 353–354.

sacred duty of the Socialists to cherish republican institutions and
to defend them against their domestic and foreign enemies.[6]

Although he did not entirely rule out the possibility of a future
social revolution, Jaurès strongly believed that the existence of political democracy in France made possible the realization of a Socialist
order without recourse to revolutionary action. Violent revolution
had largely been rendered obsolete by universal suffrage — "the
revolutionary instrument of the modern period." [7] Socialist conquest of the state's political power, the act which Jaurès considered
prerequisite for the realization of the future Socialist society, was
to be accomplished through the ballot; the assumption of power was
to be legally sanctioned at the polls. "The Socialist Revolution shall
be accomplished not by the action — the sudden surprise stroke —
of a bold minority, but by the clear and concordant will of the immense majority of the citizens." [8]

In addition to his stature as a theorist, the predominant position
which Jaurès occupied in the French Socialist movement during
the period 1893–1914 must be attributed in part to his outstanding
abilities as an orator and parliamentarian. He was indeed the hero
of the platform to the mass of Socialists. In a nation that could boast
of a galaxy of famous orators and spellbinders, Jaurès had few peers.
Friend and foe alike have recorded the opinion that he was an
orator of incomparable authority and eloquence. His speeches, rich
in verbal images, literary allusions, and emotional overtones, were
masterpieces of form and delivery. To an almost matchless degree,
Jaurès possessed, in the words of one who heard him on numerous
occasions, "the gift of identifying himself with the mood and char-

---

[6] Jaurès, "Le Socialisme et la Révolution Française," in *Oeuvres*, III, 44–46; Jaurès's
articles in the *Dépêche de Toulouse*, January 2, 3, February 20, May 29, June 26,
August 28, 1893. See also Louis Soulé, *La Vie de Jaurès* (Paris, 1921), pp. 209–212.

[7] *Dépêche de Toulouse*, April 8, 1893. See also the *Petite République*, August 21,
1901.

[8] *Petite République*, August 12, 1901. "Whoever depends on a fortunate turn of
events or the chances and hazards of physical force to bring about the Revolution
and renounces the method of winning over the immense majority of the citizens to
our ideas, renounces at the same time any possibility of transforming the social order."
See also the *Petite République*, August 26, 1901.

acter of his audience — whether a mass demonstration, a legislative gathering, or a Congress of Socialists." [9]

Jaurès was as skillful and effective a parliamentarian as he was a public speaker. His knowledge of parliamentary procedure and tactics was superior to that of any other Socialist Deputy, and he was a lion in debate. Although identified as an Independent, he provided the leadership in the Chamber of Deputies for the Socialist group as a whole. The differences among the Socialist factions did not strike Jaurès as being of great moment, for he was convinced that all essentially were in agreement on the fundamentals of Socialism and were striving to achieve the same objectives. He believed that the fusion of these factions in a unified party was the most important prerequisite for the final conquest of political power. And it was to the task of laying the foundation for this union, to the achievement of a real *rapprochement* between the representatives of the five Socialist factions in the Chamber of Deputies, that Jaurès devoted his efforts when in 1893 he returned to the Palais Bourbon as a Socialist Deputy.

Shortly after the legislative elections of September 1893, the official newspaper of the Blanquist party, the *Parti Socialiste*, proposed that the newly elected Socialist Deputies join forces to form a single bloc in the Chamber. "Without renouncing in any way their own programs," the journal suggested, "the elected representatives of the different Socialist groups should try to find *un terrain d'entente* which would permit them to act in common in the fight against the reactionary policies of the government and to work together in the crucial campaign for the enactment of the reforms contained in all the Socialist programs." [10] The Blanquist proposal

[9] Angelica Balabanoff, *My Life as a Rebel* (New York, 1938), p. 82. See also Hyndman, *The Record of an Adventurous Life*, p. 398; Edouard Berth, "Les 'Discours' de Jaurès," *Mouvement socialiste*, 14: 215 (1904); and Auclair, *La Vie de Jean Jaurès*, pp. 156–157, 239, 543–544. On the importance of oratorical skill as a requisite to party leadership, see the perceptive comments by Robert Michels in his *Political Parties*, trans. Eden and Cedar Paul (Glencoe, Ill., 1949), pp. 69–72.

[10] September 17–24, 1893. See also Vaillant's article in the *Petite République*, September 10, 1893.

received widespread support from other Socialists; and on November 8, shortly before the new Chamber of Deputies convened, a meeting of Socialist Deputies was held at the Palais Bourbon to realize this envisioned union. The meeting resulted in the formation of a new parliamentary group — the Union socialiste — which was to unify and direct the activities of the Socialist Deputies. To facilitate the work of the Union socialiste, a number of committees were subsequently set up to deal with specific legislative matters, such as finance, justice, foreign affairs, and education. Each committee was charged with the tasks of keeping the parliamentary group informed on legislative developments in its own field of concern and of drawing up bills which the group could propose in the Chamber. While the Chamber remained in session, the group held a caucus at least once a week.[11]

At the time it was organized, the Union socialiste was composed of the Blanquist, Possibilist, Guesdist, and Independent Socialist Deputies. A short time after, eight left-wing Radical-Socialists and five former Boulangists — all of whom had collaborated closely with the Socialists in the recent elections — became members.[12] The Allemanists, who were the youngest, and, from the doctrinal point of view, the most uncompromising of the Socialist factions, refused to sanction the participation of their *élus*. Allemanist leaders objected to the parliamentary group on the grounds that it admitted non-Socialists to membership and did not function in accordance with a charter of clear-cut, uncompromising Socialist principles.

[11] *Petite République*, November 9, 17, 1893. The Union socialiste was not the first organization of its kind. In 1885, eight Independent Socialist Deputies had formed a similar parliamentary group. See E. Fournière, "Revue du Mois," *Revue socialiste*, 2: 1132 (1885); and Orry, *Les Socialistes indépendants*, pp. 12–14.

[12] The following were the new members: Jean Argeliès, Thierry Cazes, Emile Compayré, Antoine Desfarges, Raymond Gendre, Claude Goujat, Emile Goussot, Léon Mirman, César Paulin-Méry, Pierre Richard, Ernest Roche, Jacques Salis, and Jean Turigny. The names of the members of the Union socialiste were affixed to the manifestoes which it issued from time to time during the years 1894–97. For the manifestoes, see the *Petite République*, April 30, May 10, June 29, July 30, 1894, January 13, 19, October 19, 1895, April 25, May 2, 1896, March 18, June 7, October 24, 1897. Some of the manifestoes are reprinted in Zévaès, *Le Socialisme en France depuis 1871*, pp, 272–277. See also H. Lagardelle, "Les Origines du socialisme parlementaire en France," *Mouvement socialiste*, 26: 87–89 (1909).

Despite the stand of their party leaders, however, the Allemanist Deputies subsequently did join the Socialist bloc.[13]

The formation of the Socialist parliamentary group had been rendered possible by the growing tendency towards unity of political action on the part of the various Socialist factions — a tendency which had been clearly manifested in the Ligue d'action révolutionnaire and in the numerous coalitions which had been formed by the various factions in the recent general elections — as well as by the more friendly feelings between the factions that had followed their victories at the polls. Moreover, as the following section will indicate, the close collaboration of the Socialist *élus* in the Chamber was greatly facilitated, if indeed not rendered imperative, by the very exigencies of parliamentary strife, by the conduct of the anti-Socialist ministries of Dupuy, Casimir-Périer, and Ribot, against which the Socialists found it expedient to unite in vigorous opposition.

The Ministerial Declaration which Charles Dupuy, the President du conseil (Premier), delivered before the new Chamber on November 21, 1893, constituted, as far as the Socialists were concerned, "a veritable declaration of war" against the Socialist movement.[14]

---

[13] See the official newspaper of the Allemanist party, the *Parti Ouvrier*, September 18–19, November 10–11, 1893, November 15–16, 17–18, 1894, January 1–2, 1896. The five Allemanist Deputies — Dejeante, Avez, Fabérot, Groussier, and Toussaint — adhered to the Union socialiste in May 1894. A few weeks later, they withdrew on orders from the General Secretariat of their party. In October 1895, on their own initiative, the five rejoined the group. Again they were compelled to withdraw. When Dejeante and Groussier broke with the party in 1896 (see above, p. 25), they were forced to give up their seats in the Chamber; however, they regained them in the fall of 1896, following their victories in special legislative elections. Both then joined the Union socialiste. Avez died in January 1896. His seat was filled by Victor Renou who enrolled in the Union socialiste. The General Secretariat of the Allemanist party responded to these developments by issuing a pamphlet which roundly denounced the group as a bizarre collection of Socialists, pseudo-Socialists, and anti-Socialists. "In this Union socialiste in the Chamber," the pamphlet charged, "there are admirers of the tricolor . . . and the red flag. There are communists, collectivists, defenders of private property, patriots, internationalists, free-traders, protectionists, partisans of the general strike, together with many of its opponents." Parti ouvrier socialiste révolutionnaire. Secrétariat Général, *La Vérité sur l'Union socialiste* (Paris, 1897), p. 9. See also the *Parti Ouvrier*, March 19–20, April 3–4, October 1–2, 1896; the *Dépêche de Toulouse*, March 19, 1896; and Lagardelle, pp. 86–87.

[14] See Guesde's comments in the *Socialiste*, November 25, 1893. See also the *Social-*

"Faithful to the spirit of the Declaration of the Rights of Man and the Citizen," Dupuy told the Chamber, "we repudiate the doctrines, which under various titles — collectivism and the like — aim at substituting the anonymous tyranny of the state for individual initiative and the free association of citizens." And the government, he added, would vigorously repress "every attempt at agitation and every act of disorder whoever may be the authors or leaders." [15]

This scarcely veiled attack on the Socialists did not go unchallenged, for immediately after the delivery of the Declaration, Jaurès and Alexandre Millerand, an Independent member of the Union socialiste, requested an interpellation on the general policy of the Dupuy Ministry. In the debate which followed, Jaurès sharply rebuked the ministry for its hostility towards Socialism. The Socialist movement in France, he asserted, had arisen not only from the economic conditions created by capitalism, but also from "republicanism" and from democratic institutions — "universal suffrage, lay education, and the trade-union laws." In order to combat Socialism, the government, Jaurès charged, would perforce have to pursue an intransigent policy of reaction in every sphere, political, educational, and industrial. The ministry would have to abandon "republican principles"; and it was to the defense of these principles, he concluded, that all Socialists were committed.[16] From this clash between the Dupuy Ministry and the Socialist Deputies, the latter emerged victorious. Weakened by internal dissension and unable to command a stable majority in the Chamber, the ministry, at the close of the debate on the Jaurès and Millerand interpellation (November 25, 1893), tendered its resignation.

The Socialist Deputies also united in strong opposition to the Ministry of Jean Casimir-Périer which was constituted in December 1893, for the new ministry was as hostile in its attitude towards Socialism as its predecessor. However, in its campaign against the

---

iste, December 2, 9, 1893; the *Parti Ouvrier*, November 23, 1893; the *Petite République*, November 23, 1893; and the *Prolétaire*, November 26, 1893.

[15] *Journal officiel. Chambre des Députés. Débats parlementaires. Compte rendu in extenso*, session of November 21, 1893, p. 78. Hereafter cited as *Journal officiel*.

[16] *Journal officiel*, November 21, 1893, pp. 80–83.

Socialists the position of the Casimir-Périer Ministry was greatly strengthened by the enactment, soon after its formation, of special legislation ostensibly intended to enable the government to curb Anarchists. In 1892 the French Anarchists, after a decade of relatively peaceful activity, had begun a campaign of "propaganda by act" — bomb-throwing. This campaign reached its height on December 9, 1893 when an Anarchist, during a session of the Chamber, threw a bomb from the visitors' gallery into the midst of the Deputies. More than a score of persons were injured. Two days after this outrage, Casimir-Périer appeared before the Chamber to request the immediate enactment of four "indispensable measures" to enable the government to act with dispatch against Anarchist terrorists and agitators who threatened the social order. Authority was sought by the government to curb the "excesses" of the radical press by imposing "preventive imprisonment" for editors and writers who sought to provoke or incite crimes against persons or property; to restrict the manufacture of explosives; and to prosecute members of any association, group, or entente formed for the purpose of "preparing or committing crimes against persons or property." Casimir-Périer also requested that the Ministry of the Interior be granted substantial funds to augment the police force at Paris and in the provinces.[17]

In the Chamber and in their press, the Socialists made a strong stand against the adoption of these measures, which they characterized as "reactionary," "dictatorial," and a menace to the individual liberties of all citizens. It was the real intention of the Casimir-Périer Ministry, they charged, to utilize the broad powers granted it by this legislation not for the avowed purpose of prosecuting Anarchist terrorists, but rather for the purpose of intimidating and persecuting republicans and Socialists.[18] Although a number of left-wing republicans joined with the Socialists in voting against the four measures, they were approved by an overwhelming majority.

[17] *Journal officiel*, session of December 11, 1893, pp. 218–219.
[18] *Journal officiel*, session of December 15, 1893, pp. 297–302, 305; the *Petite République*, December 13, 18, 22, 23, 1893; the *Prolétaire*, December 24, 1893.

Armed with the extraordinary powers conferred upon it by the Chamber, the Casimir-Périer Ministry lost little time in inaugurating its campaign against those whom it considered as enemies of law and order. On January 1, 1894, police throughout the country, acting on instructions from the Ministry of the Interior, made wholesale arrests of known Anarchists and other "agitators" and searched the domiciles of more than 2,000 persons suspected of possessing Anarchist or other "subversive" literature. As might be expected, the Socialists bitterly denounced the government for its conduct. In their speeches in the Chamber on January 27, Clovis Hugues and René Viviani, members of the Union socialiste, charged that the Casimir-Périer Ministry had wantonly violated the personal liberties of hundreds of citizens, and that it had, under the pretext of rounding up suspected Anarchists, arrested some sixty prominent Socialists at Paris, Lyons, Marseilles, Commentry, and elsewhere. In the name of their group, they introduced a resolution calling for a condemnation of the government's actions.[19] The Chamber, however, indicated its approval of the conduct of the government by rejecting the resolution. Until its fall in May 1894 the Casimir-Périer Ministry continued to harass the Socialists.

It was during the second Dupuy Ministry, which took office that same month, that the conflict between the government and the Socialist Deputies became most intense. The issue upon which the battle was joined was a demand by the Dupuy Ministry for additional anti-Anarchist legislation following the assassination of the President of the French Republic, Sadi Carnot, by an Italian Anarchist on June 24, 1894. The measure which Dupuy brought before the Chamber (July 9) proposed to make it a criminal offense to propagate "Anarchist ideas" by any means whatsoever — in the press, public speeches, private conversations, or in private letters. Persons charged with propagating such ideas (the measure did not define just what an Anarchist idea was) would be denied the usual trial by jury, for all such cases were to be transferred from Assize Courts to Correctional Tribunals. The proceedings of the latter

[19] *Journal officiel*, session of January 27, 1894, pp. 105–110, 113–115. See also the *Petite République*, January 3, 4, 1894; and the *Socialiste*, January 6, 13, 1894.

were to be closed to the public, and the publication of its proceedings forbidden.[20]

On this occasion, the Socialists were not alone in their opposition. Many Radicals (liberal republicans) also believed that the measure constituted a serious menace to civil liberties, and they joined the Socialists in efforts to defeat it. During the spectacular ten-day debate on the measure (July 17–26), leaders of the Radicals, Henri Brisson and René Goblet, as well as Jaurès, Millerand, Guesde, and other Socialists subjected the measure to cogent and often scathing criticism and bitterly denounced the Dupuy Ministry for seeking dictatorial authority.[21] Victor Dejeante, an Allemanist member of the Union socialiste, went so far as to charge Dupuy with plotting the overthrow of the Republic. "Look at the Eighteenth Brumaire and the Second of December! The makers of these *coups d'état* declared that they wished to combat the Anarchist idea, when their real objective was the destruction of the Republic. We say that the objective which you pursue by your measure is identical." [22] The majority of the Chamber, however, supported the ministry; and the measure was approved.

Against the Dupuy Ministry as well as the Ribot Ministry which succeeded it (January–October 1895), the Socialist Deputies continued their policy of intransigent opposition. They denounced the government for imprisoning Socialists, curbing freedom of the press, and infringing upon the legal rights of labor unions. They assailed it for its conduct of foreign affairs and its administration of the colonies. And in collaboration with the Radicals, they waged a vigorous, though unsuccessful, campaign for the repeal of the anti-Anarchist laws of December 1893 and July 1894 — laws which the

[20] *Journal officiel*, session of July 9, 1894, pp. 1221–1222; André Daniel, *L'Année politique, 1894* (Paris, 1895), pp. 240–241.

[21] *Journal officiel*, sessions of July 17, 1894, pp. 1354–1357, July 18, 1894, pp. 1367–1374, 1380–1381, July 19, 1894, pp. 1391–1394, 1402–1405, July 20, 1894, pp. 1415–1418, July 21, 1894, pp. 1440–1445, July 24, 1894, pp. 1519–1523, 1526–1527, 1548–1550. July 25, 1894, pp. 1570–1573, 1581–1584, 1586–1592, July 26, 1894, pp. 1625–1626. See also the manifesto of the Union socialiste against the measure in the *Petite République*, July 30, 1894.

[22] *Journal officiel*, session of July 24, 1894, p. 1539.

Socialists labeled as the *lois scélérates* (literally, wicked laws).[23] The ceaseless activity of the little group of Socialist Deputies contributed to the fall of both ministries.

During the brief tenure of the Ministry of Léon Bourgeois (November 1895–April 1896), the first all-Radical Ministry since 1876, the Socialist Deputies made a complete reversal of tactics. They abandoned the policy of implacable opposition which they had pursued during the Ministries of Dupuy, Casimir-Périer, and Ribot, and became rather loyal supporters of the government. This abrupt change was due in great measure to the character and policy of the new ministry. In contrast to the anti-Socialist policies of its predecessors, the Bourgeois Ministry, while pledged to defend private property and safeguard the existing social order, nevertheless pursued a policy of conciliation towards the Socialists and advocated, in its declaration of policy, a program of reforms which included proposals for progressive inheritance and income taxes and a broad system of workers' pensions.[24] Moreover, as gestures of friendship towards the Socialists, the Bourgeois Ministry reopened the Bourse du travail (Labor Exchange) in Paris which had been closed by the Dupuy Ministry and withdrew from the Senate a bill, introduced by the Ribot Ministry, which aimed at curbing the powers of labor unions.[25]

The Socialist Deputies, impressed by the conciliatory attitude of the Bourgeois Ministry and more than sympathetic to its reform program, joined the Radicals and a number of moderate republicans in forming a ministerial bloc in the Chamber. Gustave Rouanet, one of the prominent Independent members of the Union socialiste, set forth the policy of that group with respect to the new ministry

[23] *Journal officiel*, sessions of November 22, 1894, pp. 1952, 1968–1969, November 26, 1894, pp. 2038, 2042–2044, January 10, 1895, pp. 6–10, 15–16, May 20, 1895, pp. 1440–1442, 1458–1460, June 10, 1895, pp. 1641–1643, 1655–1657, June 29, 1895, pp. 1904–1910, 1919–1920, 1924–1927, October 24, 1895, pp. 2194–2203, October 25, 1895, pp. 2205–2212, October 26, 1895, pp. 2223–2226, 2238–2239. René Viviani, writing in the *Petite République* on July 11, 1894, declared that the anti-Anarchist laws were *lois scélérates* because "they deprive the defendants of the rights granted them by all civilizations, even the most barbarian."

[24] *Journal officiel*, session of November 4, 1895, pp. 2267–2268.

[25] André Daniel, *L'Année politique, 1896* (Paris, 1897), p. 7.

in an editorial in the Socialist newspaper, the *Petite République*, declaring that Premier Bourgeois could "count on our votes" as long as he endeavored "to carry out the positive engagements" contained in his declaration of policy: "These engagements are clear-cut. They consist of the substitution for the policy of reaction pursued until now by the preceding ministries of a policy of republican progress and the enactment of some of the social reforms on which there is complete agreement among democrats of all nuances."[26] And though they occasionally voted against the ministry (notably, against its colonial policy and its requests for military funds), the Socialists gave it unwavering support whenever its existence was threatened by a coalition of its opponents in the Chamber, in other words, the Right-Center and Rightist groups.[27]

A striking demonstration of this Socialist tactic occurred shortly after the Bourgeois Ministry took office. On November 14, 1895, in the course of the discussion of an interpellation on the general policy of the new ministry, a Rightist Deputy, Julien Dumas, demanded to know if the government intended to take the initiative in abrogating the *lois scélérates*. In his reply, Bourgeois stated flatly that the government had no such intention. He declared that while the government was opposed to these laws, which he characterized as only "temporary" legislation and as "contrary to the general principles" of the penal code, he did not believe that the public desired their abrogation.[28] Despite the fact they had waged a strong campaign for the repeal of the *lois scélérates* during the Dupuy and Ribot Ministries, the great majority of the Socialists, including Jaurès, Guesde, and Millerand, voted for a resolution approving Bourgeois's dec-

[26] November 7, 1895. See also Rouanet's article in the *Petite République*, November 16, 1895; and Jaurès's articles in the *Dépêche de Toulouse*, November 6, 21, December 4, 1895, January 15, April 8, 1896.

[27] *Journal officiel*, sessions of December 7, 1895, pp. 2769–2771, February 13, 1896, pp. 262–263, February 20, 1896, pp. 284–286, April 2, 1896, pp. 721–723. The Socialists refused to support the ministry's colonial policy and opposed its requests for military credits. See *Journal officiel*, sessions of April 2, 1896, p. 724, January 25, 1896, pp. 71–73, November 27, 1895, pp. 2568–2572, December 28, 1895, pp. 3085–3086, 3088–3089. See also the *Petite République*, April 28, 1896; and the *Parti Ouvrier*, April 11, 1896.

[28] *Journal officiel*, session of November 14, 1895, pp. 2341–2342, 2345.

laration. Viviani justified the conduct of the Socialist majority, stating that it had voted for the resolution in order to avoid a "trap" set by the "reactionaries" who were interested not in repealing the *lois scélérates*, but only in bringing about a split in the ministerial bloc in the Chamber and consequently the fall of the ministry.[29] Guesde declared that the Socialist Deputies had not desired the repeal of wicked laws at the cost of "putting wicked men in power."[30]

In May 1896, shortly after the Bourgeois Ministry left office, municipal elections were held throughout the country. As in the legislative elections of 1893, the Socialist factions — with the single exception of the Allemanists — collaborated closely, forming numerous alliances and coalitions. The Socialists registered new gains in the elections — winning a majority of seats in 150 municipal councils and a minority representation in 75 others; electing mayors in Marseilles, Lille, Roanne, and elsewhere; and polling a total of approximately 1,400,000 votes — more than twice the number obtained by the Socialist candidates in 1893.[31] To celebrate their victories, the Socialists held what came to be known as the "Saint-Mandé Banquet" in Paris on May 30, 1896. Present at the gathering were almost all the leading figures in the French Socialist movement, including Jaurès, Guesde, Millerand, Edouard Vaillant (the chief of the Blanquist party), as well as several hundred newly-elected municipal councilors and mayors. Of all the Socialist factions, only the Allemanists, who were at the time absorbed in an intraparty conflict (see page 25), did not participate.

At this victory celebration Millerand set forth a minimum Socialist program — the Saint-Mandé Program, it was subsequently called — which was to become the charter of the Union socialiste and later the basis for a union of all the Socialist forces. This speech was occasioned by a proposal concerning a point of electoral tactics that had been presented to the leaders of the Socialist factions rep-

[29] *Petite République*, November 16, 1895.
[30] *Petite République*, November 16, 1895.
[31] *Petite République*, February 29, March 3, 10, May 6, 7, 12, 1896; Adrian Veber, "Mouvement social en France et à l'étranger," *Revue socialiste*, 23: 755–757 (1896), 25: 232 (1897).

resented at the banquet. It had been suggested that in the coming legislative elections each faction run its own candidates at the first balloting but, in cases where a run-off election was required, that all support the Socialist candidate who had polled the most votes on the first ballot.[32] The question was then posed: what was the minimum program, whose acceptance was binding upon whoever claimed the title of Socialist? Millerand, chairman for the occasion, undertook to answer this question in his address.

According to him, the basis of modern Socialism, the *sine qua non* of a minimum Socialist program, was the doctrine of collectivism, of the progressive socialization of the means of production, exchange, and distribution. To Millerand this meant the transformation, not only of banks, the various means of transportation, and the mines, but also of all industries that were "incontestably ripe" for socialization. But to a "true" Socialist, this process of incorporating the great industries and monopolies (such as gas, light, and water) into "the body of socialized property" was to be a gradual one: "No Socialist has ever dreamed of transforming the capitalist regime by the stroke of a magic wand, nor of building up on a *tabula rasa* an entirely new society." To bring about the socialization of capitalist property, it was essential for the Socialists to win control of governmental power in commune, department, and state. This was to be achieved by a "majority with a purpose" relying on the ballot, not by a "rebel minority" resorting to force. "To begin, under conditions determined by the nature of things, the socialization of the means of production it is necessary and sufficient for the Socialist forces to endeavor to capture governmental power through universal suffrage." Finally, Millerand contended that Socialists were "internationalists" and sought to collaborate with the militant workers of other countries in the pursuit of common objectives. But, at the same time, Socialists were also "Frenchmen and patriots."

---

[32] Daniel, *L'Année politique*, 1896, pp. 208–209. According to French electoral procedure, if a candidate for the Chamber of Deputies failed to receive an absolute majority of the votes cast in the first balloting, a second ballot was taken for the two candidates who received the highest number of votes in the first. In the run-off election, a plurality was required for victory.

Patriots and internationalists, he noted, were two titles that "our ancestors of the French Revolution were able nobly to combine." And as for *La Patrie*, Socialists had never had "the unnatural and insane idea of destroying that incomparable instrument of material and moral progress, forged by the centuries, which is called the French fatherland."

In summary, the three points considered by Millerand "necsssary and sufficient to characterize a Socialist program" were: (1) the intervention of the state "to convert from capitalist into national property the different categories of the means of production and exchange in proportion as they become ripe for social appropriation"; (2) the conquest of governmental power through universal suffrage; and (3) the creation of an "international entente of the workers." He contended that it was the acceptance of this minimum program which would serve to identify a Socialist.[33]

Millerand's speech was well received. Guesde, Vaillant, and Jaurès, who, along with other Socialist leaders, followed Millerand in addressing the gathering, expressed approval of his remarks. Guesde enthusiastically offered toasts, first to the Union socialiste which he called the initial union of the different Socialist elements, a "union without conditions," and then to Millerand's address which, he declared, embodied the charter for a second union of the Socialist forces, a "union with conditions." Millerand, he concluded, "has indicated the necessary frontiers of a distinctly Socialist party."[34]

A few days after the banquet, the members of the Union socialiste accepted Millerand's statement of Socialist principles as their charter and the basis for parliamentary action. At a June 3 caucus of the group a resolution was approved which stated that, while the Socialist group would continue to work for the enactment of legislation aimed at ameliorating the conditions of the workers within

---

[33] For the text of Millerand's speech, see his *Le Socialisme réformiste français* (Paris, 1903), pp. 19–35. An English translation (abridged) is given in *Modern Socialism*, R. C. K. Ensor, ed. (New York, 1908), pp. 49–55.

[34] See the report of Guesde's speech in the *Petite République*, June 1, 1896. For a report of the speeches of Jaurès, Vaillant, and other leading Socialists, see the *Dépêche de Toulouse*, June 5, 1896.

the existing capitalist system, its ultimate objective was "to abolish the capitalist regime itself and to put an end to the exploitation of man by man, by means of the conquest of the governmental power by the proletariat, by the substitution of social property for capitalist property, and by the international entente of the workers." Guesde, Jaurès, Vaillant — in fact every Guesdist, Blanquist, Possibilist, and Independent Socialist who had attended the caucus — voted for this resolution. Only the Radical-Socialists and ex-Boulangists who had joined the Union socialiste soon after it was formed in 1893 refused to subscribe to collectivism and abstained from voting. To maintain group unity, the Independent Socialists proposed a second resolution which declared that the abstention of these members did not reflect on the necessity for the union "of all in parliamentary and political action . . ." This resolution was adopted unanimously.[35]

The approval accorded both resolutions by the Guesdists, their acceptance of the Saint-Mandé Program, which Lafargue was later to characterize as a program "that contained only radical ideas clad in Socialist phraseology,"[36] and their approval of collaboration with left-wing republicans and former Boulangists, who were, after all, bourgeois Deputies, clearly demonstrated that they had substantially modified and attenuated — if indeed they had not abandoned entirely — many of the revolutionary doctrines that they had expounded during the decade of the eighties. At that time the Guesdists had rejected without qualification such reformist notions as the gradual socialization of the means of production and exchange within the framework of the existing social order; the conquest of governmental power by peaceful, democratic means; and collaboration for purposes of political action with elements of the bourgeoisie. Nevertheless, by their unqualified support of the two resolutions the Guesdists had explicitly declared their adherence to these same notions.

[35] The text of the resolutions is given in the *Petite République*, June 5, 1896.

[36] *Petit Sou*, November 12, 1900. Lafargue, in a letter to Guesde (July 11, 1898), spoke contemptuously of "the three dogmas of the Gospel of Saint Mandé." Guesde Archives.

The retreat of the Guesdists from their early revolutionary ideology, a retreat rendered manifest by the conduct of the Guesdist Deputies, was a development of major importance in the history of the modern French Socialist movement. Why did the Guesdists, ostensibly exponents of orthodox Marxism in the eighties, definitely cease to be revolutionary Socialists in the nineties? Evidence seems to indicate that this retreat from orthodoxy, this drift toward reformism, was due in large measure to the active participation of the Guesdists in politics — participation not simply to propagate the party doctrines and recruit new members, but primarily to win political power. The taming, the domestication of the Guesdist party was one of the unanticipated consequences of its quest for votes and political offices.

The Guesdists had taken the initial step toward reformism in 1891. As was described (page 27), at the party's national congress at Lyons, the Guesdists, desiring to emulate the electoral successes of the Possibilists, had adopted a municipal reform program which they believed would win the votes of sections of the petite bourgeoisie (artisans and small merchants) as well as the urban proletariat. Encouraged by victories in the municipal elections of 1892, their first real electoral triumphs, the Guesdists had adopted a reform program designed to appeal to sections of the agrarian population. The Guesdist leadership, in adopting these programs, had been motivated by the desire to exploit to the fullest the opportunities which republican institutions offered for creating a mass social movement. In stressing legal political methods, in accepting the Republic as the institutional framework within which they were henceforth to function, the Guesdists had not intended to abandon extralegal methods of action in promoting the class struggle, nor had they intended to dilute their revolutionary ideology.[37]

What the Guesdist leadership did not anticipate was that their party would be influenced by the milieu, the structured political order within which it functioned. Gradually, almost without being aware of the process, these leaders, under the demands made by the

[37] See Guesde's articles in the *Socialiste*, December 26, 1891, March 13, May 15, September 25, 1892.

institutional structure of political democracy, in response to the day to day pressures of political action, modified the doctrine and objectives of their party.[38]

These modifications were many and varied. For example, the attitude of the Guesdists toward the state. In the eighties the Guesdists had conceived of the state as an instrument of power manipulated by the ruling bourgeois class to serve its own interests. "As long as the bourgeoisie shall exist," the *Socialiste*, had declared on June 19, 1886, "the governing class will be the bourgeois class. The state, whether it be called monarchy, empire, or republic, will serve the capitalists and crush the workers." Lafargue, in 1888, had asserted: "The state is a machine cleverly organized to serve the interests of the capitalists and to repress and enslave the proletarian mass." This bourgeois state would have to be smashed before a collectivist society could be realized.[39] Now, however, the Guesdists had come to view the existing state — that same bourgeois institution — as the instrument to be employed by Socialists in the pursuit of their goal; and they ceased to speak of the destruction of the state as a party objective.[40] This change of position was dictated by the logic of the situation. The adoption of specific reform programs by the Parti ouvrier français committed the Guesdists in their day to day activities to a policy of "gradualism," to the piecemeal reform of the existing social order, and thus to the acceptance of the bourgeois state as the essential instrument for social transformation. These programs were based on the tacit assumption that the Guesdist *élus*, upon their entrance into political office in the commune, department, and state, would utilize the governmental power *here and now* for the realization of social reforms. This policy implied the preservation and even the strengthening of the bourgeois state, of the bourgeois governmental power, rather than its destruction. In this

[38] This paragraph embodies ideas expounded by Professor Seymour M. Lipset in a lecture which he gave in a course in Political Sociology at Columbia University on December 7, 1950.

[39] *Socialiste*, January 21, 1888. See also the *Socialiste*, June 19, 1886, September 5, 1889.

[40] *Parti Ouvrier*, August 22–23, 1892, August 16–17, 1896.

instance, short-term objectives, immediate aims, involved the recession, if not the abandonment, of ultimate, long-range goals.

Other modifications involved the attitude of the Guesdist party on such questions as patriotism and the process by which the future Socialist order was to be realized. Regarding both matters, the pressure of electoral considerations forced the Guesdists to attenuate their former revolutionary stand. Their position on the question of patriotism had been stated rather succinctly in an editorial on the subject which appeared in the *Socialiste* in 1886: "*La Patrie* is today simply a word devoid of meaning. The workers, dispossessed of the soil and the instruments of production of their native land (factories, mines, banks, railways, mills, ships, and so forth), have only one *Patrie* — the social revolution, which will free them from the cosmopolitan exploitation of the capitalists. And this *Patrie* is not contained within the frontiers of one nation, but comprises all the workingmen of the universe." [41] But now that they were seeking to win the support of wide sections of the electorate, patriots as well as antipatriots, the Guesdists found it politically expedient to abandon this intransigent antipatriotism. Shortly before the general elections of 1893, the Guesdists declared that internationalism and patriotism were complementary rather than mutually exclusive ideals; and they identified themselves as loyal and patriotic Frenchmen. In a manifesto which appeared in June 1893, the National Council of the party denounced the "reactionaries" for their frequent assertions that the Socialists were indifferent to the "grandeur" and "destiny" of their country. It declared that the Guesdists wished to see France "great and strong" capable of defending her republican institutions against "the monarchist leagues" and, looking ahead, capable of maintaining the future "Social Republic" against a coalition of all the remaining capitalist countries of Europe if necessary. [42] And at the national congress of the Parti ouvrier français in that same year,

---

[41] March 13. See also Lafargue's articles in the *Socialiste*, August 20, October 15, 1887.

[42] See the text of the manifesto in the *Socialiste*, June 17, 1893. See also the *Socialiste*, May 27, June 10, September 9, 1893; and Conseil national du Parti ouvrier français, *Aux Travailleurs de France* (Paris, 1901), pp. 31–35, 45–46.

the delegates adopted a resolution written by Guesde himself which concluded: "But, not any more than working class solidarity excludes the right of workers to defend themselves against other workers who are traitors to their class *does international solidarity exclude or limit the right and duty of a nation to defend itself against any government whatever which betrays the peace of Europe. France, if attacked, would have no more zealous defenders than the Socialists of the Workers' party, convinced as they are of the great role which is reserved to France in the next social revolution.*" [43] Guesde's speeches in the Chamber of Deputies reiterated these views, stressing the patriotic sentiments of the Socialists and insisting that if France were attacked, the Socialists would place themselves in the avant-garde of the republican army. [44]

The stand of the Guesdists on the question of the method by which the transformation of the existing capitalist order into the future collectivist society was to be realized underwent a similar change. Up to about 1891, they had repudiated the notion of the reformist Socialists of the Possibilist variety that in a democratic state, universal suffrage could serve as the instrument for the emancipation of the proletariat, and they had contended that participation in legal political action was useful for purposes of propaganda and recruitment and as a means for ascertaining the strength of the party. During the eighties the Guesdists had expounded a clear-cut doctrine of class struggle, stressing the view that the transformation of the capitalist order into a collectivist society was to be achieved through revolutionary action, through the overthrow of the exist-

---

[43] The text is given in *Onzième Congrès national du Parti ouvrier, tenu à Paris du 7 au 9 octobre 1893* (Lille, 1893), p. 12. The emphasis is in the text. See also Weinstein, *Jean Jaurès*, pp. 66–68. In a speech which he delivered in Paris in July 1893, Guesde declared that his party was "the only truly patriotic party" in the country. *Petite République*, July 29, 1893.

[44] *Journal officiel*, sessions of June 15, 1896, p. 939, April 10, 1895, p. 1285, July 11, 1895, p. 2089, June 22, 1896, p. 1030, February 20, 1897, pp. 484–485. See also Lagardelle, pp. 185–188. In this connection it is noteworthy that when Guesde ran for re-election in 1898, one of the pieces of campaign literature used by his electoral committee was a sticker which was addressed to the "Patriotes de Roubaix et de Wattrelos" and which carried the following statement: "Voter pour Jules Guesde, c'est voter pour l'Alsace-Lorraine." Guesde Archives.

ing order by the force of arms.[45] Between 1892 and 1896, however, the Guesdists ceased to be ardent revolutionists. Having committed themselves to legal political activity, to the democratic process of seeking votes, the Guesdists were forced to trim their sails to the democratic winds. Like any other political party, the Guesdists had to attract a following and secure electoral majorities; this could hardly be done if the party were to continue to disparage democratic political methods. Thus, instead of appeals to revolution and class warfare, the Guesdists began to emphasize in glowing terms the value of universal suffrage as a means of capturing political power and of achieving the peaceful transformation of the existing social order. In their electoral manifestoes which, significantly enough, they now addressed to sections of the peasantry, to small merchants and artisans, as well as to the urban workers, the Guesdists called upon the voters to use the ballot as a legal weapon in the struggle against reaction and for the realization of the "Social Republic." [46] Immediately after his election to the Chamber of Deputies in 1893, Guesde issued a statement in which he declared: "Legally, by means of your will become law, the social transformation shall be accomplished." [47] In his speeches in the Chamber during 1894–1896, Guesde, as spokesman for his party, repudiated the idea of violent revolution, characterizing his organization as the "party of order and social peace" and the "party of reforms." He made it clear that, as long as the government respected the social reforms and the rights and liberties of the individual which had already been secured, the Socialists would continue to seek the realization of their programs through legal political processes. He asserted that universal suffrage rendered revolution "unnecessary"; that it was the unique instrument "for solving pacifically all questions." With supreme confidence, he told the Deputies that by means of universal suffrage

---

[45] *Citoyen*, October 1, 1881, January 4, 25, 1882; *Egalité*, November 5, 1882, February 11, 18, 23, 1885, February 11, March 1, 1889; the *Socialiste*, October 17, 31, December 19, 1885; Jules Guesde, *Le Socialisme au jour le jour* (Paris, 1899), pp. 341, 397, 423. See also above, pp. 17–18.

[46] The manifestoes are reprinted in *Aux Travailleurs de France*, pp. 18–19, 40, 44–45, 57, 59–62. See also the *Petite République*, April 6, 1894.

[47] *Petite République*, August 30, 1893. See also Lagardelle, pp. 171–174.

(*cette arme légale*) alone, the Socialists would before long win control of the government, and would then proceed to institute a collectivist society.[48] Other Guesdist leaders expressed similar views.[49] Thus, by 1897, the Guesdists, with respect to doctrine and tactics, had ceased to be revolutionists.

The Parti ouvrier français was not the only Socialist faction in France to turn away from its initial revolutionary beliefs during the 1890's. The Blanquist Comité révolutionnaire central also had attenuated its revolutionary ideology and adopted a conciliatory attitude toward existing social and political institutions. Like the Guesdists, whose lead they frequently followed and with whom they collaborated closely in the eighties and nineties, the Blanquists came to accept democratic institutions as the milieu within which they would function. They too sought to utilize to the greatest possible extent legal methods for the attainment of their objectives.[50] And, as in the case of the Guesdists, success at the polls in 1892 and 1893 aided the drift toward reformism. To improve their position in electoral contests, the Blanquists also adopted a municipal reform program and entered into electoral coalitions with other parties, non-Socialist as well as Socialist.[51] Blanquist approval of the Saint-Mandé Program pointed up, as it did in the case of the Guesdists, the extent to which they had come to terms with political democracy.

Parenthetically, it should be noted that this shift toward reformism by left-wing Socialists was not unique to the French Socialist

[48] *Journal officiel*, sessions of November 20, 1894, pp. 1911–1912, July 11, 1895, pp. 2088–2089, July 19, 1894, pp. 1393–1394, November 22, 1895, pp. 2466–2467, June 15, 1896, pp. 934, 939–940, June 25, 1896, pp. 1055, 1068. See also Jules Huret, *Enquête sur la question sociale en France* (Paris, 1897), pp. 361–362.

[49] *Petite République*, February 6, 1896; Gabriel Deville, *Socialism, Revolution, and Internationalism*, trans. Robert R. La Monte (New York, 1900), pp. 51–53, 57–59.

[50] Compare, for example, Vaillant's articles in the *Homme Libre*, June 25, August 20, 1888, and the *Cri du Peuple*, September 3, 1888, January 24, 31, 1889, with his later articles in the *Petite République*, July 3, 26, 1893, and the *Parti Socialiste*, September 10–17, 1893.

[51] For the text of the program, see the *Petite République*, February 3, 1896. See also the *Petite République*, August 31, September 1, 2, 3, 4, 1893, April 22, 1896; and the *Parti Socialiste*, September 3–10, 1893.

movement. Elsewhere in Europe where representative parliamentary institutions existed, the self-styled revolutionary Socialist parties tended increasingly to function as legal, reformist political organizations toward the close of the nineteenth century.[52]

The retreat of the Guesdists and Blanquists from revolutionary collectivism altered the relations among the various French Socialist factions. Their adoption of moderate reform programs and their acceptance of legal political action as the means *par excellence* for transforming the existing capitalist order narrowed considerably the gulf between the left- and right-wing sections of the Socialist movement. The significant distinctions between the Guesdists and Blanquists on the one hand and the Possibilists and Independent Socialists on the other, in terms of both doctrine and tactics, were becoming less and less marked. This trend toward conformity in views led, in turn, to a *rapprochement* between the diverse Socialist factions during 1891–1896.

This *rapprochement* was manifested in various ways. In political campaigns, for example, the Socialist factions entered into electoral coalitions with one another for the mutual support of their candidates. This form of collaboration, as has been noted, was common in the legislative elections of 1893 and in the municipal elections of 1896; and the agreement on electoral tactics arrived at by the leaders of the major Socialist factions at the Saint-Mandé celebration in May 1896 served to reinforce this trend toward unity on the level of political action. This tendency was also indicated by the formation in 1892 of the Fédération des conseillers municipaux socialistes de France et des colonies (Federation of Socialist Municipal Councilors of France and the Colonies). At congresses of the Fédération, held regularly until 1899, members of municipal councils and mayors who were adherents of the various Socialist factions met to discuss common problems relating to the administration of public office and to formulate practical reform projects dealing with such matters of general public concern as education and sanitation.[53]

[52] See G. D. H. Cole, *Socialism in Evolution* (Harmondsworth, England, 1938), pp. 47, 52, 161–163.
[53] Adrien Veber, "Mouvement social en France et à l'étranger," *Revue socialiste*,

The collaboration in the Chamber between the Socialist Deputies of all nuances during 1893–1897 greatly strengthened this trend toward unity. Although they did not arrive at a common understanding on many issues,[54] the Socialist Deputies in a single parliamentary bloc showed considerable cohesion and accord, uniting on vital matters; by that very fact they were able to exercise a significant influence in the Chamber. As has been shown, the Guesdist, Blanquist, Allemanist, Possibilist, and Independent Socialist Deputies joined forces to present a united front of vigorous opposition to the ministries of Dupuy, Casimir-Périer, and Ribot. They also worked together to maintain the Bourgeois Ministry in power. Moreover, Socialist Deputies gave united support to the bills and resolutions presented to the Chamber by members of the Union socialiste.[55] Rouanet, the Independent Socialist Deputy, explained the union of Socialists in the Chamber during this period: "Unity of thought and doctrine alone reigned in the discussions in which the members of the diverse factions took part. Spontaneously, under the fire of the enemy, Socialism drew up a united front of battle; and Jules Guesde, Vaillant, Jaurès, or Viviani could speak in the name of the Socialist forces without fear of disavowal." [56]

16: 358, 480–481 (1892); Rodolphe Simon, "Congrès des conseillers municipaux socialistes de France et des colonies," *Revue socialiste*, 22: 354–368 (1895); Adrien Veber, *Le Socialisme municipal* (Paris, 1908), p. 20.

[54] In this connection, see the rather detailed examinaton of the voting record (December 11, 1893 to March 29, 1897) of members of the Union socialiste in *La Vérité sur l'Union socialiste*, pp. 11–32.

[55] See the *Petite République*, November 20, 1893, January 15, February 10, October 26, 1894, July 12, 1897. See also Eugène-Melchior de Vogüé, "Explorations parlementaires," *Revue des deux mondes*, 125: 214 (1894); and André Liesse, "Les Travaux parlementaires de la Chambre des Députés, 1893–1894," *Journal des économistes*, 20: 4 (1894). The Socialist Deputies also maintained unity of action outside the Chamber, often appearing together at mass meetings and collaborating in political campaigns. In this connection, see the *Petite République*, December 13, 1893, June 22, December 29, 1894, October 20, 28, 1895, April 26, July 14, 1896.

[56] "Le Parti socialiste français en 1898," *Revue socialiste*, 28: 93 (1898). See also Jaurès's article in the *Dépêche de Toulouse*, January 24, 1894; Vaillant's article in the *Petite République*, October 20, 1894; Léon de Seilhac, "L'Organisation socialiste," *Revue politique et littéraire* (*Revue bleue*), 4: 558 (1895); J. Bourdeau, "Revue du mouvement socialiste," *Revue politique et parlementaire*, 12: 142 (1897); and Lagardelle, pp. 85–86.

Thus, as the result of the growing conformity of views and action among the several Socialist factions — a conformity brought about in large measure by the common pressures and exigencies of political life — the outlook for the unification of the French Socialist movement appeared brighter by 1897 than at any time since the schism of the first Post-Commune Socialist party in 1882. There remained, of course, certain distinctions of doctrine between the factions. But these were vaguely defined, and, at least in 1897, did not appear to Jaurès, Guesde, or any other Socialist leader to constitute insurmountable obstacles to the formation of a unified Socialist party.[57] It was to the task of bringing about this consolidation of the Socialist forces that these leaders now devoted their efforts. However, before much could be done in this direction, the Socialists were caught up in the agitation surrounding the Dreyfus Affair, which dominated the French political scene during the year 1898 and for some time thereafter.

[57] See the articles by Jaurès, Millerand, Vaillant, Guesde, Sembat, and Deville respectively in the *Petite République*, May 20, 22, September 13, 1897, *Almanach du Parti ouvrier pour 1896* (Lille, 1895), p. 15, and the *Petite République*, February 28, 1894, January 29, 1896.

Chapter 3

The Dreyfus Affair
and the Socialists

The Dreyfus Affair, world-wide *cause célèbre* which brought France almost to the brink of civil war, began in December 1894, when Alfred Dreyfus, an army officer, was tried by a Court Martial on a charge of having procured secret military documents for a foreign power (Germany), found guilty, and sentenced to military degradation and imprisonment for life. For a time after the condemnation of Dreyfus, sections of the French press, particularly Edouard Drumont's anti-Semitic newspaper, the *Libre Parole*, which made capital out of the fact that Dreyfus was a Jew, continued to play up the case; but the public soon lost interest, and it appeared that the matter was over and done with.

During the years 1896–1897, however, new evidence brought to light reawakened public interest. For one thing, the legality of the Court Martial procedure was impugned by the disclosure that Dreyfus had been convicted principally on the strength of certain evidence which had not been revealed to either him or his counsel — evidence which had been submitted to the judges in secret. Of far greater significance was the discovery, by Lieutenant Colonel Picquart, who had been appointed Chief of the Intelligence Branch of the French General Staff shortly after the Dreyfus conviction, that the author of the famous *bordereau* (a memorandum listing the secret documents allegedly procured by the traitor for Germany), the only definitely incriminating evidence presented at the Court Martial, was not Dreyfus (as the judges had believed), but Walsin-Esterhazy, a French army officer. Convinced that Esterhazy was guilty of the crime for which Dreyfus had been condemned, Picquart sought to have a retrial, or revision, of the case. But the General Staff was determined not to allow the case to be reopened, believing that to impugn the verdict of the Court Martial, hence, the guilt of Dreyfus, by instituting a retrial, would endanger the honor and prestige of the army. Picquart was summarily removed from his post, sent to Tunis, and told to keep the information concerning Esterhazy's implication to himself. The information leaked out, however, and when the Dreyfus family and others who believed in Dreyfus' innocence — such as Auguste Scheurer-Kestner, the highly esteemed First Vice-President of the Senate — demanded that the case be reopened, the General Staff was forced to act. In January 1898, Esterhazy was tried by a Court Martial but was acquitted.[1]

At the moment, when it appeared to all but the most stubborn Dreyfus supporters that all was lost, Emile Zola published (January 13, 1898) in the newspaper, *Aurore*, "J'accuse." This famous article, in the form of an open letter to Félix Faure, President of the French Republic, almost immediately made the Dreyfus Affair the paramount political issue of the day. After presenting the first complete exposé of the Affair to appear in the French press, Zola accused two ministers of war and several prominent members of the General Staff of having collaborated to bring about the conviction of Dreyfus by means of an irregular trial and on false evidence, and later of having concealed evidence which would have established his innocence. He accused the military authorities of having waged in certain newspapers "an abominable campaign" aimed at misleading the public and concealing the "errors" of the war office. Finally, Zola

[1] For the details of the Dreyfus Affair, see Armand Charpentier, *The Dreyfus Case*, trans. J. Lewis May (London, 1935); Alfred and Pierre Dreyfus, *The Dreyfus Case*, trans. and ed. Donald C. McKay (New Haven, 1937); and Guy Chapman, *The Dreyfus Case: A Reassessment* (New York, 1955).

accused the first Court Martial "of having violated the law by condemning an accused person on the strength of secret documents,"
and the Second Court Martial, "of having covered this illegality, in
obedience to orders, committing in turn the judicial crime of know-
ingly acquitting a guilty man." [2]

The publication of Zola's article created a sensation throughout
France, provoking new interest in the Affair, and causing large
sections of the public, hitherto indifferent, to take sides. Before long,
those who took an interest in the case were grouped in two opposing
camps. On the one side stood the Dreyfusards or "Revisionists"
(those who demanded a retrial of the case), on the other the Anti-
Dreyfusards or "Anti-Revisionists."

The ranks of the Dreyfusards were composed on the whole of
liberal intellectuals, Protestants, Jews, Freemasons, radicals of all
nuances, republican political leaders like Georges Clemenceau and
Paul Painlevé, and other Frenchmen who either were convinced
that Dreyfus was a victim of injustice or were opposed to the notion
that the military authorities were infallible. The Anti-Dreyfusard
camp consisted mainly of politically conservative Catholics and a
large part of the Catholic clergy, Anti-Semites, Monarchists, Nationalists, high-ranking army officers, and others who either were
convinced that Dreyfus was guilty of treason or were determined
to see to it that the honor and prestige of the army were maintained
at all costs. [3]

It was at the beginning of the crisis precipitated by the appearance
of Zola's article that an important section of the Socialist leadership
formally made known its stand on the Dreyfus Affair for the first
time. On January 19, 1898, the Socialist group of the Chamber of
Deputies issued a manifesto to the workers of the country calling
on them to abstain from taking sides in the struggle between the

[2] Zola's article is reprinted in *Le Procès Zola devant la Cour d'Assises de la Seine
et la Cour de Cassation, 7 février–23 février — 31 mars–2 avril 1898* (2 vols., Paris,
1898), I, 3–14. For an English translation, see Matthew Josephson, *Zola and His Time*
(New York, 1928), pp. 437–445.

[3] *Aurore*, January 14, 15, 16, 17, 18, 19, 20, 1898; Charles Seignobos, *L'Evolution
de la 3ᵉ République* (Paris, 1921), p. 197; Charpentier, *The Dreyfus Case*, pp. 144–
145.

Dreyfusards and the Anti-Dreyfusards. According to the manifesto, the Affair was essentially a conflict betwen rival bourgeois factions, the "Opportunists" and the "Clericals." The issue at stake in this conflict was not the guilt or innocence of Dreyfus — this was but a pretext. These bourgeois factions, the manifesto charged, were really fighting over the distribution of the "booty" obtained through the exploitation of the proletariat and the Republic by the capitalist class as a whole. On one side stood the Clericals who sought to exploit the conviction of Dreyfus in order to smear and discredit all Jews and with them "all Protestants and Freethinkers." If the Clericals were successful in whipping up an anti-Semitic campaign, they would be able to eliminate "all their rivals from the high judicial and administrative posts, from all high offices, ranks, and honors; and all France would be handed over, as booty, to the Clerical bourgeoisie." This was the tactic and objective of the Anti-Dreyfusard forces. On the other side stood the Jewish capitalists who, "after all the scandals which have discredited them, have need, in order to keep their part of the spoils, to rehabilitate themselves at least to some extent." If these were able to show that Dreyfus had been the victim of a judicial error and of public prejudice, they would obtain "through this direct rehabilitation of a member of their class — and in accord with their Opportunist allies — the indirect rehabilitation of all the *groupe judaïsant et panamisant.*" And just as the Clericals covered their "sorry lusts" with patriotic declarations and slogans, so the Opportunists and Jews sought to bring about their own "political and moral resurrection" by invoking "the sacred right of defense, the legal guarantees due all men." Hence, both Dreyfusards and Anti-Dreyfusards sought to dupe the public through lies and hypocrisy: "The Clericals lie when they call their shameful hunger for positions and stipends 'patriotism.' The Opportunists lie when they invoke, in order to save themselves, the rights of all men. . . ." The manifesto concluded by admonishing the workers to stand aloof from "this bourgeois civil war" between Dreyfusards and Anti-Dreyfusards, to repudiate anti-Semitism, and to carry on an incessant class war against the Clericals, the army chiefs, and the capitalists, both Jewish and Christian: "Unite and fight openly for the Social Republic against Dogma, Sabre, and Capital." Affixed to this arresting manifesto were the names of the Guesdist, Possibilist, Allemanist, Blanquist, and Independent Socialist Deputies in the Chamber.[4]

The united front of this section of the Socialist leadership on the Dreyfus Affair was soon broken, however, when Jaurès abandoned the position of rigid abstention advocated in the manifesto of the Socialist parliamentary group and identified himself with the Dreyfusard cause. At the very beginning of the Affair, Jaurès had believed that Dreyfus was without a shadow of doubt guilty of treason. Indeed, in a speech delivered in the Chamber of Deputies on December 24, 1894, he criticized the army for its relative leniency in punishing Dreyfus.[5] Two days later, in the newspaper, *Dépêche de Toulouse*, he stated that there was "absolutely nothing political" about the case: "Dreyfus handed over secret documents for money — that's all there is to it." The new evidence concerning the conduct of the first Court Martial, made public a few years later, led Jaurès, with others, to wonder if justice had really been done. Writing in the *Petite République* on November 27, 1897, he disclosed that he was no longer as certain as he had once been that Dreyfus was guilty, asserting that more light on the whole matter was necessary before the guilt or innocence of Dreyfus could definitely be established. Several days later, in the same newspaper, he declared that even though the Affair appeared to be little more than a family squabble between factions of the bourgeoisie, the proletariat should nevertheless follow it with interest. If Dreyfus had not received a fair trial, if his legal rights as a citizen had been violated as the Dreyfusards charged, then indeed the proletariat was concerned. "For the working class," Jaurès affirmed, "not only has for its mission the assumption of power and the creation of a more equitable social order, but it also should have, while awaiting the inevitable hour of social revolution, the mission of safeguarding all that is good and noble in *le patrimoine humain*." He then called upon the government to de-

[4] The text is given in the *Lanterne*, January 20, 1898.
[5] *Journal officiel*, session of December 24, 1894, pp. 2320–2322.

clare once and for all whether Dreyfus had or had not been convicted on the basis of secret documents.[6]

The appearance of Zola's "J'accuse" with its striking revelations and indictments inspired Jaurès to an even more serious interest in the Affair. Encouraged by Lucien Herr and Lucien Lévy-Bruhl, who were fellow *normaliens* and active Dreyfusards, he undertook a thorough study of all aspects of the case. He became convinced that Dreyfus had been irregularly and unjustly condemned. Moreover, he came to the conclusion that the Affair was not simply a struggle concerning the guilt or innocence of a single army officer, but a decisive struggle between the progressive forces of the country and the "military and clerical reaction"; between democrats who believed in the principles of the Declaration of the Rights of Man and antidemocrats who repudiated them; between the supporters and opponents of the Republic itself. Convinced that the triumph of the militarists and clericals in this struggle would result in the suppression of liberty and justice, the subordination of civil to military power, and the overthrow of republican institutions, Jaurès, in the spring of 1898 joined with the Dreyfusards in waging a vigorous campaign for a review of the Dreyfus trial and for the defense of the Republic.[7]

The response of the Socialists to Jaurès's conversion to *Dreyfusisme* was a mixed one. Most Possibilists and Allemanists followed his lead and joined the ranks of the Dreyfusards. As in the Boulanger crisis a decade earlier, the Possibilists were motivated principally by their desire to defend the Republic, while the Allemanists were prompted to identify themselves with the Dreyfusards in accordance with their principles of intransigent antimilitarism and anticlerical-

---

[6] *Petite République*, December 11, 1897. See also Jaurès's article in the *Dépêche de Toulouse*, January 13, 1898.

[7] See articles by Jaurès in the *Lanterne*, January 20, 21, 22, February 10, 13, 18, 20, 1898; the *Dépêche de Toulouse*, January 22, 28, February 16, March 10, June 29, 1898; and the *Petite République*, January 22, February 12, 19, May 17, June 7, 1898. See also *Journal officiel*, sessions of January 22, 1898, pp. 159–160; January 24, 1898, pp. 161–165; Paul Fesch, ed., *L'Année sociale en France et à l'étranger 1898* (Paris, 1899), pp. 20–21; and Léon Blum, *Souvenirs sur l'Affaire* (Paris, 1935), p. 28.

ism.[8] Jaurès's adherence to the Dreyfusard cause, however, created division within his own faction, the Independent Socialists. The majority of the rank and file of the Independents, sharing his concern over the growing threat of the Anti-Dreyfusard militarists to civil liberties, enlisted in the Dreyfusard army; but a number of leading Independents refused to follow suit. For one thing, some of them, like Gabriel Deville (the former Guesdist) and Georges Renard, were not at all certain, despite the revelations of Zola, that Dreyfus had not received a fair trial; for them his guilt or innocence remained an open question. Other Independent Socialists, like Millerand, did not consider it politically expedient to become involved in the controversy, apparently believing that if they were to identify themselves with the Dreyfusard cause, which was an unpopular one in the spring of 1898, they might compromise their chances for success in the approaching general elections.[9] On the basis of considerations such as these, both groups of Independent Socialists maintained for some time a position of neutrality in the struggle between the Dreyfusard and Anti-Dreyfusard forces.

Jaurès's conversion also failed to sway the majority of the Guesdists and Blanquists, and both parties continued to pursue a policy of non-intervention. Although Guesde, Vaillant, and other party leaders personally agreed with Jaurès that Dreyfus was innocent and applauded his efforts on behalf of justice, they nevertheless admonished their followers to stand aloof from the controversy. This official policy of abstention was justified on the basis of the arguments which had been set forth in the manifesto of the Socialist parliamentary group.[10] Not all Guesdists and Blanquists, however,

[8] See Humbert, *Les Possibilistes*, pp. 78–79; the manifesto on the Dreyfus Affair of the Union fédérative du centre of the Allemanist party in the *Lanterne*, January 22, 1898; Allemane's article in the *Parti Ouvrier*, February 26, 1898; and the report of an interview with Allemane in *Aurore*, March 20, 1898. See also the *Parti Ouvrier*, February 5, 12, 1898; and Charnay, *Les Allemanistes*, pp. 95–101.

[9] See the *Petite République*, January 24, 25, 26, 28, February 16, 20, 24, March 6, 1898; *Aurore*, July 15, 1898; the *Lanterne*, July 9, 1898; Gabriel Deville, "L'Affaire Dreyfus et le Parti socialiste," *Devenir social*, 4: 786 (1898); and J.-B. Séverac, "Der Fall Dreyfus und die französischen Sozialisten," *Sozialistische Monatshefte*, 3: 351 (1899). See also Zévaès, *Sur l'Ecran politique*, p. 272.

[10] *Petite République*, February 5, 17, 1898. See also Alexandre Zévaès,"Jules

followed this policy. Some members of both parties joined the Dreyfusard camp, while a few Blanquists, motivated perhaps by much
the same patriotic sentiments that had led members of their party to
support General Boulanger a decade earlier, identified themselves
with the Anti-Dreyfusards.[11]

Despite the divisions within their ranks over the Dreyfus Affair,
the various Socialist factions collaborated rather closely in the general elections which took place in May 1898. As in the 1893 elections, the factions often supported coalition candidates. This collaboration was facilitated by the fact that the great majority of the
Socialist candidates campaigned on similar programs. Not one of
the factions took an official stand on the question of reopening the
Dreyfus case, and only a few Socialist candidates made this an
electoral issue. The elections registered an increase in Socialist
strength. Socialist candidates of all factions received approximately
800,000 votes, roughly 200,000 more than in 1893. Forty-two Socialists, five more than in 1893, were elected Deputies: twenty Independent Socialists, ten Guesdists, eight Blanquists, two Allemanists,
and two members of the Alliance communiste révolutionnaire faction (see page 25). On the debit side of the ledger there were these
entries: the Possibilist party failed to win a single seat in the Chamber, and two of the leading figures in the Socialist movement, Jaurès
and Guesde, failed to retain theirs. Both were defeated by candidates
who had the strong support of Nationalists and conservative Republicans.[12]

Guesde et Jean Jaurès," *Revue de Paris*, 4: 93 (1936); and Zévaès, "L'Affaire Dreyfus:
quelques souvenirs personnels," *Nouvelle Revue*, 141: 105–106 (1936).

[11] See Jean Longuet's article in *Aurore*, August 8, 1898; G. Rouanet, "La Crise du
Parti socialiste," *Revue socialiste*, 30: 212 (1899); and J. Bourdeau, "Revue du mouvement socialiste," *Revue politique et parlementaire*, 18: 437 (1898).

[12] *Petite République*, May 5, 10, 11, 12, 18, 20, 24, 25, 28, 1898; *Aurore*, May 11,
12, 1898; Marcel Fournier, "Après les élections générales: situation des partis et
direction politique," *Revue politique et parlementaire*, 16: 491–493 (1898). See also
Alexandre Zévaès, *L'Affaire Dreyfus* (Paris, 1931), pp. 121–122. The following Social-
ists were elected Deputies: Gaëtan Albert-Poulain, Basly, Boyer, Calvinhac, Chassaing,
Pierre Colliard, Marius Devèze, Eugène Fournière, Grousset, Charles Gras, Hugues,
Jourde, Labussière, Millerand, Paul Narbonne, Henri Palix, Renou, Rouanet, Vaux,
Viviani (Independent Socialists); Jean Bénézech, Bernard Cadenat, Maximilien Car-

During the summer of 1898 the Dreyfus Affair monopolized public interest, while within the ranks of the Socialists debate over it became more intense. The Guesdists and Blanquists, who had hitherto taken little interest in the matter, began an active campaign to frustrate and counteract the efforts of Jaurès and other leading Socialists to win the workers to the Dreyfusard cause. The leaders of the Guesdist and Blanquist factions were convinced that the success of these efforts which was becoming increasingly apparent during the summer of 1898, could serve only to distract the workers from what they believed to be the pressing, indispensable task of creating a strong, disciplined, working-class party. Believing also that the growing collaboration of workers and progressive elements of the bourgeoisie in support of Dreyfus would result in the total negation of the idea of class struggle, they undertook to discredit his cause and impress upon the workers the need for rigid abstention.

On July 24, the National Council of the Guesdist Parti ouvrier français issued a manifesto cautioning the workers not to take sides in the conflict between the Dreyfusards and Anti-Dreyfusards — "both equally enemies of our class and of Socialism." This conflict, the manifesto reiterated, was a quarrel of rival bourgeois factions that did not concern the proletariat. Why should the workers, it queried, trouble themselves about the fate of a rich army officer who was, after all, a member of the privileged bourgeois class — the class that ruthlessly exploited the proletariat? And what was the significance of the injustice suffered by a single officer as compared with the injustices suffered by the "millions who constituted the working class?" The workers had their own interests to look after. They were obliged to seek justice not for an individual, but for their class. It was their duty to struggle unceasingly for the abolition of the social

---

naud, Jacques Dufour, Prosper Ferrero, Philippe Krauss, Hégésippe Légitimus, Ulysse Pastre, Sauvanet, Zévaès (Guesdists); Maurice Allard, Jules-Louis Breton, Chauvière, Coutant, Stéphane Létang, Sembat, Vaillant, Walter (Blanquists); Lamendin, Jean Lassalle (Allemanists); Dejeante, Groussier (Alliance communiste révolutionnaire). In February 1899, Joseph Ferroul, a Guesdist, was elected Deputy in a special election in Narbonne. This gave the Socialists forty-three seats in the Chamber. These Socialist Deputies alone comprised the membership of the Union socialiste when it was reconstituted shortly before the new Chamber was convened in June 1898.

and economic iniquities of which they were victims. And since this objective could only be realized by the concerted effort of the proletariat alone organized in a disciplined political party, it was incumbent upon the workers and Socialists in the present situation not to abandon even for a moment the all important "class struggle for the emancipation of labor and humanity" in order to save Dreyfus.[13] The Blanquist Parti socialiste révolutionnaire (formerly the Comité révolutionnaire central, the party label having been changed in June 1898), in a manifesto formulated by its Administrative Committee, likewise endeavored to impress upon the workers the need to stand aside from the struggle. It called upon them to rally around "the Socialist banner" and to devote their efforts to the crucial struggle for social emancipation.[14]

But hardly had the Guesdists and Blanquists begun their campaign to win the workers to a policy of rigorous abstention, when they found themselves under fire from Dreyfusard Socialists. This counterattack was spearheaded by Jaurès, who was now one of the recognized leaders of the Dreyfusard forces. To begin with, Jaurès took exception to the notion that the Dreyfus Affair concerned only the bourgeois class. It was true, he granted, in one respect it was a struggle for "the direction of the Republic" between two factions of the bourgeoisie. But the very fact that the bourgeoisie was divided was reason enough for the workers to intervene in the controversy, as it was to the advantage of the working class to capitalize on this division in order to press "the struggle against militarism and reac-

---

[13] The text is given in the *Socialiste*, July 24, 1898. In later years, Guesde denied that the manifesto had advocated a policy of abstention. In a public debate with Jaurès in Lille in November 1900 (reported in the *Petite République*, November 30, 1900), Guesde asserted that his party, in its manifesto, "recalled the workers to their class obligations, but did not advocate disinterestedness or abstention. The declaration stated unmistakably: 'Prepare yourselves to turn against the capitalist class and capitalist society the scandals of a military Panama joined to a financial Panama.' What we saw, in reality, in the Dreyfus Affair were the egregious disgraces which overtook and ruined the capitalist regime itself. In these scandals one had a new and powerful weapon with which one was able and with which one ought to strike the entire bourgeoisie, instead of immobilizing the proletariat behind a faction of the bourgeoisie. . ." Nevertheless, in the summer of 1898 the Guesdist manifesto was universally construed as advocating an abstentionist policy.

[14] The text is given in Zévaès, *Le Socialisme en France depuis 1871*, pp. 285–286.

tion." Yet the only way that the workers could do this was to "participate in a Socialist sense and for revolutionary ends in the struggle which one faction of the bourgeoisie was obliged to wage at the present time against militarism." Although the bourgeoisie under capitalism formed "a single conservative class," it was at the same time divided into rival factions. One of these factions, which comprised the ranks of the Anti-Dreyfusards, was identified with the old counterrevolutionary interests, while the other faction, the Dreyfusards, was still attached to the ideals of the French Revolution. If the Socialists and workers abstained from collaborating with the latter, they would, in reality, be giving aid and comfort to the counterrevolutionary bourgeoisie, which, "supported by the nobility, the army chiefs, and the clergy," would "get mastery over the bourgeois minority faithful to the spirit of the Revolution." [15]

Jaurès also challenged the view that the proletariat should have no interest in the fate of Dreyfus because he was an army officer and a member of the privileged bourgeois class. If Dreyfus had been condemned for a crime of which he was innocent, he was no longer either an officer or a member of the bourgeoisie. By the very extremity of his sufferings, he was "stripped of all class distinctions" becoming "humanity itself on the highest plane of despair and misery that it is possible to imagine." Since he had been condemned contrary to law, condemned falsely, it was ridiculous to still count him among the privileged. "He is no longer an officer of that army which, by a criminal error, has degraded him. He no longer belongs to those ruling classes which by the cowardice of their ambition hesitate to reestablish legality and truth on his behalf." Dreyfus had become an example of human suffering "in its most

[15] Jaurès, "Revue politique," *Revue socialiste*, 28: 387 (1898). In the Lille debate referred to above, Jaurès declared: "Society is today divided into capitalists and proletarians. But at the same time it is menaced by the aggressive revival of all the forces of the past — by the aggressive revival of feudal barbarism, by the whole power of the Church — and it is the duty of the Socialists, when the liberty of the Republic is in danger, when freedom of conscience is threatened, when old prejudices are being resurrected which revive once more the race hatreds and the atrocious feuds of centuries ago — it is the duty of the Socialist proletariat to march together with those factions of the bourgeoisie which have no wish to revert to the past." Jaurès's speech was published in the *Petite République*, November 29, 1900.

poignant form" and a living witness to "military lies, political cowardice, and to the crimes of the authorities." Whatever his class origin, he had become, as a consequence of his illegal condemnation by bourgeois society, "a bitter protest against this social order." Because this society persisted in its "criminal treatment" of him, Dreyfus had also become *un élément de Révolution*. Certainly, Jaurès insisted, the Socialists and workers could, without contradicting Socialist principles, without neglecting the class struggle, "listen to the dictates" of their pity: "We can, for all our revolutionary struggle, retain our sense of human compassion. We are not bound, for the sake of remaining inside Socialism, to place ourselves outside of humanity."

Finally, Jaurès maintained that by joining the ranks of the supporters of Dreyfus, the workers would not only be serving humanity and defending the cause of justice, but would be serving their own class interests as well. It was the proletariat that was most menaced by the "arbitrary action of the Generals" and by the "constantly glorified violence of military repression." It was, therefore, a matter of vital concern to the proletariat to see to it that the "illegalities" and "outrages" of the Court Martial were curbed once and for all before such practices became "a sort of custom accepted by everyone." It was of the utmost importance to the workers "to hasten the moral discredit and the fall of those high reactionary officers who are ready to shoot down the workers tomorrow." [16]

While this controversy was going on within the Socialist ranks,

[16] See Jaurès's article in the *Petite République*, August 10, 1898. His stand on the Dreyfus Affair was approved almost unanimously by the leadership of the international Socialist movement. In the summer and fall of 1899, the *Petite République* conducted a poll of leaders of the Socialist parties of Europe on the following question: "Is it possible for the Socialist proletariat to intervene in the conflicts between rival bourgeois factions, either to preserve political liberty, or, as in the Dreyfus Affair, to defend humanity, without abandoning the principle of the class struggle?" Of the thirty-one Socialists polled, including such leading figures as August Bebel, Karl Kautsky, Eduard Bernstein, Rosa Luxemburg, Wilhelm Liebknecht, George Plekhanov, Enrico Ferri, Henry Hyndman, and Tom Mann, only one — Liebknecht — opposed such intervention, contending that it did indeed constitute a violation of that principle. The responses were published in the *Petite République*, September 14, 16, 21, 22, 25, 26, 28, 29, October 3, 4, 5, 6, 11, 22, 28, 29, November 15, 19, 26, December 9, 31, 1899.

important developments in the Dreyfus Affair were taking place. On July 7, 1898 the Minister of War in Henri Brisson's Radical Cabinet, Godefroy Cavaignac, in a forthright speech delivered in the Chamber of Deputies, disclosed new evidence which he declared constituted absolute proof of Dreyfus's guilt. The principal piece of evidence which the Minister of War presented to the Chamber was an alleged code letter from the correspondence of the Italian and German Military Attachés in Paris in which reference was made to Dreyfus as the traitor. Cavaignac told the Chamber that he had considered "both the material and moral authenticity of this document" and had found them to be irrefutable.[17] The Deputies were so impressed by the speech of the Minister of War that they voted overwhelmingly to have it printed and placarded in every commune in France. The Anti-Dreyfusards were exultant. Again it appeared that the Affair was closed.

The leaders of the Dreyfusards, however, did not believe that their cause was lost. Instead of acknowledging defeat, they endeavored to discredit the new evidence by challenging its relevance and authenticity. In a series of cogently written articles which appeared in the *Petite République* in the summer of 1898, Jaurès undertook to prove that two of the three new documents cited by Cavaignac in no way served to incriminate Dreyfus and that the third, and principal piece of evidence, was a complete forgery. This document, in which Dreyfus's name appeared, had been concocted, Jaurès contended, by someone connected with the Ministry of War for the purpose of positively establishing his guilt, thus preventing a review of the case and protecting the honor of the army.[18]

Jaurès's contentions were dramatically and unexpectedly confirmed. On August 30, 1898, Lieutenant-Colonel Henry, head of the Intelligence Bureau of the General Staff, confessed that he forged

---

[17] *Journal officiel*, session of July 7, 1898, pp. 1956–1958, 1968–1969. Twenty-eight Socialists, including Boyer, Dufour, Millerand, Rouanet, Viviani, and Zévaès, voted with the majority.

[18] Jaurès, *Les Preuves* (Paris, 1898), pp. 174–226. This book is a collection of the articles on the Dreyfus Affair which Jaurès wrote for the *Petite République* in the summer of 1898. See also the report of an interview with Jaurès in *Aurore*, July 8, 1898.

the principal document cited by Cavaignac and was placed under arrest. The following day Henry was found dead in his cell, an apparent suicide. Henry's confession and death shocked the nation. Public opinion shifted rapidly in favor of the Dreyfusards, and the Brisson Ministry, taking cognizance of the new state of affairs, set in motion the legal procedure for review of the case by submitting (September 26th) an appeal of the decision of the 1894 Court Martial to the Court of Cassation, the highest court of appeal in France.

Despite this dramatic turn of events which made the triumph of the Dreyfusard cause appear inevitable, certain elements in the Anti-Dreyfusard camp refused to lower their standard. Some of their newspapers admitted that Henry's forgery rendered their position untenable and justified a reopening of the Dreyfus case. But other sections of the Anti-Dreyfusard press insisted that the forgery provided no new grounds for such action. Indeed, an attempt was made to justify the forgery and to represent Henry as a true patriot and national hero. Charles Maurras, the future leader of the Action Française movement, came forth with the story of the "patriotic forgery." According to Maurras, Henry had concocted his forgery as a substitute for certain authentic documents which positively identified Dreyfus as the traitor — documents which could not be made public without risking a war with Germany. In perpetrating his forgery, Henry acted as a true patriot, seeking to protect the honor of the army and save his country. Maurras's justification of Henry's activities was accepted without question by a great many extreme Nationalists, Anti-Semites, and Royalists.[19]

These elements now opposed the Dreyfusards with renewed vigor. A number of nationalist and anti-Semitic organizations were formed, including the old Ligue des patriotes, which was revived under the leadership of Paul Déroulède, "the Don Quixote of Nationalism," and the Ligue antisémitique de France. In the fall and winter of 1898 these groups held numerous mass meetings protesting the reopening of the Dreyfus case. Not all of the Anti-Dreyfusard agitation, however, took the form of such relatively peaceful public

[19] *Aurore*, September 2, 28, 1898; the *Lanterne*, September 2, 1898; Charpentier, *The Dreyfus Case*, p. 193; Zévaès, *L'Affaire Dreyfus*, p. 133.

demonstrations. With an aggressiveness and audacity born of desperation, bands of Nationalists and Anti-Semites roamed the streets of Paris and other cities and towns shouting their battle cries "Vive l'Armée!" and "Mort aux Juifs!" and breaking up the public meetings of the Ligue pour la défense des droits de l'homme et du citoyen, an organization which served to rally Dreyfusards around the democratic ideals of the French Revolution. Under the eyes of the police, who did little to curb their acts of intimidation and violence, it appeared that these bands were rapidly becoming masters of the streets.[20]

Just at this critical time a series of major strikes broke out which exacerbated an already tense and ominous situation. Late in September several thousand workers in the building trades in Paris went on strike. In a show of solidarity, thousands of workers in other trades joined the walkout. To strengthen the position of these strikers, the organization of railway employees decided to call a nation-wide strike. The government immediately took energetic measures to cope with these strikes which it believed threatened public order. Early in October, almost a complete army corps, mobilized from the neighboring departments, moved into Paris and took up positions on the main streets and boulevards. At the same time, troops occupied important railway stations and junctions throughout the country.

The presence of a large body of troops in Paris, the occupation of railway stations, the unrest and disorder created by the strikes, and the increasingly tumultuous demonstrations of the Anti-Dreyfusards in the streets served to excite public opinion and gave rise to widespread apprehension and alarm. Rumors spread throughout Paris like wildfire. It was alleged and widely believed that a *coup d'état* by army chiefs was imminent. According to one version, the Military Governor of Paris, General Zurlinden, and the Commandant of the Fourth Army Corps, General Mercier, were hatching a plot to overthrow the Republic and establish a military dictatorship. This *coup d'état* was to be brought about by having the troops in Paris provoke

[20] *Petite République*, September 15, 19, 20, 22, 27, October 4, 1898; *Aurore*, October 3, 8, 9, 1898; the *Lanterne*, October 4, 19, 27, 1898.

the strikers into committing acts of violence which would furnish the military with a pretext for taking over control of the government.[21]

To the mass of Socialists, whose distrust of the military was deep-rooted and traditional, these rumors appeared entirely credible. Convinced that the Republic was now more endangered by reactionary forces than at any time since its formation, they openly affirmed their allegiance to republican institutions and their determination to crush any attempt at a putsch. On October 13, the Socialist Deputies met at the Palais Bourbon and unanimously adopted a resolution protesting against "the state of siege" to which they charged Paris was "arbitrarily subjected," and they censured the government for moving troops into the capital.[22] Three days later, a Guesdist spokesman, writing in the party journal, called upon the Socialists to "redouble their vigilance" and to make it clear to all that they would not tolerate "the slightest aggression of the counter-revolutionaries, whoever they be." [23]

Many Socialists believed, however, that in the existing grave situation it was necessary to do more than just issue declarations. If the menace to the Republic were to be dealt with effectively, it was essential that all Socialist factions join to present a united front. Division and dissension were luxuries which they could no longer afford.[24]

Ironically, it was the Guesdist faction which took the lead in bringing about such a union. After having advised Socialists and workers to have nothing to do with the conflict between the Dreyfusards and the Anti-Dreyfusards, after having energetically opposed the efforts of Jaurès to rally the masses to the Dreyfusard cause, in the

---

[21] *Socialiste*, October 16, 23, 1898. See also *Aurore*, October 14, 15, 16, 25, 1898; the *Lanterne*, October 16, 1898; and Zévaès, "L'Affaire Dreyfus," *Nouvelle Revue*, 141: 200–201 (1936). In September and October 1898, German diplomatic circles in Paris also believed that a military *coup d'état* might take place. See Max J. Kohler, "Some New Light on the Dreyfus Case," in *Studies in Jewish Bibliography and Related Subjects in Memory of Abraham Solomon Freidus* (New York, 1929), p. 303.

[22] *Petite République*, October 15, 1898.

[23] *Socialiste*, October 16, 1898.

[24] See Léon Gérault-Richard's article in the *Petite République*, October 15, 1898.

fall of 1898 the Guesdist leaders became convinced that the Anti-Dreyfusard forces did constitute a real threat to civil liberties and the Republic, and they moved to abandon their policy of abstention. At their national congress, held at Montluçon in September, the Guesdists took a new position and adopted a resolution which opened the way for the collaboration of the party with the Dreyfusards. The party, the resolution declared, should use the Affair with its "military, judicial, and governmental scandals" for agitation in such a manner "as to complete the Socialist and revolutionary education of the proletariat." At the same time, the congress called for the formation of a permanent central organ to federate the various Socialist elements on the minimum basis provided by the Saint-Mandé Program. This organ, to be composed of representatives of these elements, was to meet whenever political developments demanded "a common decision or a unity of action" on the part of the Socialist forces.[25] It was this unity of action that the Guesdists leaders now sought to realize.

On October 14, the National Council of the Guesdist party summoned the Socialist Deputies, the representatives of the various Socialist organizations, and the directors of the Socialist newspapers, to a special meeting to consider steps to meet the present crisis. Socialist response to this call was favorable; and on October 16 an unprecedented meeting took place, with Jaurès as chairman. Following a brief convocation address by Guesde, in which he declared that the purpose of the meeting was "to give the country the impression of a Socialist party that was united and determined to face all eventualities," the delegates, representing every shade of Socialist opinion, decided to establish a Comité de vigilance (Vigilance Committee). The function of this Comité would be to examine the political situation and to recommend a common program of action with respect to it. Composed of two delegates from each of the organizations and newspapers represented at the meeting, it constituted a

[25] See the report of the congress in the *Socialiste*, September 18–25, 1898. In a letter to Guesde (September 27, 1898), Lafargue emphasized the propaganda value of the Dreyfus Affair, declaring that it would prove as "useful" to Socialism as the Panama scandal. Guesde Archives.

veritable "Who's Who" of French Socialism, including such notables as Allemane, Brousse, Guesde, Jaurès, Millerand, Vaillant, and Viviani. At the conclusion of the meeting, the delegates issued a manifesto which asserted that all the Socialists were now united and "prepared to face all eventualities." The Socialist forces "will not permit the militarist conspiracy to touch the too few republican liberties and will not leave the streets to reaction and its violences." It concluded with the declaration that, despite the faults and short-comings of "bourgeois governments," the Socialists believed that it was incumbent upon the workers "to defend the Republic." [26] This manifesto was published in all the Socialist journals and subsequently placarded throughout Paris.

It is noteworthy that in forming the Comité the delegates of the various Socialist organizations and journals had intended to create an organ concerned only with the existing crisis. Provisional in character, it was to be dissolved as soon as the crisis was over. Many Socialist leaders, however, desired a permanent central organ which would examine all questions of interest to Socialists;[27] less than a month after the formation of the Comité, a movement was under way to establish such an organization. Under the leadership of the Allemanists, representatives of the different Socialist factions held a series of meetings in November and December 1898 for the purpose of studying ways and means of bringing about a closer union of the nationally constituted Socialist organizations than that provided by the Comité. At the last of these meetings (December 11), the representatives decided by unanimous vote to dissolve the Comité and replace it with a new central organization, the Comité permanent de rapprochement socialiste (Permanent Committee for Socialist Reconciliation). According to its constitution, the chief objectives of the new organ were to facilitate joint action by the affiliated organizations and to work for the creation of a unified So-

<hr />

[26] See the *Socialiste*, October 23, 1898, for an account of the meeting and the text of the manifesto.

[27] *Petite République*, November 15, 17, 20, 29, 1898; the *Lanterne*, November 29, 1898; Albert Richard, "La Marche de l'esprit socialiste en France," *Revue politique et parlementaire*, 21: 50–51 (1899).

cialist party. The authority of the Comité permanent was circumscribed by the stipulations in its constitution which stated that it could not modify anything in "the internal operations of the affiliating organizations," and that these organizations were to be bound by their delegates on the Comité permanent only "to the direct extent to which the organizations will have authorized them." The Comité permanent was to be composed of seven delegates from each of the nationally constituted Socialist parties. The Independent Socialists were also to be represented on the Comité permanent as soon as they had organized themselves on a national level.[28]

In order to participate in the work of the Comité permanent, the great majority of the Independent Socialists, who hitherto either had been free of any group affiliation or had formed autonomous local units, immediately undertook to meet the membership requirement. On December 4, a number of them met in Paris to organize the Fédération des Groupes socialistes révolutionnaires indépendants (Federation of Independent Revolutionary Socialist Groups). At the same time the Independent Socialist Deputies and the Fédération républicaine socialiste de la Seine (Republican Socialist Federation of the Seine), the largest autonomous Independent Socialist group in France, took the lead in organizing the Fédération des Socialistes indépendants (Federation of Independent Socialists). The charters of both Independent Socialist organizations were based on the statement of principles set forth in the Saint-Mandé Program. A close relationship was soon established between the two national federations; and while the question of their merger was being considered, they were represented on the Comité permanent by a single group of delegates.[29]

The Comité permanent, which in December 1898 was renamed the Comité d'entente socialiste (Committee for Socialist Entente) began to function in January 1899; during the next six months it served as the central coordinating agency for Socialist action. The Comité d'entente socialiste was handicapped in its work to some

---

[28] *Petite République*, November 29, 1898.

[29] *Petite République*, December 3, 7, 1898, January 4, 1899; Orry, *Les Socialistes indépendants*, pp. 39-40.

extent by the fact that all decisions required the unanimous approval of the delegates of each of the five affiliated national organizations. Despite this encumbrance, which sometimes rendered its deliberations tedious and sterile, the committee, whose membership included Jaurès, Guesde, Vaillant, and Brousse, was able to realize to a great extent the purposes for which it had been formed. At Paris, Marseilles, Lyons, Grenoble, and elsewhere, the Comité d'entente socialiste organized public demonstrations at which speakers representing all the Socialist factions made common appeals for the defense of the Republic.[30] The most significant effort of this kind which it undertook was the great mass demonstration of Socialist and republican forces at Longchamps in June 1899, following the assault upon President Loubet by a Royalist. The success of the Comité d'entente socialiste in promoting unity of action by the Socialist forces was also indicated by the fact that for the first time, all the Socialist factions marched together in the 1899 May Day celebration.

The *rapprochement* between these factions led many to believe that the time was ripe for the formation of a unified Socialist party. By the spring of 1899 a movement led by Jaurès, to convoke a congress of all Socialist organizations for this purpose, was well under way. In an arresting article which appeared in the first issue (January 1899) of the *Mouvement socialiste*, a bimonthly journal edited by Hubert Lagardelle, a recent recruit to the Socialist ranks, Jaurès argued the case for Socialist unity. He declared that the movement toward the merger of the Socialist forces was "irresistible," that the continued existence of autonomous Socialist "sects" and parties could no longer be justified, and that the formation of a single party similar to the Socialist parties in Germany and Belgium should be realized as soon as possible.

The movement toward unity, Jaurès asserted, had been clearly manifested in the formation of the Socialist parliamentary group, the Union socialiste, in the Chamber of Deputies in 1893, in the

---

[30] For the activities of the Comité, see the *Petite République*, January 17, February 7, 21, March 7, 8, 14, 22, May 3, 30, 1899; Zévaès, *L'Affaire Dreyfus*, pp. 142-143, n.; and Paul Dramas, "La Politique en France," *Mouvement socialiste*, 1: 607 (1899).

acceptance of the Saint-Mandé Program by the great majority of Socialists three years later, and in the recent formation of the provisional Comité de vigilance, and its successor, the Comité d'entente socialiste. Each of these developments marked an advance toward the ultimate objective — "the complete and manifest unification of the Socialist movement." Jaurès pointed out that the existing Socialist factions represented "a period or an aspect of Socialist action" and that they had at one time made important contributions to the Socialist movement. But, just as these factions "represented historical forces, historical moments," so the movement "which today brings them together and which tomorrow will unify them is also an historical force."

Jaurès took exception to the view that unity would result in complete uniformity with respect to doctrine and tactics and the total abolition of organizational autonomy within the framework of a centralized party. He believed that the projected party would embody the "rich traditions" of French Socialism and would "harmonize" all the various elements of the Socialist movement. "Like the child whose complex physiognomy reflects a multiple ancestry, unified French Socialism will express the diverse traditions out of which it has emerged." Indeed, the very "diversity of its origins" and the "great variety of its constituent elements," would oblige the unified party "to allow the most liberal expression of all it forces." In the projected party there would be "harmony, not annihilation or uniformity."

The formation of a single party, he maintained, would greatly increase the strength and influence of the Socialist movement. In the face of the "growing disorganization of all authority" the Socialists would be able to "stand together, visibly united." Moreover, the formation of such a party would enable the Socialists to deal more satisfactorily with the multitude of problems which contemporary political and social developments were incessantly creating. It was no longer possible for them merely to repeat "two or three elementary formulas in order to resolve all problems." The adaptation of these formulas to the course of events, "their incessant confrontation with the facts," required "a constant vigilance of thought." To cope successfully with the countless issues "so diverse, so pressing, so vast," posed for the Socialists by events, which they were obliged to resolve "under pain of disgrace," it was necessary that "all the active forces of Socialism and of the proletariat be summoned together for deliberation" at national congresses. At these gatherings "all questions of doctrine, method, and tactic which are of immediate interest to Socialism — that is to say, to humanity itself — would be openly discussed." And, in addition to enabling the Socialists to deal effectively with immediate problems, these convocations would also prepare "the revolutionary proletariat for its great future role." It was, therefore, a necessity for the Socialists to "bring about the creation of a unified party and the organization of periodic national congresses."

To realize these objectives, Jaurès proposed that the Comité d'entente socialiste, convoke a congress of all Socialist forces. Socialist unity of spirit and action already existed; all that was needed was an organization to express it. He concluded by recalling the fact that to French Socialists had been delegated the task of organizing the next congress of the Socialist and Labor International, which was to be held in Paris in 1900, and he urged the various French Socialist elements to give that congress "the spectacle of perfect harmony" — to present it with a unified party.[31]

The fact that Jaurès could speak of the formation of a united party as an imminent possibility was a significant indication of the extent of the confluence of the diverse Socialist forces in the course of several months. In July 1898, division on the Dreyfus Affair had definitely impeded the Socialist unity movement which up to that time had been gaining ground. The confession of Colonel Henry in August and the rise of the antirepublican menace in the fall put an end to this division and brought about a united front of Socialist forces in defense of civil liberties and the Republic. Thus, the Drey-

[31] "L'Unité socialiste," *Mouvement socialiste*, 1: 6–15 (1899). For other articles by Jaurès on the unification of the Socialist movement, see the *Dépêche de Toulouse*, May 22, 1898, and the *Petite République*, June 3, 4, 7, 14, 30, July 23, 1898. See also the report in the *Petite République*, June 8, 1898, of the speech on this subject which Jaurès delivered at a mass meeting of Socialists in Tivoli-Vaux Hall (Paris) in June 1898.

fus Affair — which at first had split the Socialists into Dreyfusards and abstentionists — had, by the beginning of 1899, served to bring about a closer alliance than had ever existed before. This was the most important effect of the Dreyfus Affair on French Socialism.

The Dreyfus Affair had at least two other important effects on the Socialist movement. For one thing, the political and social crisis associated with the Affair, particularly in the summer and fall of 1898, forced the Socialists to think and act realistically — to consider the actual facts of the situation, rather than rely on a few preconceived Socialist formulas. As Jaurès pointed out in his article on Socialist unity, there was a tendency in some sections, particularly among the Guesdists and Blanquists, to interpret all political and social developments in terms of a limited number of elementary formulas, to fit these developments into a few set categories. Thus, the same formulas, the same categories were applied to all situations almost without modification. Slogans and catch phrases were more often than not substituted for a thorough study and analysis of the facts themselves. The Dreyfus Affair drove home to many Socialists the fact that life was infinitely more complex than the categories of the Guesdists or Blanquists seemed to indicate. It made them aware that, as Lagardelle put it, "the movement of history did not resemble a chain of theorems." [32] The concept of class struggle as expounded by the Guesdists and Blanquists is a case in point. Until the confession and death of Colonel Henry, both factions had admonished their followers to abstain from taking sides in the conflict between the Dreyfusards and Anti-Dreyfusards. As justification for this stand, they had argued that the two camps were composed of members of the bourgeoisie and thus equally enemies of the proletariat and of Socialism. It was not until the menace to the Republic from the extreme Right became too evident to be ignored by anyone that the Guesdists and Blanquists modified their notion of what class struggle really meant and joined with the Dreyfusard Socialists and republicans, even though the latter were members of the hated bourgeois class. Truly, as Lagardelle declared, "In the Dreyfus

[32] Hubert Lagardelle, "Le Socialisme et l'Affair Dreyfus," *Mouvement socialiste*, 1: 297 (1899).

Affair, formulas ran up against the facts and the formulas flew to pieces." [33]

It should not be assumed that as a consequence of the Affair all intransigent Socialist formulas and slogans were abandoned. A number of Socialists, particularly the members of the old guard, continued to repeat the old formulas. Yet the Affair initiated the process of educating the more indoctrinated Socialist elements to the complexity of the realities of political and social life and the constant need for fitting formulas to life rather than the reverse. In brief, it led many Socialists to reconsider the validity and applicability of some of their basic doctrinal and tactical conceptions in the light of actual historical developments.

The Affair influenced the Socialist movement in another respect in that it strengthened and broadened it by bringing many new recruits into the ranks. The strong stand of the Socialists in defense of civil liberties and the Republic attracted many who hitherto had taken little interest in politics, much less Socialism. Conversions occurred among the bourgeoisie as well as the working class. One historian has observed: "Thousands of younger aesthetes and scholars — students whose lives had seemed to have no meaning, whose sensibilities and interests seemed to lack any connection with the social world — found themselves during the Affair, and became first Dreyfusards, then Socialists." [34] Although a large number of these recruits abandoned the Socialist movement during the years immediately following the Affair, a good many retained their affiliation and, like the recruits Léon Blum and Francis de Pressensé, came to play a significant part in the development of contemporary French Socialism.

The person responsible for winning many of these converts to Socialism during the Affair was Jaurès. He, perhaps more than anyone else, had identified the Affair as a crucial struggle for human rights and republican institutions, as an all-out battle between progressive and reactionary forces for control of the state. It was his linking of Socialism with the welfare of all humanity, his eloquent

[33] Lagardelle, p. 297.
[34] Jackson, *Jean Jaurès*, p. 82.

defense of truth and justice, his courageous campaign of public meetings, and his cogent, stimulating articles which had exercised a
powerful, if not decisive, influence on public opinion. These had
won, for him and for the Dreyfusard and Socialist movements, the
allegiance of the mass of workers and of sections of the younger
generation of bourgeois intellectuals. They hailed Jaurès as leader,
teacher, and prophet.[35]

The entry of these recruits gave a strong impetus to the campaign
for the formation of a unified Socialist party. Full of enthusiasm for
their new-found faith, anxious to see an end to the dissipation of
strength that was a consequence of division and factional bickering
within the movement, they gave full support to the drive for the
convocation of a congress of all the Socialist forces. However, in the
late spring of 1899, while this unity movement was gaining ground
and plans for a congress were being formulated, the Socialist forces
were confronted with a crisis of unprecedented severity. This crisis
not only caused the miscarriage of the unity movement, but also
created divisions within the Socialist ranks that were to delay for
years the formation of a unified party.

[35] See Albert Léon Guérard, *French Civilization in the Nineteenth Century* (New
York, 1914), p. 208; Jackson, pp. 81–82; and Hubert Bourgin, *De Jaurès à Léon
Blum, l'Ecole Normale et la politique* (Paris, 1938), p. 190.

Chapter 4

The Millerand Case

The most critical phase of the Dreyfus Affair, the period during which the assault of the forces of reaction on republican institutions in France reached its height, began in the late spring of 1899. That June the Court of Cassation, which for several months had been considering the question of reopening the Dreyfus case, finally announced its decision. By unanimous vote the Court annulled the sentence of condemnation given against Dreyfus by the Court Martial in December 1894 and ordered a retrial of the case.

The Court's decision served to heighten partisan passions. The extreme Nationalists and their allies were infuriated, and their agitation grew more violent than ever. As soon as the judgment of the Court became known, streets in Paris were invaded by bands of Nationalists, Royalists, and Anti-Semites who demonstrated against the judgment, which they denounced as an insult to the honor of the army, and against the Court itself, which they condemned as a "tool" of the "Jewish Syndicat" and other "betrayers" of France. Some Anti-Dreyfusard newspapers openly called for action by the army against the government. Drumont, writing in the *Libre Parole*, declared that an army that did not know how to defend its honor against "a band of Jews" certainly would not know how to defend the country againse a foreign invasion. Paul de Cassagnac, a prominent Nationalist, expressed similar sentiments in his newspaper *Autorité*, promising his readers that the army would

have the last word in the matter.[1] The partisans of disorder, however, did not confine their agitation to verbal remonstrations. On
June 4, the day following the announcement of the Court of Cassation's judgment, the President of the Republic, Emile Loubet, was
assaulted by a Royalist, Baron de Christiani, who struck him with
a cane.

The assault on President Loubet, known for his staunch republicanism and Dreyfusard sympathies, pointed up most dramatically
the aggressive character of the antirepublican elements and led the
Socialists and republicans of all shades of opinion to form a closer
union than had existed hitherto. On June 5, members of the Moderate Republican, Radical, Radical-Socialist, and Socialist groups in
the Chamber of Deputies sent a letter of condolence to Loubet, expressing their "absolute devotion to republican institutions." At the
same time representatives of these groups, together with representatives of the republican groups in the Senate, organized a committee
to coordinate the activities of the republican forces in both Cham-
bers.[2]

This working alliance of Socialists and republicans for the purpose of defending republican institutions was also manifested outside the Palais Bourbon. The Comité d'entente socialiste joined with
a number of republican groups of Paris to stage a mass demonstration in reply to the attack on President Loubet at Auteuil. On June
11 more than a hundred thousand Parisians marched in formation
to the Longchamps racecourse where they acclaimed Loubet, who
was present, with cries of "Vive le Président!" and "Vive la République!" The Dupuy Ministry, determined to prevent disorder,
had sent a large contingent of troops and police (two regiments of
infantry, twenty squadrons of cavalry, and several hundred special
guards) to Longchamps. This display of armed force, which the
demonstrators construed as an attempt on the part of the government to intimidate them, provoked rather than prevented disorder;

[1] Joseph Reinach, *Histoire de l'Affaire Dreyfus* (7 vols., Paris, 1901–1911), V, 110.
See also André Daniel, *L'Année politique, 1899* (Paris, 1900), p. 203.
[2] *Petite République*, June 4, 7, 1899; Daniel, p. 214.

and before the demonstration ended, several clashes occurred between police and crowds.[3]

The following day, in the Chamber of Deputies, Vaillant, in the name of the Socialist parliamentary group, interpellated the government on "the violence of the police against the Republicans and Socialists" at the Longchamps demonstration. Vaillant denounced the Parisian police for their "brutality" and "antirepublican sentiments," asserting that, while they showed considerable "gentleness and kindness" in dealing with those who endangered the Republic, the police, in the streets of Paris and at the Longchamps racecourse, "brutally assaulted" the Socialists — "the true defenders of the Republic." It was imperative, Vaillant concluded, that the Ministry inform the country whether the police were henceforth to protect the Republic "against the conspirators of reaction" or were to be at the disposal of these conspirators for use against the supporters and defenders of the Republic.[4] In his brief response, Dupuy declared his complete satisfaction with the conduct of the Parisian police and asked for a vote of confidence. Instead of complying with his request, the Chamber approved a resolution declaring that it would only support a ministry "determined to defend energetically republican institutions and to maintain public order."[5] The Dupuy Ministry thereupon resigned.

The fall of the Dupuy Ministry initiated a major ministerial crisis, perhaps the most momentous since the establishment of the Third Republic. For a period of ten days thereafter, while political unrest increased and the Nationalists and their allies spoke openly of a *coup d'état*, President Loubet sought desperately to find a parliamentary leader capable of forming a ministry. On June 13 he called on Raymond Poincaré to make an attempt, but after six days of fruitless negotiations the latter gave up. Loubet then entrusted René Waldeck-Rousseau, a *Progressiste* (conservative Republican) and former colleague of Gambetta and Ferry, with the mission. Convinced that the very existence of the Republic was at stake and that

[3] *Socialiste*, June 18, 25, 1899; Daniel, pp. 215–216.
[4] *Journal officiel*, session of June 12, 1899, pp. 1640–1642.
[5] *Journal officiel*, p. 1648.

only a coalition cabinet of the parties of the Left could cope successfully with the antirepublican menace, Waldeck-Rousseau undertook
to form a "ministry of republican defense" which would include a
representative of the Socialist group in the Chamber.

Once he had decided on this tactic, it was not surprising that
Waldeck-Rousseau should have selected Alexandre Millerand for a
portfolio. Millerand was the spokesman for the Socialist parliamentary group, now that Jaurès and Guesde were no longer in the
Chamber. Moreover, he was recognized as one of the leaders of the
reformist wing of the Socialist movement. Millerand's brand of Socialism, as embodied in his Saint-Mandé Program — generally
acknowledged as being one of the truly classic expressions of reformist Socialism — was of the most moderate variety. Waldeck-Rousseau
could hardly have selected a member of the Socialist bloc with a less
"revolutionary" stance.[6]

Furthermore, Millerand was known to be favorably disposed
toward the notion of a coalition ministry composed of representatives of all the parties of the Left. In the late spring of 1899, when
a military *coup d'état* appeared to many to be imminent, he re-
peatedly called for a concentration of all Socialist and republican
elements. In the newspaper, the *Lanterne*, on June 4, he declared:
"This is not the time for recriminations . . . All the republican
forces ought to make a united front against the enemy." A few days
later he wrote: "All the republican forces express a common desire
. . . for unity." On June 16, in the midst of the ministerial crisis, he
pledged the support of the Socialist group to any republican coalition ministry that might be formed. "No one within the republican
ranks dreams of quibbling over the details of the declarations of
the politicians who will take power . . . No matter what the political label of the premier may be, the cabinet is certain to be supported by a unanimous republican party."[7] Millerand not only

---

[6] A lawyer by profession, Millerand began his political career as a Radical. A combined Radical and Socialist vote sent him to the Chamber of Deputies in 1885. In
1891, he declared himself a Socialist and identified himself with the Independent
faction. During the years 1893–1896, he edited the *Petite République*.

[7] All the quotations are taken from Zévaès, *Sur l'Ecran politique*, pp. 273–274.

wrote about the need and feasibility of a coalition ministry; he actively intervened in the course of the ministerial crisis in an effort to realize it. In June 1899, when President Loubet had called upon Poincaré to form a ministry, Millerand sought out Poincaré, informing him that, with the gravity of the situation, in the Socialist view, it was indispensable to appeal to all republican forces, including the Socialists, in the formation of a cabinet. Millerand then proposed that Poincaré offer a portfolio to a member of the Socialist parliamentary group. But Poincaré did not believe that the political situation warranted such a cabinet, and turned down this proposal.[8]

Waldeck-Rousseau, however, was prepared to see such a concentration; when he received a mandate to form a ministry, he entered into negotiations (June 18) with Millerand. But these negotiations had to be abandoned since his own party was opposed to the constitution of a ministry which would include a Socialist, even one as moderate and well-behaved as Millerand. On June 19, therefore, Waldeck-Rousseau informed Loubet that he was unable to form a ministry and resigned his mandate.[9] The ministerial crisis continued.

At a caucus of the Socialist parliamentary group on June 21, Millerand disclosed the fact, hitherto unknown to many, that he had been offered a post in a projected ministry, but that nothing had come of it as the negotiations had proved fruitless and the ministry had miscarried. He then put the following question to his colleagues: What would they think of his accepting such a post if another offer were made? In the discussion that followed, it appeared that none of the members of the group had any real objection to Millerand's acceptance of a future offer so long as it was clear that he was acting

---

In this connection, see also Millerand's statements in the *Lanterne*, October 19, 1898, February 11, 18, June 10, 11, 14, 15, 17, 18, 19, 20, 21, 1899.

[8] Poincaré disclosed this episode in a speech which he delivered at Nancy in May 1901. His speech was reported in the *Petit Sou*, May 14, 1901. See also Reinach, *Histoire*, V, 162–164.

[9] Daniel, pp. 221–222; Rudolph A. Winnacker, "The Influence of the Dreyfus Affair on the Political Development of France," *Papers of the Michigan Academy of Science, Arts and Letters*, 21; 473 (1935).

on his own responsibility and that his action did not involve the group in any formal manner. Bernard Cadenat, a Guesdist, wanted the group to take an official position on the question, arguing that, since it asserted that Millerand could accept a ministerial post, there was no reason why it should not adopt a resolution to that effect. If Millerand were to accept a post, he should do so with the approval of the Socialists. However, Vaillant and Marcel Sembat, also a Blanquist, believed that Millerand should act independently since there was no unified party which could sanction his acceptance of office in the name of all Socialists. Millerand then intervened, declaring that, since some of the members of the group preferred not to engage it officially, he would take upon himself full responsibility for accepting a future offer. This ended the discussion.[10]

In the light of subsequent developments, it is important to note that during this meeting nothing was said about Socialist doctrine. None of those present raised the fundamental question posed by Millerand's query — namely, whether a Socialist could participate in a bourgeois ministry without violating the principle of the class struggle. Alexandre Zévaès, who attended the caucus, has supplied what might be a partial explanation for the failure of the group to examine the issue of ministerial participation thoroughly. He observed that the offer of a portfolio to Millerand was viewed as "une chose rétrospective," a thing of the past, and that the participation of Millerand in a cabinet in the foreseeable future was believed by the Socialist Deputies to be "beyond all possibility." [11] In this instance, however, the ostensibly impossible occurred, and with disastrous consequences for the Socialist unity movement.

On the day after the caucus of the Socialist group, Waldeck-Rousseau, who had again undertaken to form a ministry, offered Millerand the post of Minister of Commerce and Industry. Without con-

---

[10] See the conflicting accounts of this caucus in Georg von Vollmar, "A Propos du cas Millerand," *Mouvement socialiste*, 5: 20–21 (1901); Vaillant, "L'Entrée de Millerand au ministère," *Mouvement socialiste*, 5: 204–207, 516–521 (1901); and Jaurès, "L'Entrée de Millerand au ministère," *Mouvement socialiste*, 5: 451–458 (1901). See also Vaillant's article in the *Petit Sou*, April 26, 1901.

[11] Zévaès p. 280. See also Vaillant, p. 205; and Lagardelle, "Sur l'Article de Kautsky," *Mouvement socialiste*, 4: 601 (1900).

sulting the Socialist parliamentary group or the Comité d'entente socialiste, he accepted it immediately. The following day Waldeck-Rousseau publicly announced his ministry of republican defense, which included, in addition to Millerand — the first Socialist ever to enter a ministry under the Third Republic — representatives of all the republican factions in the Chamber of Deputies and a General, the Marquis de Galliffet. Galliffet was famous for the part he had played in the suppression of the Paris Commune, and among Socialists and radicals generally, he was known as the "Butcher" and the "Bloodhound" of 1871.[12]

The news of the Waldeck-Rousseau-Millerand-Galliffet Ministry electrified the country. In some quarters it was hailed as a Ministry of All the Talents, and in other quarters it was denounced as a Ministry of All the Contradictions. Within the Socialist ranks, Millerand's presence elicited conflicting responses of approbation and condemnation. Right-wing Socialists, particularly Possibilists and Independents, strongly approved of the new government. Jaurès, who once had been opposed to the entry of a Socialist into a bourgeois ministry,[13] was displeased, to say the least, to find Galliffet holding a portfolio side by side with Millerand; nevertheless, he hastened to give his blessing to the latter. Jaurès declared in the *Petite République*, on the very day the new ministry was announced, that the exigencies of the political crisis rendered indispensable a ministry drawn from all the groups of the Left, and he praised Millerand for having the courage to participate in a "ministry of combat." If the peril of the Republic, he asserted, "is only a fiction, then this ministerial combination is a monstrosity and a scandal." But, "if there is truly, as we firmly believe, danger for the Republic, it would be unfortunate if the Socialist forces did not take, in a forthright fashion, part of the burden of responsibility in the struggle." That Waldeck-Rousseau had found it necessary to call upon the

---

[12] Zévaès, pp. 286–296.

[13] In an article in the *Dépêche de Toulouse* on September 10, 1893, Jaurès had stated that a Socialist in a ministry, the majority of whose members represented bourgeois political parties and interests, would be a "captive" of the ruling class. See also his article in the *Lanterne*, May 1, 1898, on the same topic.

Socialists to aid the bourgeoisie in saving the Republic from the menace of the "military conspiracy" was to Jaurès a fact of paramount importance: it was a clear recognition of the strength and influence of the Socialist movement. And the Socialists, he concluded, ought not to neglect "these challenges of destiny, these overtures of history." [14] Brousse, the Possibilist leader, likewise approved Millerand's decision, declaring: "The safety of the country is the supreme law. When it is in danger, it is necessary to exhaust all measures of defense, equally the legal arms as well as the revolutionary means." [15]

However, many left-wing Socialists, notably the leaders of the Guesdist and Blanquist parties, received the news of Millerand's action with extreme consternation. Even before the official announcement, Vaillant, the Blanquist leader, having heard that Millerand and the hated General had accepted portfolios, on June 22 dispatched a *pneumatique* (special delivery letter) asking Millerand if it was true that he had agreed to participate in a ministry which included Galliffet, the man who represented "all the crimes and violence of Versailles." Vaillant asked to be reassured that nothing "so repugnant, so ignoble" had taken place.[16] Interestingly enough, Vaillant made no mention whatsoever of the class struggle or other Socialist principles as arguments against ministerial participation. The following day, shortly after the formation of the Waldeck-Rousseau Ministry was officially announced, Vaillant joined with a number of his colleagues in issuing a statement declaring that the Deputies of the Blanquist party and the Alliance communiste révolutionnaire had withdrawn from the Union socialiste and were henceforth to constitute a new autonomous group in the Chamber — the "Revolutionary Socialist" parliamentary group. Although it did refer to Galliffet as the "Massacrer" of Communards, the state-

[14] June 24, 1899. See also Jaurès's article in the *Petite République*, June 27, 1899; and the articles by Viviani and Rouanet respectively in the *Lanterne*, June 24, 25, 1899.

[15] *Petite République*, August 7, 1899, quoted in Humbert, *Les Possibilistes*, pp. 80–81.

[16] See the text of the telegram in Zévaès, p. 281.

ment gave no clear-cut explanation for the withdrawal.[17] But it was obvious that the action had been taken in order to separate the Blanquist and Alliance communiste révolutionnaire Deputies from those members of the Union socialiste, particularly the Independents, who had approved of Millerand's conduct.

Coincident with this statement was the rather equivocal manifesto issued (June 23rd) by the Guesdist Deputies. They asserted that the doctrine of the class struggle made it impossible for them "to join forces with a ministry which is headed by Waldeck-Rousseau, the man of big business and high finance, and which includes General de Galliffet, the Slaughterer of the Republican and Socialist Paris of 1871." Nevertheless, in order to "safeguard the Republic, the necessary instrument for social transformation, against the attacks of militarism and clericalism," the Guesdists affirmed that they would support "energetic republican policies directed against the conspiracies of seditious Generals, Jesuits, and of all reactionaries." [18] In the light of subsequent developments, this manifesto is of particular interest for it indicates that the first response of these Deputies to the Waldeck-Rousseau Ministry was one of conditional support. The manifesto, however, did not meet with the approval of Guesde, Lafargue, and other party leaders; and before long these Deputies were directed to adopt a new line.

On the evening of the eventful June 23, at the instigation of Jaurès, the Comité d'entente socialiste met to consider Millerand's entry into the Waldeck-Rousseau Ministry — a development which soon came to be known as the "Millerand Case." Following an inconclusive discussion, the Comité, attempting to end controversy and division within the Socialist ranks, adopted a compromise resolution which declared that it was "solely on his own personal responsi-

---

[17] The text of the statement is given in Rouanet, "La Crise du Parti socialiste," *Revue socialiste*, 30: 203–204 (1899). Some of the Deputies whose names were affixed to the declaration later charged that they had not been consulted by Vaillant or anyone else with regard to the question of withdrawing from the Union socialiste. It would appear that the authors of the declaration had listed the names of these Deputies without prior consent. See Rouanet, p. 204; and J.-L. Breton, *L'Unité socialiste* (Paris, 1912), pp. 11–12.

[18] For the text of the manifesto, see the *Socialiste*, July 2, 1899.

bility that a Deputy of the [Socialist] party has entered the new ministry" and which affirmed that the Comité would "energetically maintain its union in order to combat military, clerical, and capitalist reaction and to defend the Republic and the working class against all its enemies." [19]

The Comité, however, failed to achieve its purpose. Two days later the National Council of the Guesdist party held a meeting of its own to take up the Millerand Case. After adopting a resolution stating that the Guesdist Deputies had "nothing in common" with a ministry which included Galliffet, the Council ordered its Deputies to withdraw at once from the Union socialiste and form their own parliamentary group. At the same time the National Council instructed that when the Waldeck-Rousseau Ministry presented itself to the Chamber, party Deputies were either to vote against it or to abstain; but that in no case were they to give it their support. It delegated Guesde, Lafargue, and Zévaès to formulate a manifesto which would offer a full explanation for the withdrawal of the party Deputies from the Union socialiste and present the Guesdist argument against ministerial participation.[20]

On June 26, when the Waldeck-Rousseau Ministry made its initial appearance in the Chamber, several Guesdist and Blanquist Deputies greeted Galliffet with jeers and cries of "Vive la Commune!" "A bas l'Assassin!" While Waldeck-Rousseau read his Ministerial Declaration, which outlined the principal task of the new ministry as one of restoring public order and defending the Republic against the menace of reaction, these continued to jeer. When Waldeck-Rousseau concluded, Vaillant arose to state that he and his colleagues in the Revolutionary Socialist parliamentary group would not support the new ministry because it contained Galliffet — "the assassin of the Commune and the massacrer of the Communards." [21] Later, Zévaès took the floor to set forth the attitude of the Guesdist Deputies. He made it clear that they would not support a ministry which had responded to the "admirable republican demonstration

[19] See the report of the meeting in the *Petite République*, June 25, 1899.
[20] *Socialiste*, July 2, 1899.
[21] *Journal officiel*, session of June 26, 1899, p. 1679.

of the people of Paris at the Longchamps racecourse by entrusting the post of Minister of War to the violent suppressor of the Republican Paris of 1871." Zévaès pointed out, however, that while the Guesdists would not support the ministry, they did not intend to identify themselves with the antirepublican groups of the Right by voting against it; rather they would abstain when the ministry requested a vote of confidence. "Our abstention will signify," he told the Deputies, "that we do not wish to have anything in common with the different bourgeois and reactionary parties represented in this Chamber, and that we recognize no other struggle but that of the working class against the capitalist class until the coming triumph of the Social Republic." [22]

At the close of this stormy session, when a resolution expressing confidence in the new government was put to a vote, all the Blanquist Deputies, the two Deputies affiliated with the Alliance communiste révolutionnaire, and a majority (seven) of the Guesdist Deputies abstained. Nineteen Independent Socialist Deputies, the two Allemanist Deputies,[23] and four Guesdist Deputies joined with republican groups to form the majority (twenty-five votes) approving the resolution, making it possible for the Waldeck-Rousseau Ministry, which was destined to remain in power for a longer period than any previous ministry in the history of the Third Republic, to continue in office.[24] This vote of confidence also promoted the creation of the coalition of groups in the Chamber that came to be known as the Bloc des gauches (Left Bloc). This Left Bloc, which united Moderate Republicans, Radicals, Radical-Socialists, and a majority of the Socialists in a defense of republican institutions, was to dominate the Chamber from 1900 to 1905.

On July 14, three weeks after the confidence vote in the Chamber, the National Council of the Parti ouvrier français (Guesdists), the Administrative Committee of the Parti socialiste révolutionnaire

[22] *Journal officiel*, p. 1681.

[23] The Allemanist party had not taken a definite position on the question of Millerand's participation in the Waldeck-Rousseau Ministry. In this connection, see the manifesto of the Paris section of the party in the *Parti Ouvrier*, June 30, 1899.

[24] *Journal officiel*, pp. 1692–1693.

(Blanquists), and the General Secretariat of the Alliance communiste révolutionnaire issued a joint manifesto explaining the withdrawal of the members of these three factions from the Socialist
parliamentary group. According to this, action had been rendered
imperative by the need to draw a sharp distinction between the
members of these factions and those of the Union socialiste who
actively supported the Waldeck-Rousseau Ministry and who had
endeavored for a long time to substitute a "counterfeit Socialist political method, consisting of compromises and deviations" for "the
class and hence revolutionary political method of the militant proletariat and the Socialist party." There could be no accord with members of the Socialist parliamentary group who, by their approval of
Millerand's participation in a ministry which contained Galliffet,
had "compromised the honor and interests of Socialism." In sharp
and caustic language, the manifesto condemned the participation
of a Socialist in a bourgeois ministry as a violation of fundamental
Socialist principles. It asserted that the Socialist party — meaning
the Socialist forces as a whole — was a party of "intransigent opposition" to the existing bourgeois order, and that it could not become
a "ministerial party" without suffering complete *embourgeoisement*
in the process. "The Socialist party is not able to share political
power with the bourgeoisie, in whose hands the State can be nothing
but an instrument of conservatism and of social oppression." The
imperative task of the Socialist party was to seize control of the
state from the hands of the bourgeoisie and to make of it an instrument of liberation and of social revolution: "Party of opposition we
are and a party of opposition we shall remain, sending our representatives into Parliaments and other elective assemblies as into
an enemy state — only in order to fight the enemy class and the
various political groups that represent it." [25]

[25] For the text of the manifesto, see the *Socialiste*, July 16, 1899. The manifesto
is reprinted in Zévaès, *Le Socialisme en France depuis 1871*, pp. 311–313. The names
of the following Deputies were affixed to the manifesto: Bénézech, Cadenat, Carnaud,
Dufour, Ferrero, Ferroul, Krauss, Légitimus, Pastre, Sauvanet, Zévaès (Guesdists);
Allard, Breton, Chauvière, Coutant, Létang, Sembat, Vaillant, Walter (Blanquists);
Dejeante, Groussier (Alliance communiste révolutionnaire). Ferrero, Ferroul, Krauss,
and Pastre had voted in favor of the Waldeck-Rousseau Ministry on June 26.

This manifesto, with its sweeping indictment of the policy and tactics of the Union socialiste (which actually indicted the Independents who had dominated the Socialist parliamentary group since 1893), as consisting of "compromises and deviations," and its strong reaffirmation of class warfare, of intransigent opposition to the existing bourgeois state, created a sensation within the Socialist ranks and gave rise to lengthy and acrimonious debate. One of the leading Independent Socialists, Rouanet, writing in the *Revue socialiste*, assailed its authors for seeking to "excommunicate" the Independents from the Socialist movement for their alleged "heretical" beliefs and practices. What, indeed, he asked, were these compromises and deviations attributed to the Independents by the Guesdists, Blanquists, and their allies? Since 1896, the Socialist parliamentary group had consistently pursued the program and tactics outlined by Millerand in his Saint-Mandé Program. If that program and the "political activities undertaken by the parliamentary representatives of Socialism in conformity with it" together constituted the compromises and deviations, the heretical practices and beliefs for which the authors of the manifesto reproached the Socialist parliamentary group, then the Guesdists and Blanquists were likewise guilty of having deviated from and compromised with the fundamental Socialist principles which they now invoked. They, too, were guilty of heretical beliefs and practices because they had accepted the Saint-Mandé Program and had participated in the political activities of the Socialist parliamentary group since its formation in 1893. It seemed a case of the pot calling the kettle black.

Rouanet cited specific instances in which the Guesdists, in flagrant violation of the conception of the class struggle which they, for the first time since the late 1880's, now reaffirmed with such passion, had allied themselves with progressive bourgeois groups in both municipal and legislative elections in order to ensure the success of Guesdist candidates. Indeed, he charged that since the early 1890's, when they achieved their first real success at the polls, the Guesdist party had been "a reformist and parliamentary party." The same could be said for the Blanquists. As for the question of ministerial participation, he maintained that Millerand's presence in the Waldeck-Rousseau Ministry could be justified on the grounds of political expediency. For the past two years all the reactionary forces of the country — "the clergy, the army, and the feudal and aristocratic elements" — had openly affirmed their intention of destroying democratic institutions. In the presence of this menace, the Socialists could not remain indifferent. It was their duty to enter into the arena of combat and to join forces with the liberal bourgeoisie in defense of democracy; and from the point of view of strengthening this collaboration, Rouanet asserted, the participation of Millerand in the new ministry was a desirable and logical development.[26] Other reformist Socialists also attacked the authors of the July 14th manifesto.[27]

On July 17, the Possibilist party intervened in the growing controversy in the role of peacemaker. In a statement which it issued, the National Council of the Fédération des travailleurs socialistes pleaded for the immediate cessation of the "fratricidal conflict" within the Socialist ranks and called for the amicable resolution of all the disputes arising from Millerand's entry into the Waldeck-Rousseau Ministry. "We request," the Council declared, "that these disputes be submitted for examination and arbitration either to a general congress of the Socialist forces or to the Comité d'entente socialiste." [28]

The response of the various Socialist factions to this appeal was completely affirmative. The day after it appeared in the press, the National Council of the Guesdist party, the Administrative Council of the Blanquist party, and the General Secretariat of the Alliance communiste révolutionnaire, in a note addressed to the Possibilist party, expressed their willingness to submit their dispute with the "Ministerial" Socialists (those who approved of Millerand's presence in the Waldeck-Rousseau Ministry) to arbitration. They proposed that the Comité d'entente socialiste be given the task of con-

---

[26] Rouanet, "La Crise du Parti socialiste," pp. 347–371.

[27] See Jaurès's articles in the *Petite République*, July 15, 16, 17, 18, August 3, 1899. See also the *Petite République*, July 19, 20, 21, 22, 1899; and Anthelme Simond, "La Crise socialiste," *Mouvement socialiste*, 2: 162 (1899).

[28] See the text in the *Petite République*, July 17, 1899.

voking a "General Congress of French Socialism" which would consider the Millerand Case and determine "if the class struggle, which is the very basis of Socialism, permits the entry of a Socialist into a bourgeois government." [29] The fact that the leaders of these three parties responded favorably and with such alacrity to the Possibilist proposal of arbitration clearly indicated that they did not accept their break with the Ministerial Socialists as complete and final. Their willingness to arbitrate was prompted in part by certain developments which were taking place within their own organizations. The rank and file of the Guesdist, Blanquist, and Alliance communiste révolutionnaire factions, like the rank and file of the other Socialist organizations, earnestly desired the unification of the Socialist forces. The manifesto of July 14, which announced the severance of relations with the reformist Socialists and which envisioned the partition of the Socialist movement into two opposing camps, had not received anything like unanimous approval. Its appearance led many prominent members of the Guesdist and Blanquist parties, including five Guesdist Deputies, to disassociate themselves from the position taken by their leaders. At the same time many local groups affiliated with one or another of the three factions withdrew from the national organization in protest.[30] Thus the Guesdist, Blanquist, and Alliance communiste révolutionnaire leaders, whatever their personal sentiments with regard to the arbitration proposal of the Possibilists, to some extent were motivated to accept it by the need to appease dissident elements

[29] For the text of the note, see the *Socialiste*, July 23, 1899.

[30] *Petite République*, July 16, 18, 19, 20, 21, 22, 23, 24, 25, 26, 1899; the *Lanterne*, July 18, 19, 20, 21, 22, 23, 25, 26, 27, 28, 1899. See in this connection the *cahier* entitled "Groupes du Parti: ordres du jour défavorable" in the Guesde Archives. This *cahier* is full of press clippings that reported the opposition of various sections of the Guesdist party to the July 14th manifesto. An extremely hostile response to the manifesto was that of Raymond Lavigne, the party militant from Bordeaux. In a letter to Guesde (July 16, 1899), Lavigne assailed the latter for "brutally unleashing a war" against Jaurès and Millerand; and in a letter to another prominent figure in the party, Edouard Fortin (September 5, 1899), Lavigne disassociated himself entirely from Guesde, Vaillant, and those who followed their lead, declaring that they were all possessed with "l'idée fixe de faire du mal" to Jaurès, Millerand, and their friends on the *Petite République*. Both letters are in the Guesde Archives.

within their own organizations. Refusal to arbitrate the Millerand Case might well have been construed by the rank and file of these factions as added proof that their leaders were indifferent or hostile to the common desire for Socialist unity; this would probably have led to further losses in party memberships.

A few days after these factions declared their willingness to submit the Millerand Case to arbitration, the Allemanists and Independent Socialists announced similar decisions. In its response to the Possibilist proposal, the Independent faction demanded that the projected congress be authorized not only to consider the Millerand Case, but also the question of Socialist unity and the formation of a single Socialist party.[31] Jaurès, who had helped to formulate the Independent declaration, asserted in a *Petite République* article that it was inconceivable that the congress of all the Socialist forces should only concern itself with a single question however important it be. "The Guesdists and Blanquists have sought to restrict in advance the agenda of this general congress," he asserted, "but once assembled, the delegates of all the Socialist forces will be sovereigns, and they will not disperse without having rendered impossible for the future the lamentable conflicts which have always plagued us."[32] The Guesdists and Blanquists, however, hastened to express their willingness to have the question of Socialist unity placed on the agenda; and the Comité d'entente socialiste immediately began to arrange for the convocation of this unprecedented congress — a congress which one Socialist leader hailed as the "Estates General of the French Socialist movement."[33]

In preparation for this event, the Guesdist leadership convoked a congress of their own party at Epernay in mid-August. At this congress, the National Council, dominated by Guesde and Lafargue, endeavored to win the approval of the entire party for its conduct in the Millerand Case and for its July 14th manifesto. The Epernay

---

[31] *Petite République*, August 6, 1899. See also Allemane's article in the *Parti Ouvrier*, July 21, 1899.

[32] July 21, 1899. See also Jaurès's articles in the *Petite République*, July 22, 23, 1899; and Rouanet's article in the *Lanterne*, July 23, 1899.

[33] L. Gérault-Richard in the *Petite République*, July 21, 1899.

Congress, however, proved to be sharply divided on this matter. Some of the delegates — notably Edouard Delesalle, one of the party leaders in the department of the Nord, and Calixte Camelle, a party militant from Bordeaux — strongly criticized the manifesto and expressed approval of Millerand's conduct. After a lengthy debate which went on for two days and two nights, the delegates adopted an equivocal resolution on the question of Socialist tactics. The first part expressed the attitude of intransigent "Antiministerialists" like Guesde and Lafargue. It affirmed that by the conquest of governmental power the party "has always understood the political expropriation of the capitalist class, and that that expropriation might take place peacefully or violently; that it is, furthermore, only the elective positions that the party may capture by its own forces, i.e., the workers organized as a class party." But its concluding part was not consistent with this attitude: "It leaves, for the future, to the National Council the task of considering, on the occasion and in accord with the circumstances, whether, without quitting the terrain of the class struggle, other positions may be occupied." [34]

The ambiguity contained in this resolution is readily apparent. First, the principle is set forth that Socialists were permitted to occupy only those elective positions which could be won directly by Socialist votes. Hence, the occupation of a ministerial post would be a departure from this principle. Then this principle is apparently repudiated by the assertion that under certain conditions and in accordance with certain stipulations a Socialist might, after all, be permitted to occupy a nonelective position — a ministerial post perhaps. The adoption of this resolution, coming as it did after the National Council of the party had taken an intransigent stand on ministerial participation, was something of a defeat for Guesde. This failure to secure the unqualified support of the entire party was certain to weaken the position of Guesde and other rabid Antiministerialists at the coming congress of the Socialist forces.

At long last, on the morning of December 3, 1899, some 670 delegates gathered in the poorly-heated Salle Japy in Paris for the open-

[34] The text is given in the *Socialiste*, August 20–27, 1899.

ing of the First General Congress of French Socialist Organizations. It was a memorable occasion, for never before in the history of French Socialism had representatives of so many different shades of opinion come together for common deliberation. The Guesdist faction had the largest representation, holding 530 out of a total of 1,452 mandates that had been distributed among the major Socialist parties and organizations. The Blanquists and their close allies, the Alliance communiste révolutionnaire delegates, together had the second largest representation with 300 mandates. The Independents were third with 250, while the Allemanists and Possibilists held 200 and 100 mandates respectively. Several autonomous regional and departmental Socialist organizations as well as a number of independent labor *syndicats* and cooperative groups that were Socialist in character also held mandates at the congress.[35]

After dealing with preliminary organizational matters, the congress turned to the consideration of the first question on the agenda, the all-important question of class conflict and the conquest of governmental power. On this, concretized in the Millerand Case, the Socialist forces were most sharply divided; and the debate which took place was acrimonious. Indeed, in the course of the debate, two delegates came to blows, and on one occasion the presiding officer was forced to adjourn a session to prevent the proceedings from degenerating into an open brawl. Yet its discussion merits close examination for it contained rather extensive expositions of the arguments of both the Ministerial and Antiministerial Socialists.

Jaurès opened the debate with a strong defense of ministerial participation. He began with the argument that Millerand's entry into the Waldeck-Rousseau Ministry was a direct and natural consequence of the active Socialist participation in the political life of the nation. With the growth of their movement, Socialists had not hesitated to enter the bourgeois municipal government and the Chamber of Deputies where they shared with bourgeois politicians the "heavy responsibilities and obligations" of public office. All Socialist parties and factions had engaged, and continued to engage,

[35] *Congrès général des organisations socialistes françaises, tenu à Paris du 3 au 8 décembre 1899* (Paris, 1900), pp. 417–477; the *Socialiste*, December 3–10, 1899.

in such political activity. Why, therefore, should a Socialist hesitate to enter a bourgeois ministry, since ministerial participation was analogous to participation in municipal councils and in the Chamber. Jaurès maintained, as he had previously, that the exigencies of republican defense rendered essential Millerand's presence in the Waldeck-Rousseau Ministry. He reminded the delegates that all Socialists accepted the view that the Republic was the indispensable instrument for the realization of the Social Republic and that to prepare the way for "social justice" and to become the "masters in the factories and in the shops" the workers ought to begin by becoming masters of the Republic. Consequently, to endanger republican institutions was to jeopardize the hope of attaining this future Socialist order. "And if the proletariat, which today is a force and which, being a force has a responsibility; if this proletariat, by being disinterested in the struggle [against the menace of reaction] and by not dispatching one of its representatives to the post of combat, had compromised the Republic, the proletariat," he declared, "would have gone against its own interest, against the revolution, and that would have been a true deviation from fundamental Socialist principles and practices."

Jaurès approached the question of ministerial participation from still another angle. He argued that if the Socialists were certain of the exact date that would mark the collapse of the existing capitalist order, then it would be "useless and dangerous for them to involve themselves in all the political and social movements of present-day society." Indeed, were they certain of that fateful date, their only task would be to prepare themselves and the proletariat for the great day of "decisive action" which would witness the replacement of capitalism by a collectivist society. He insisted, however, that no one could say with certainty just when the overthrow of capitalism was to take place; therefore, it was the duty of the Socialists, "while preparing themselves for future revolutionary action," to press day-by-day for the enactment of immediate social reforms within the existing bourgeois society. And there was no valid reason why Socialists should not use a ministerial post for that purpose. State power could be utilized here and now to obtain progressive legislation, and it was only that many Socialists still held to the "false notion" of the state as the impenetrable bulwark of capitalism that prevented them from grasping that significant fact. "We have been obliged to abandon the false hypothesis of the iron law of wages, which had prevented the workers from struggling for the immediate amelioration of their condition; we must now abandon the iron law of government, which still sets the revolutionaries in opposition to the bourgeois state."

Jaurès conceded that ministerial participation involved the dangerous possibility that a Socialist seated in a predominantly bourgeois ministry (such as the Waldeck-Rousseau) might be deterred from his duties and responsibilities as a representative of Socialism by "personal ambitions and temptations." But he maintained that such dangers could be overcome by having the united Socialist party, which he hoped would be formed in the near future, stipulate that a Socialist could accept a portfolio only with its prior consent and only on the conditions laid down by the party. Once in office, the Socialist Minister would be subject to strict, constant supervision of that party. "I am sure," he told the delegates, "that your growing force will soon be such that the bourgeoisie, in an hour of crisis, will be obliged to accept the conditions which you will attach to the collaboration — which is at the same time governmental and revolutionary — of the organized working class." [36]

Viviani, in his defense of ministerial participation, argued that the rules of the game of politics, the logic of political action, made it necessary for the Socialists to draw distinctions between the different factions of the bourgeoisie and forced the Socialists to collaborate with the liberal bourgeois elements in order to maintain republican institutions and to promote the particular interests of the proletariat. The Antiministerial Socialists believed that the principle of the class struggle forbade such collaboration; but it was impossible that this intransigent conception be maintained in the existing political situation. When the very existence of the Republic was at stake, menaced by the "reactionary elements of the bourgeois class," it was essential that the Socialist forces "collaborate with the

[36] *Congrès*, pp. 58–63.

most liberal factions of the bourgeois class which, for the present at least, wish to defend the Republic, without which there can be no Social Republic." Similarly, the collaboration of Socialists and bourgeois liberals in the Chamber of Deputies was rendered imperative by the very exigencies of political action. In the Chamber the Socialists, in order to repulse attacks from the Right on a republican ministry, often joined forces with progressive bourgeois elements. Failure of the Socialists to collaborate would have meant the fall of the republican ministry and its replacement by a reactionary ministry. Political considerations rendered the collaboration of Socialists and bourgeois liberals on the ministerial level indispensable. To accept the interpretation of the class struggle as set forth by the Antiministerial Socialists, to prohibit collaboration between Socialists and non-Socialists, would render ineffectual any further political action on their part. Viviani recommended that the Socialists abandon unrealistic formulas and seek instead to fit their theory to the "facts of political life." "The Socialist party," he concluded, "ought to be not only a party of doctrine, but also a party of action." [37]

In the debate on tactics, the antiministerial case was set forth with vigor and cogency by Vaillant, Lafargue, Zévaès, and Guesde. Vaillant argued that the participation of a Socialist in a bourgeois ministry constituted an egregious violation of the fundamental doctrine of the class struggle, which, he insisted, distinctly prohibited any form of collaboration between the proletariat and the Socialists on the one hand and any factions of the bourgeois class on the other. It was this fundamental doctrine which characterized the Socialist party, which marked it off from all other parties in the political arena. It was this conception of the Socialist as a distinct class party, concerned primarily with the battle against the bourgeoisie for the emancipation of the proletariat which induced workers to join. Vaillant also asserted that the presence of a Socialist in a bourgeois ministry, far from advancing the cause of the proletariat, could only serve to promote the particular interests of the bourgeois ruling class. Once he entered a ministry dominated by representatives of the bourgeoisie, a Socialist became "a hostage." Holding a portfolio, he

[37] *Congrès*, pp. 140–146.

was obliged to work with the government, and the government was essentially a class instrument of power which represented only "capitalist interests, the interests of the bourgeoisie." As long as the capitalist order existed it was impossible for the government to "be anything else." It followed, therefore, that a Socialist Minister, though sincerely devoted to the welfare of the working class, soon discovered that, owing to his role as an administrator, he had to participate along with his bourgeois colleagues in the "reactionary acts" of the government and was obliged to share the responsibility for maintaining the capitalist regime. As an illustration, Vaillant pointed out that when the government sent troops against strikers, the ministry as a whole took responsibility for the move. Hence, to retain his post, a Socialist participating in the ministry would have to give his approval to the employment of such troops. Just how long, Vaillant queried, would the workers have confidence in a Socialist party which sent "into the bourgeois government one of its representatives who would merely be able to act in support of the capitalist regime against the emancipation of the working class?" The workers "would come to doubt the value of Socialism and they would end by saying: 'That is the negation, the renunciation, the desertion of Socialism.'" It was impossible, therefore, for anyone to participate in a bourgeois ministry, "without losing his identity as a Socialist."

Rejecting ministerial participation, Vaillant asserted that the Socialist party must remain, with respect to the capitalist regime, a party of intransigent opposition, "the party of the struggle of the working class against the capitalist class — in other words, the party of revolution." In pursuing a policy of revolutionary action, of incessant opposition to the existing bourgeois order, the Socialists, "must endeavor to seize governmental power, not in order to maintain the capitalist regime and not in order to associate ourselves with efforts to maintain it, but only in order to overthrow this regime and to install in its place, during the revolutionary crisis, the regime of the working class, master of governmental power through its impersonal dictatorship, so as to smash all resistance to the revolution and to institute the Social Republic." [38]

[38] *Congrès*, pp. 90–95.

Lafargue sought to prove that the formation of a government which included a Socialist was not, as the Ministerial Socialists claimed, a victory for the Socialist movement, but rather a crafty policy employed by the ruling bourgeoisie to serve its interests. He pointed out that in 1848, Ledru-Rollin, spokesman for the bourgeois republicans, had invited the labor leader Albert Thomas and the Socialist Louis Blanc to participate in the Provisional Government. At that time the workers had considered it a "victory for Socialism because the bourgeoisie had permitted a Socialist to be seated in a governmental chair." But, while Louis Blanc was holding conferences on the organization of labor at the Luxembourg Palace, "the bourgeoisie was organizing the massacre of the workers and was bringing back from Africa the Cavaignacs, the Lamoricières, and the other butchers of June." The sole purpose of the bourgeoisie in admitting a Socialist and a labor leader into the inner circle of the government, had been to neutralize the Socialist forces and prevent the workers from taking action, while the bourgeoisie devoted itself to consolidating its position. Lafargue insisted that once again a Socialist had been summoned to serve the interests of the bourgeois class. Waldeck-Rousseau, the new spokesman for the bourgeoisie, had taken Millerand into his ministry in order to utilize the powerful Socialist forces which Millerand represented for the defense of the existing political order. "The country knows today," he remarked ironically, "that it is to the Socialists, whom the bourgeoisie denounced as antirepublicans, whom the bourgoisie abused, insulted, and imprisoned — it is to this rabble that the bourgeois republicans are obliged to turn in order to defend their Republic."

Lafargue asserted that if Millerand's entry into the Waldeck-Rousseau Ministry had been considered as an "exceptional action," the Antiministerial Socialists would have let it pass "without saying a word." But unfortunately this was not the case, for there were many Socialists who wished to make Millerand's action "a point of departure of a new method of political action" which they hoped to impose upon all the Socialist forces. The supporters of ministerial participation, the new method of "political opportunism," were the bourgeois intellectuals and radicals who had joined the Socialist ranks in recent years. "These new recruits, instead of taking their places in the ranks as comrades and assimilating the theories of International Socialism," he declared, "have set themselves up as reformers, seeking to change the established political method [the class struggle] . . ." These recruits had joined the Socialist movement not to advance the cause of the proletariat, but to "exploit" the movement for their selfish political interests, to gain governmental posts and stipends. To prevent these elements from realizing their purposes, from compromising the Socialist cause, it was imperative that their "opportunistic" methods of political action be repudiated once and for all.[39]

Zévaès attacked the view that the participation of a Socialist in a bourgeois ministry was analogous to the participation of Socialists in the municipal government and in the Chamber of Deputies. He contended that there was an essential difference between a Socialist who was sent into a municipal council or into the Chamber "by the workers exercising universal suffrage — that is to say, by the workers organized in a class party relying upon their own electoral strength," and a Socialist Minister who was, after all, "summoned to power not by the proletariat, but by the most eminent representative of the capitalist bourgeoisie — by the President of the Republic." He pointed out that when Socialists entered the Chamber they made no long-term alliances with any political groups present there. "We do not distinguish between the different political groups represented in Parliament. We fight all the bourgeois factions without exception, those on the extreme Left as well as those on the extreme Right." The situation of a Socialist in a predominantly bourgeois ministry was quite different. By the very nature of his office a Socialist Minister must "collaborate with all his bourgeois colleagues." In contrast to a Socialist Deputy, who was free to fight the bourgeois ruling class at all times, a Socialist Minister was a "prisoner" of that very class, forced to do its bidding as long as he retained his portfolio.[40]

Guesde maintained that the "most sinister" consequence of minis-

[39] *Congrès*, pp. 111–115.
[40] *Congrès*, pp. 131–135.

terial participation was that it would ultimately destroy the international solidarity of the proletariat and paralyze the efforts of the workers and Socialists to prevent war. He contended that a new era of capitalist wars was opening, "the era of commercial and colonial wars, wars for markets and for profits." In the face of this menace, it was necessary for workers and Socialists of all countries to pool their strength and form a strong international entente. But if the Socialists of all countries, as in France, were to share governmental power with the enemy bourgeois class, the warmaking class — if, in addition to "a French Millerand," one had "an English Millerand, an Italian Millerand, and a German Millerand" — then all workers and Socialists would find themselves tied to the bourgeoisie and supporting its war policies. As a result the international entente of the proletariat would be destroyed, and the workers and Socialists of the various countries, no longer able to offer effective opposition to the war policies of their respective governments, would be pitted against one another. "The day when the Millerand Case becomes a general practice," Guesde declared, "it will be necessary to say adieu to all internationalism." [41]

After more than a score of delegates had spoken on the question of the class struggle and the conquest of governmental power, the debate was brought to a close. The committee on resolutions which was composed of an equal number of Ministerial and Antiministerial Socialists was then instructed to prepare a policy statement on the question. The resulting resolution constituted neither a clearcut approbation nor a repudiation of ministerial participation. It declared that while "exceptional circumstances might arise" in which the Socialist forces should examine the question of Socialist participation in a bourgeois government, it was nevertheless true that in the existing state of capitalist society and of the Socialist movement, all Socialist efforts "ought to be devoted to the conquest, in the commune, department, and in the state, of only elective offices which the proletariat, organized as a party of class, can secure by its own efforts: offices and positions which, by installing itself in them, the proletariat begins legally and peacefully the political ex-

[41] *Congrès*, pp. 187–188.

propriation of the capitalist class which will terminate in revolution." [42] The committee submitted this resolution, which was simply a restatement of the equivocal resolution on tactics which had been adopted by the Guesdist party congress at Epernay a few months before, to the plenary session of the congress.

Before the resolution was finally acted upon, however, Guesde, in the name of his party, requested that the delegates vote on the following amendment to it: "Does the class struggle prohibit the entry of a Socialist into a bourgeois government?" Guesde declared that the adoption of his amendment would put the congress on record as being opposed to the principle of ministerial participation — its rejection would, of course, signify the opposite. The amendment was adopted. The congress then approved the resolution submitted by the committee.[43]

Given the wide divergence of opinion between the supporters and the opponents of ministerial participation, it was not surprising that the congress should have taken an equivocal position on this question by adopting both the amendment and the resolution. Partisan passion, as the debate had clearly demonstrated, was such that had the congress approved the amendment and then rejected the resolution, or vice versa, it might well have witnessed a major schism. In the existing situation a clear-cut decision on the question simply was not possible.

Having devoted most of the sessions scheduled for the congress to consideration of the Millerand Case and its implications, the delegates found themselves pressed for time and were able to deal with other questions on the agenda in only a summary fashion. The congress did give serious attention, however, to the important question of Socialist unity. More than a score of speakers, all affirming the necessity and the desirability of a close union of the Socialist forces, participated. In the discussion, which was singularly free of recrimination and invective, there appeared to be but one major point of dispute: the basis upon which the unified party was to be organized.

[42] *Congrès*, pp. 263–264.
[43] *Congrès*, pp. 272–285.

Some of the speakers who represented large national organizations argued that the new party should be based on a *federation* of the existing national and departmental organizations; with each organization, for the time being at least, retaining a considerable degree of autonomy. They believed that the formation of an organic union of the Socialist forces was a long-term proposition, that the fusion of the diverse factions into which the Socialist movement was divided would require a good deal of time, and that to abolish with one stroke the existing Socialist organizations would impede, rather than hasten, this fusion. As Guesde put it: "To demand too much would be to run the risk of obtaining nothing." Other speakers argued that the new party should be based on a complete *fusion* of all existing national and local Socialist organizations. They maintained that the present national organizations only served to perpetuate obsolete and irrelevant theories and keep the movement divided. They could find no rational grounds to justify their continued existence. "The formation of absolute unity, of unity without reservations," observed one delegate, "demands the death of the nationally constituted organizations." From discussion on the question it was apparent that the strongest pressure for the formation of a single party came from the "grass roots" of the Socialist movement — the provincial groups. These cared little for the long-standing conflicts between the major Socialist factions — conflicts over doctrine and tactics which had, in their opinion, served only to weaken the Socialist movement, to dissipate its energies. The formation of a democratically controlled, unified party appeared the primary task of the hour. The leaders of the major Socialist factions likewise desired unity, but unity with conditions. Some of these leaders — Guesde was perhaps the best example — did not want to sacrifice their dominant positions in the Socialist movement; and the possibility existed that in a unified party so organized as to be largely free of bureaucratic control, their powers, quite extensive within their own organizations, might be seriously restricted.[44]

[44] *Congrès*, pp. 194–199, 307–354. On the unity question, see also the *Petite République*, July 12, 1899; J. Bourdeau, "Revue du mouvement socialiste," *Revue*

At the close of the discussion on Socialist unity, the committee on resolutions brought before the plenary session a plan for unification. According to the scheme, the new party, called the Parti socialiste français (French Socialist party), was to be founded on the basic principles set forth in Millerand's Saint-Mandé Program. The party was to be given direction, its policies and tactics were to be defined, by a national congress convened annually. In the period between these congresses, the party was to be administered by a central organ, the General Committee, vested with considerable authority. It was to exercise "direct supervision" over the party *élus* in the Chamber of Deputies, seeing to it that they, organized in a single parliamentary group, conducted themselves in accordance with the general principles of the party and that, as far as possible, they voted in unison. Just how the General Committee was to deal with cases of discipline involving party Deputies was not made clear. The General Committee was also to supervise the Socialist press. The party was not, at least for the time being, to have an official organ; but all the journals published by organizations affiliated with the party were to insert official communications from the central organ. These were to have "freedom of discussion with regard to questions of doctrine and method," but "with regard to action," they were to "conform strictly to the decisions of the national congress as interpreted by the General Committee." Should the latter find that a journal was violating "the decisions of the party or compromising the interests of the proletariat," it was empowered to suppress it and to exclude from the party the organization or organizations responsible for its publication. Finally, the Committee was authorized to arbitrate disputes between organizations affiliated with the party. Until the unified party was actually constituted, the Socialist organizations that were to be incorporated in it were to retain their identity.[45]

The reception which the delegates accorded the plan of unification was quite remarkable. Considering the importance of the ques-

---

politique et parlementaire, 23: 441–443 (1900); and P. Landrieu, "Les Fédérations départementales," *Mouvement socialiste*, 3: 200–206 (1900).

[45] *Congrès*, pp. 401–404.

tion of unity and given the differences of opinion which had previously been manifested with regard to it, one might well have expected that the plan would be examined in considerable detail. Yet at the plenary session there was almost no discussion of the scheme. After spokesmen for many of the organizations and groups represented at the congress expressed their unqualified approval of it, the delegates, by unanimous vote, adopted the plan as the constitution for the new federated Socialist party.[46] Undoubtedly the vote was an expression of the deeply felt desire of the mass of the Socialist forces for unity.

As soon as the plan of unification was approved, the work of the congress was declared at an end. At that moment, with the First General Congress of French Socialist Organizations soon to pass into history, an unforgettable demonstration of comradeship took place. In various parts of the great hall, moved as if by a single impulse, delegates started to sing "L'Internationale" and, with red flags and banners in hand, began to march in file around the hall. A number of Socialist leaders, including Guesde, Jaurès, Vaillant, and Brousse, together with many militants of the Socialist movement who had participated in the Paris Commune, marched in a body to the podium. There, standing side by side, their arms locked around one another, they joined with the hundreds of other delegates in singing the revolutionary refrain:

> C'est la lutte finale,
> Groupons-nous, et demain,
> L'Internationale,
> Sera le genre humain.

It appeared that the unification of the Socialist movement had at last been achieved.

[46] *Congrès*, p. 404.

Chapter 5

The Era of Schisms

Shortly after the conclusion of the First General Congress, while the memory of that moving demonstration of fraternal affection and good will which marked its closing was still fresh, the first steps in the implementation of the unity plan were undertaken. Late in December 1899 the central organ of the new federated Socialist party — the General Committee — was constituted. At the same time the Socialist Deputies, who had formed two separate factions in the Chamber since the previous summer, joined in reestablishing a single parliamentary group.

The General Committee was composed of fifteen delegates from the Guesdist party, seven from the Blanquist party, six from the Independent factions, four from the Allemanist party, three from the Possibilist party, one from the Alliance communiste révolutionnaire, and twelve delegates from other affiliated organizations (autonomous federations, labor unions, and cooperative societies). On the General Committee were many of the most prominent figures in the French Socialist movement, including Jaurès, Guesde, Lafargue, Vaillant, Brousse, Allemane, and Viviani. Of the forty-eight members of the General Committee, more than half were delegates from organizations which opposed ministerial participation.[1]

[1] For the membership of the General Committee, see the *Petite République*, December 22, 24, 1899. The national organizations were represented on the General Committee in proportion to the number of mandates which each held at the General Congress of 1899. The Antiministerial Socialist majority was made up principally

It will be recalled that according to the unity plan, the General Committee had been granted rather broad, though in certain matters not precisely defined, authority. It could arbitrate disputes between the federated organizations, organize and direct propaganda activity, and supervise the party *élus* and the press. Taking its duties seriously, too seriously perhaps, soon after its formation, the General Committee made its first attempt to bring the Socialist parliamentary group under its control. On January 31, 1900, the General Committee sent a circular to each member of the parliamentary group requesting that he place himself "at the disposal" of the General Committee for propaganda work. Each was instructed to submit to the Committee a written statement of his willingness to participate in this work.[2]

The response of the Socialist parliamentary group to the circular, which was rather haughty in tone, was mixed. Most of the Guesdist and Blanquist Deputies, accustomed to strict party discipline, acceded without hesitation to the request. But the Allemanists and Independent Socialists, who were used to freedom of action, construed the circular as an attempt on the part of the General Committee to subjugate the group, and many did not bother to reply. Some of the Deputies were so offended that they made it quite clear that they would not have anything to do with the propaganda work carried on by the General Committee. For instance, when, on March 12, the Committee asked Marius Devèze to address a mass meeting of strikers at Floing and again, on March 19, when it called on Jean Bénézech to undertake similar propaganda work at Montchanin, both flatly refused to do so.[3] The reception given the circular by the Independent Deputies was the first overt manifestation of opposition within the Socialist parliamentary group to the General Committee; but as the Committee made further attempts to impose its

---

of the Guesdist, Blanquist, and the Alliance communiste révolutionnaire delegations. In this connection, see the *Lanterne*, December 24, 1899.

[2] The text of the circular is given in the *Petite République*, February 3, 1900.

[3] *Petite République*, April 11, 21, 26, 1900. For the membership of the parliamentary group, see the *Petite République*, December 14, 1899. Only the Socialist Deputies were admitted to the group.

authority upon the group, opposition became more and more pronounced.

On February 21 the General Committee sent another circular to the parliamentary group setting forth the regulations which were to govern its conduct in the Chamber. According to this, individual members were to inform the Committee concerning all bills and resolutions they intended to bring before the Chamber. In addition, they were instructed not to introduce a bill or a resolution nor "to engage in any parliamentary negotiations" without prior discussion of the matter by the entire group. The purpose of these preliminary discussions was "to realize as far as possible the unity of vote of the parliamentary group, in conformity with the statutes of the party as established by the General Congress of Socialist Organizations." The circular stated that allowance would be made for those proposals which were "provoked by incidents arising during the course of a parliamentary session or by unforeseen critical developments." Yet even in such cases, "it should often be possible for one to communicate the text of a proposal to most of the members of the group." To make certain that the activities of the Socialist Deputies received wide publicity, the circular instructed them to inform the General Committee of all their votes in the Chamber. The General Committee was in turn to submit this information to the Socialist journals for publication.[4]

The Socialist parliamentary group discussed this circular at two caucuses which took place on March 2 and March 8. Most of the Guesdists and Blanquists found nothing to criticize and accepted the instructions without reservation. The Independent Socialists, however, were up in arms. The General Committee, they charged, had exceeded its rights in seeking to supervise the parliamentary action of the group. Eugène Fournière, an Independent Deputy, argued that it had endeavored "to assume a directoral authority which did not belong to it." Others insisted that on many specific issues it was impossible to realize anything like a unity of vote on the part of the entire parliamentary group, that allowances had to

[4] See the text of the circular in the *Petite République*, February 25, 1900. See also the *Lanterne*, February 26, 1900.

be made for some diversity of opinion and action within the group. Finally, the group adopted two resolutions. The first declared that while the General Committee had for its mission "the task of bringing about an entente of all the militants with regard to doctrine," supervision of the acts of the individual *élu* belonged "only to universal suffrage and to his electoral committee." In other words, the Deputy was accountable to the local group that had sponsored him and to the voters who had sent him to the Chamber and to no one else. This was a clear declaration of independence on the part of the parliamentary group, and strongly suggests that the majority of the Deputies considered themselves as constituting a sort of "party" within the party. The second resolution strengthened this impression, for it stated that each member was at liberty to act as he saw fit regarding the matter of informing the General Committee of his voting record.[5]

The response of the parliamentary group to the General Committee strained relations between the two, and during the spring of 1900, matters went from bad to worse. During that period the Socialist Deputies failed to vote together on many important issues, and the Ministerial Socialists followed a policy of close collaboration with republican groups in the Left Bloc in support of the Waldeck-Rousseau Ministry. The most striking instance of this policy — indeed, the one case which more than any other helped to bring about a complete rupture in relations between the Socialist parliamentary group and the General Committee and which split the Socialist ranks wide open — was the alliance of Ministerial Socialists and republicans in support of the government when it was under sharp attack from many quarters for its conduct in the famous Chalon-sur-Saône strike.

Late in April 1900, a strike broke out in a factory in Chalon-sur-Saône in the department of the Saône-et-Loire. As was customary, armed forces were dispatched to the area. On June 2, a clash occurred between strikers and the guardians of order; three strikers were shot dead and several more were seriously wounded. The bloodshed created widespread indignation, and on June 15, a Radi-

[5] *Petite République*, March 20, 29, 1900; the *Lanterne*, March 28, 1900.

cal-Socialist Deputy, Julien Simyan, requested an interpellation of
the government on its conduct in the strike. At the close of the
discussion of the interpellation, several resolutions were brought
before the Chamber. The first, introduced by Zévaès, the Guesdist
Deputy, and André Berthelot, a Radical-Socialist, called for an investigation of the tragic incident by a parliamentary committee.
When this resolution was put to a vote, sixteen Socialists, construing
it as a censure of the government (which had previously promised
to undertake its own investigation), cast their votes against it. The
votes of the Ministerial Socialists defeated the Zévaès-Berthelot resolution.[6] Another resolution, introduced by Simyan, read as follows:
"The Chamber, counting on the government to prosecute all the
responsibilities that may be established by a judicial investigation,
passes to the order of the day."[7] Waldeck-Rousseau declared that
his ministry was prepared to accept this resolution. But before
it could be voted on, a Nationalist Deputy, Joseph Massabuau, offered the following amendment to be tagged on to the Simyan
resolution: "and condemning the collectivist doctrines which deceive the workers, passes to the order of the day." The Simyan
resolution alone was put to a vote and carried. The Massabuau
amendment alone was likewise adopted, with all but two of the
Socialist Deputies (Millerand and Vaux, who abstained) voting
against it.[8] The joint Simyan-Massabuau resolution was then brought
before the Chamber for a vote.

The Ministerial Socialist Deputies now found themselves forced
to make a most difficult decision. If they were to pursue their tactic
of supporting the government, they would find themselves in the
anomalous position of voting a condemnation of their own doctrines. On the other hand, were they to oppose the resolution, they
would be placing the ministry in a most precarious position owing
to the fact that its enemies in the Chamber (the conservative and

[6] *Journal officiel*, session of June 15, 1900, pp. 1494–1503, 1506–1507.

[7] *Journal officiel*, p. 1503. The motion was called an "order of the day" from
the fact that after the Chamber expressed its opinion (or lack of opinion) on the
matter under consideration, the interpellation would be declared close, and the Chamber would then take up the next item on the order of the day (agenda).

[8] *Journal officiel*, pp. 1503, 1509–1510.

reactionary groups of the Right Center and the Right), eager to exploit the discontent aroused by the tragedy, were prepared to vote in a bloc against the government; and there was a strong possibility that with the votes of the Socialists they would succeed in reversing the ministry. Convinced that the continuance in power of the Waldeck-Rousseau Ministry was of the utmost importance, that the long-term benefits to be secured by collaboration with that government would more than compensate for any single act of indiscipline however disconcerting and compromising it might be, nineteen Socialists decided to support the ministry; and they broke rank to vote for the Simyan-Massabuau resolution. The resolution was approved by a rather close vote, thus enabling the ministry to continue in office.[9]

The votes of the Ministerial Socialists on the Zévaès-Berthelot and the Simyan-Massabuau resolutions created a storm within the Socialist ranks and brought to a head the longstanding conflict between the General Committee and the Socialist parliamentary group. On June 22 the General Committee met to consider the conduct of the Ministerial Socialist Deputies. This furnished the occasion for an angry debate between the critics and the defenders of the Ministerialists. Several members of the General Committee bitterly denounced the Ministerial Socialists for their "betrayal" of the proletariat and for their repudiation of party doctrines. Defenders of the Ministerial Socialists argued that their votes were justified by the exigencies of republican defense, by the need to support the Waldeck-Rousseau Ministry when it was threatened by a coalition of its enemies in the Chamber. Referring to the Zévaès-Berthelot resolution, Viviani declared: "If the investigation had been voted, what would have been the result? We would have given our votes to those men who are our most avowed adversaries, and consequently the ministry would have been overturned!" He pointed out that, when the Massabuau amendment denouncing collectivist doctrines had been put to a vote, all the Ministerial Socialists had voted against it; this was proof of the integrity of the Ministerialists. As for their stand on the joint Simyan-Massabuau resolution, Viviani, who had him-

[9] *Journal officiel*, pp. 1510–1511.

self voted for it, contended that the addition of the amendment to the Simyan declaration of confidence was simply a "parliamentary trick" employed by the enemies of the ministry in the hope of separating the Socialists from their republican allies, thus destroying the ministry's majority in the Chamber. And, with the very existence of the ministry at stake, "it was necessary for us to be crafty too." Jaurès conceded that the Ministerial Socialists had to some extent compromised themselves by their acceptance of the Simyan-Massabuau resolution, but he too argued that the exigencies of parliamentary strife rendered it necessary for them to take the position they did. Yet the "painful situation" in which the Ministerialists had found themselves could have been avoided had the Socialist Deputies decided on a common tactic prior to the vote on the resolution. "If the parliamentary group had been united, if its various elements had consulted and come to terms with one another," he declared, "the group would certainly have found the means of frustrating the Nationalist maneuver while still proudly affirming collectivist doctrines." Rather than censure the Ministerial Socialists, the General Committee should recommend to the parliamentary group that it form a closer working unit in the Chamber and that it adopt "a common plan of action" to guide it in all subsequent parliamentary activity.

The critics of the Ministerial Socialists far outnumbered their defenders, however; and at the end of the discussion, by an overwhelming majority (forty-three to three), the General Committee approved a resolution which concluded: "The General Committee censures these Socialist Deputies [the Ministerialists] for having sacrificed for the sake of political considerations the superior principles of Socialism, formulated at the General Congress of December 1899. The General Committee also decides to submit the case to the next General Congress, in order that it may give final judgment and take the necessary measures to assure the unity of vote of the Deputies with regard to the principles and the general policy of the Socialist party." [10]

[10] *Lanterne*, August 28, 30, September 1, 2, 1900. See also the *Socialiste*, June 24, 1900; and the *Petite République*, June 25, 1900.

A few days after the General Committee meeting, stung by its rebuke, the Socialist parliamentary group met at the Palais Bourbon. At the close of a discussion which had fairly bristled with insults hurled at the General Committee, the group, by a vote of twenty-one to sixteen, approved a resolution which set forth the views of its Ministerial majority concerning the now-famous vote of June 15. As might be expected, the Ministerial Socialists were completely exonerated. Their repudiation of the Zévaès-Berthelot resolution was justified on the grounds that they "had refused to lend themselves to the crafty parliamentary maneuver which had as its sole objective the triumph of the adversaries of the republican regime." The support given the Simyan-Massabuau resolution was justified on the same grounds.[11]

In a sense, the opposing resolutions adopted by the General Committee and the Socialist parliamentary group were declarations of war. Before many weeks had passed, the two organizations were engaged in an acrimonious battle of words: the casualty was the cause of Socialist unity. More and more Socialists became involved in the controversy, and, as at the time of Millerand's entry into the Waldeck-Rousseau Ministry in the spring of 1899, the Socialist forces split into two hostile and uncompromising camps. The line-up was identical with that of 1899. On the one side stood the great majority of the Independents, Allemanists, and the Possibilists, all of whom opposed the "dictatorial" pretensions of the General Committee and approved of the policy of the Ministerial Socialists. Opposing them were principally the Guesdists and Blanquists, who supported the position of the General Committee (which they happened to control), and denounced the policy of consistent collaboration of Socialists with bourgeois republicans in support of a non-Socialist government as a flagrant violation of "orthodox" Socialist principles. The Ministerialists waged battle with the *Petite République*, the

---

[11] The text of the resolution together with an account of the caucus is given in the *Petite République*, June 28, 1900. The following voted for the resolution: Albert-Poulain, Boyer, Cadenat, Calvinhac, Carnaud, Colliard, Gras, Chassaing, Devèze, Ferrero, Ferroul, Fournière, Jourde, Krauss, Labussière, Narbonne, Palix, Pastre, Rouanet, Vaux, and Viviani.

Lanterne, and the *Revue socialiste*, while the Antiministerialists fired broadsides from the pages of the *Socialiste* and a new daily, the *Petit Sou*.[12]

By the late summer of 1900, that *rapprochement* between Socialist elements, achieved at the First General Congress a year earlier, was gone. The opposing factions now looked forward to a fight to the finish on the question of Socialist method and tactics at the two congresses that were scheduled to take place shortly in Paris — the Fifth Congress of the Socialist and Labor International and the Second General Congress of French Socialist Organizations.

On September 23, 1900, more than 800 delegates representing Socialist parties and organizations of twenty-one different nationalities gathered in the Salle Wagram in Paris for the Fifth Congress of the Socialist and Labor International (the Second International). In keeping with established procedure, each national delegation met shortly before the first plenary session of the congress for the purpose of validating credentials. For the French delegation this meeting provided the occasion for an unprecedented demonstration of factional bickering and vindictive animosity. The Ministerial and Antiministerial blocs accused one another of having falsified the number of their mandates in order to achieve a majority within the delegation as a whole and thereby control its votes at the congress. There was some justification for these mutual accusations. Both factions — the Antiministerialists to a greater extent than their opponents — had engaged, prior to the congress, in the now time-honored practice of creating fictional local party groups in order to increase their delegations. At last, however, after a discussion devoted in the main to exchanging insults, the factions arrived at a working agreement. It was decided that, with certain exceptions, each would verify its

---

[12] See the *Lanterne*, July 2, 14, August 9, 19, 22, 26, 29, September 1, 5, 6, 16, 18, 1900; the *Petite République*, July 15, August 12, 15, 23, 29, September 16, 22, 23, 1900; the *Socialiste*, June 14, July 1, 15, 1900; the *Petit Sou*, September 19, 22, 27, 1900; and G. Rouanet, "Le Congrès de 1900," *Revue socialiste*, 32: 344–346 (1900). The newspaper, the *Petit Sou*, had recently been founded by a wealthy, new recruit to the Blanquist ranks, Alfred Edwards.

own mandates, and that each was to exercise one of the two votes assigned to the delegation as a whole. The Ministerial bloc, composed largely of Independents, Allemanists, Possibilists, and the great majority of the autonomous federations, verified a total of 1,600 mandates. The Antiministerial bloc, comprising the Guesdists, Blanquists, the delegates of the Alliance communiste révolutionnaire, and the delegates of a few autonomous federations, verified 1,083 mandates.[13]

The conflict over the verification of mandates was only the first of a number of clashes within the French delegation. From time to time the proceedings of the congress were interrupted by displays of "Gallic fraternity" which Henry Hyndman, a member of the British delegation, declared "could scarcely be distinguished from a keen disposition for mutual slaughter." [14]

The most important matter taken up by the international congress, certainly the most relevant from the point of view of the French delegation, was the question of ministerial participation, listed on the agenda as: "The conquest of governmental power and alliances with bourgeois parties." To examine this matter in detail and to formulate a party statement concerning it, a committee, including Guesde and Jaurès, was set up. This engaged in lengthy discussion but was unable to resolve the question of ministerial participation in a manner acceptable to all concerned. As a result, the committee submitted two reports to the plenary session of the congress.

The majority report was presented by Emile Vandervelde, the distinguished Belgian Socialist. Vandervelde informed the delegates that on the second part of the question, alliances with bourgeois parties, all the members of the committee, "no matter the nationality or the Socialist orientation to which they belong," were in funda-

---

[13] *Cinquième Congrès socialiste international, tenu à Paris du 23 au 27 septembre 1900* (Paris, 1901), pp. 20–29. At this time there were twenty-six autonomous federations. For their Socialist orientation, see Paul Dramas, "Chronique sociale," *Mouvement socialiste*, 4: 373 (1900).

[14] Henry M. Hyndman, *Further Reminiscences* (London, 1912), p. 116. See also the *Lanterne*, September 25, 26, 1900; and the *Petit Sou*, September 26, 28, October 2, 1900.

mental agreement. The committee believed that under ordinary circumstances alliances between Socialist and bourgeois political parties should be prohibited and even when "exceptional circumstances" rendered them indispensable, they were to be employed "with an extreme prudence." On the first part of the question, the conquest of governmental power, the committee was divided. The attitude of the majority, Vandervelde reported, was given expression in a resolution which had been formulated by Karl Kautsky, the well-known German Socialist. After affirming that in a modern democratic state the conquest of governmental power by the proletariat "must be the result of a long and painful work of proletarian organization on both economic and political levels . . . of the gradual conquest of municipalities and legislative assemblies," the Kautsky resolution stated that in countries where the governmental power was centralized, it could not be "conquered fragmentarily." In such countries, the entry of a single Socialist into a bourgeois government could not be viewed as "the normal beginning of the conquest of political power, but only as an expedient, imposed, transitory, and exceptional." The question of ministerial participation, the resolution continued, was one of tactics, not of principle, and therefore not a matter upon which an international congress must declare itself. In any event, the participation of a Socialist in a bourgeois government would not "permit the expectation of good results for the militant proletariat except when the Socialist party, by a large majority, authorizes the action and the minister remains at the command of the party." Vandervelde cautioned the delegates against construing the Kautsky resolution as either "a condemnation or a tacit approbation" of the conduct of any group of French Socialists. (He meant, of course, the Ministerial Socialists.) The international congress, he contended, was not a court of justice empowered to stigmatize or to pronounce "decrees of excommunication." Rather, its task was to promote "tolerance and conciliation." What the majority of the committee had in mind in submitting the Kautsky resolution, he pointed out, was to have the congress make "a formal declaration on questions of principle, but to leave complete liberty to the nationalities on questions of tactic." And it was the opinion of the majority that the "question of *Ministérialisme* is a question of tactics and not of principle." [15]

The committee's minority report was presented by Enrico Ferri, the Italian Socialist leader. The entry of a Socialist into a bourgeois government, he argued, paralyzed the revolutionary activity of the Socialists and placed them at the bidding of the ruling class. He cited the fact that the majority of the French Socialist Deputies, in order to keep the Waldeck-Rousseau-Millerand Ministry in office, had voted funds for the government's imperialist ventures in China. This sort of behavior, which involved a compromise with fundamental Socialist principles, was the natural consequence of ministerial participation; and it was for that reason that a minority of the committee had taken the position that the participation of a Socialist in a bourgeois ministry should be absolutely prohibited.[16]

Such a prohibition was contained in a resolution which Ferri and Guesde called upon the congress to approve. "Under the bourgeois regime, the conquest of governmental power permits occupation only of those elective offices which the party may win by means of its own forces, that is, the workers organized in a class party, and forbids necessarily all Socialist participation in bourgeois governments against which the Socialists must maintain an unwavering opposition." [17]

Following a brief discussion of the Vandervelde and Ferri reports by the delegates, the Kautsky resolution was approved by an overwhelming vote. This resolution, like the one on ministerial participation passed by the First General Congress in 1899, was ambiguous and equivocal; like the earlier resolution, it failed to put an end to the conflict between the French Ministerialists and Antiministerialists. Its ambiguous character is patent. On the one hand it stated that, in those countries where governmental power was centralized, as in France presumably, power could not be conquered in a piecemeal manner. Ostensibly this was intended as a repudiation of the

[15] See Vandervelde's report in *Cinquième Congrès*, pp. 57–64. The text of the Kautsky resolution is given in the report.

[16] Ferri's report is given in *Cinquième Congrès*, pp. 65–72.

[17] *Cinquième Congrès*, pp. 81–82.

principle of ministerial participation, since, as a matter of fact, almost all Ministerial Socialists sought to justify their stand on the grounds that the entry of a Socialist into a bourgeois ministry was actually a partial conquest of governmental power by the Socialist and labor forces. On the other hand the resolution declared that, given certain undefined political circumstances, the participation of a Socialist in such a ministry could be justified as a "transitory and exceptional" expediency. Thus, having thrown out ministerial participation in principle, the resolution allows ministerial participation in practice to enter by the back door.

On the day after the conclusion of the international congress, the Second General Congress of French Socialist Organizations opened (September 28) in the same Salle Wagram. From the outset, sharp hostility between the Ministerialists and Antiministerialists was in evidence. The question of the verification of mandates provided the initial clash. At the first session of the congress, the committee for the verification of mandates reported that, of the 2,748 mandates examined by it, 2,509 had been validated, 81 had been rejected outright, while 158 mandates required further investigation before their validity could be established. Of the 2,509 validated mandates, 1,266 were held by delegates identified with the Ministerialist camp, while the opposing faction held the remaining 1,243. To complete the task of verification, a committee of Ministerialists and Antiministerialists was set up. After laboring for some time, this committee informed the congress that it had been able to resolve the validity of only 22 additional mandates, lacking data to declare with any degree of certainty on the validity of the remaining 136 mandates, all of which were claimed by Ministerial delegates. Nevertheless, in its report to the congress, the committee recommended that these mandates be validated *en bloc*.[18]

The question then arose: How was the congress to vote on the report of the committee? Was it to vote by mandate or by delegate? The Guesdists insisted that the vote be by mandate, pointing out that the circular of convocation of the congress, which had been

[18] *Deuxième Congrès général des organisations socialistes françaises, tenu à Paris du 28 au 30 septembre 1900* (Paris, 1901), pp. 4, 15–22.

formulated by the General Committee, clearly stipulated that during the proceedings of the congress vote by mandate was to be employed "whenever it shall be demanded." The Independent Socialists insisted with equal vigor that the vote be by delegate, arguing that the stipulation in the circular applied only to questions of principle and not to questions of procedure, and that in any case the congress, being a sovereign body, could make its own rules of procedure.[19]

Actually at stake was the control of the congress itself. The Antiministerialists were anxious to have the committee's report rejected for it recommended the validation of 136 mandates claimed by Ministerial delegates. True, even without these mandates, the Ministerialists held a majority of the validated mandates. But since the number of validated mandates held by the Antiministerialists was almost equal to those held by their opponents, there was the possibility that given its superior organization and tighter discipline, the Antiministerial bloc would be able to reject the report of the committee by a solid phalanx of votes if balloting by mandate were employed. Rejection of the report would serve to indicate that the power of decision in the congress lay within this bloc. After a stormy debate, the congress decided that the vote on the report was to be by delegate. The report was accepted, and the control of the Ministerialists in the congress was thereby secured. The Guesdist delegation, maintaining that the Ministerial Socialists had obtained a "factitious majority" by means of an invalid and irregular procedure, refused to recognize the congress as a legally constituted authority; with a single exception, they abstained from all subsequent voting.[20]

With the question of mandates out of the way, the delegates turned to a consideration of the conflict between the General Committee and the Socialist parliamentary group. In this connection, reports were presented by Louis Dubreuilh, for the General Committee; Alexandre Bracke, for the Commission for Supervision of the Press, Élus, and the Militants — a subgroup of the General Committee; Victor Andrieux, for the Commission for Propaganda —

[19] *Deuxième Congrès*, pp. v–ix, 36–45.
[20] *Deuxième Congrès*, pp. 31–46. The Guesdists joined in the unanimous vote of the congress approving a resolution which called for the repeal of the *lois scélérates*.

another subgroup; and by Gustave Rouanet, for the Socialist parliamentary group.

Dubreuilh, the Blanquist executive secretary of the General Committee, reviewed the work of the General Committee since its formation. Without attempting to attribute blame, he gave a detailed account of the gradual deterioration of the relations between the General Committee and the parliamentary group. Bracke, the Guesdist secretary of the Commission for Supervision, likewise submitted a rather objective account of the work of his group. He cited numerous instances in which the parliamentary group had failed to achieve unity of action in the Chamber, and he stressed the need for greater discipline. However, in his report, Andrieux, the Guesdist secretary of the Commission for Propaganda, disclosed a marked bias against some of the Ministerial Socialist Deputies, contending that they alone had hindered the work of his Commission.[21]

Rouanet, reporting for the parliamentary group, staunchly defended the conduct of the Ministerial Socialist Deputies. He repudiated the notion that the Antiministerial Deputies alone were loyal and sincere Socialists and that the Ministerial Deputies were rogues, opportunists, and betrayers of Socialism and the working class. He insisted that all the Socialist Deputies adhered faithfully to the fundamental principles of the federated party as defined at the First General Congress of 1899: it was only that the Ministerial and the Antiministerial Deputies interpreted the principles differently. "On the application of these principles to the facts and developments of everyday politics," the Socialist Deputies "have been and still remain in the same state of uncertainty as the diverse organizations of the present party which interpret these principles each according to a different criteria and, hence, starting from identical principles, sometimes wind up in actual practice with contradictory and opposing actions."

The fundamental division within the Socialist parliamentary group, as within the party itself, was, in Rouanet's opinion, on the attitude that the Socialists should take toward the government. It was the absence of agreement on this point which accounted in

[21] The reports are given in *Deuxième Congrès*, pp. 107–132.

large part for the opposing votes of the members of the parliamentary group. The Antiministerialists maintained that the doctrine of class struggle implied on the part of Socialists an "indifference with regard to the form of government" and also that "to fight for the maintenance or for the accession of one of these forms was to misguide the action of the proletariat against phantoms." [22] But the Ministerialists were not indifferent to the fate of republican institutions. "We have always repudiated as an insult and a calumny the accusation of the bourgeoisie sometimes directed against the Socialist party — the accusation of holding cheaply the Republic and civil liberties, of being a party of economic demands exclusively, of being indifferent to the maintenance of the republican form of government. . ." Since they first entered the Chamber in force, Socialists of various shades of opinion had reiterated in word and deed their determination to defend the Republic and to aid in the development of liberal institutions. In 1895–1896, all the Socialist Deputies had joined forces with Radicals and other republican elements in the Chamber in supporting the Bourgeois Ministry "because they saw in it the possibility of developing our institutions more democratically."

At the close of his report, Rouanet commented briefly on the relations between the Socialist parliamentary group and the General Committee. He indicted the latter for its arbitrariness and accused it of seeking to humiliate and subjugate the members of the group. He charged that the General Committee not only had taken impor-

---

[22] In an article published in the *Petit Sou* on September 19, 1900, Guesde, reverting to a position he had held in the 1880's, declared that as long as capitalism continued to exist, it made no difference to the proletariat whether their government be republican or monarchical in form, since the government in a class-stratified society (such as France) was always an instrument of the bourgeois ruling class: "None of the changes in the form of government can be beneficial to the workers as long as the same class, the capitalist class, remains in power. Under the Republic as under the Monarchy, the workers are equally exploited and annihilated; for whether it be elective or hereditary, the control of the government remains in the hands of the exploiting bourgeoisie." In his famous Introduction (March 1891) to Karl Marx's, *The Civil War in France* (New York, 1940, page 22), Friedrich Engels had declared: "In reality, however, the state is nothing but a machine for the oppression of one class by another, and indeed in the democratic republic no less than in the monarchy."

tant decisions bearing on the activity of the group without previous consultation with it, but, having taken these decisions, had communicated them to the Socialist Deputies "in terms which seemed to some of them to be a deliberate slight on their dignity as men and as chosen representatives." "But even granting that the General Committee had the right to dictate categorical orders to each of us," he went on, "still it would have been more suitable to employ terminology which did not appear to impose a rigorous and puerile subordination on the Deputies." He expressed the hope that the congress would replace the existing General Committee with a new organ which would treat the parliamentary group with proper regard for the "dignity of a Socialist Deputy." To this last remark, delegates seated on the Guesdist benches retorted: "You are our servants!" [23]

The presentation of the four reports served to heighten partisan passions, and during the course of the discussion that followed, Andrieux, who had reported for the Commission for Propaganda, was assaulted and stabbed in the hand by an unidentified delegate. Confusion reigned and it appeared for a moment that the congress would degenerate into an open brawl. But, as it turned out, sober and responsible leaders of the opposing factions were able to hold their followers in check. When order was restored, Lucien Roland, in the name of the Guesdist delegation, introduced a resolution calling for the expulsion of the unfraternal delegate who had committed the outrage. The resolution was defeated, whereupon the entire Guesdist delegation stood up and with shouts of "Assassins! Assassins!" marched out of the hall.[24]

The Guesdists had undoubtedly been aroused by the attack upon a member of their own delegation and by the refusal of the congress to vote the expulsion, an action which they construed as tantamount to an approbation of the outrage itself. This alone does not explain

[23] Rouanet's report is given in *Deuxième Congrès*, pp. 90–102. Bracke later characterized the report as a "cynical apology for those Deputies who, for the love of a ministry of assassins, had rejected a proposal for a parliamentary investigation of the massacre of workers at Chalon-sur-Saône." *Leur Congrès à la Salle Wagram* (Paris, 1901), p. 54. See also Lafargue's article in the *Petit Sou*, October 3, 1900.

[24] *Deuxième Congrès*, pp. 158–160.

why they bolted; a more fundamental reason appears to have been the fact that they were a minority at the congress, lacking the power of decision. From the opening session, the Guesdists were aware that they were outnumbered and would not be able to impose their views on the congress and, hence, on the party. Unwilling to accept the fact that their opponents were in control, they had declared that the congress was without legal authority. The refusal of the delegates to vote the expulsion of the assailant served as an excuse for withdrawing from a congress where they could expect to achieve little if anything. This is by no means mere conjecture. On at least one other occasion the Guesdists had left a congress in which they were a powerless minority — the Saint-Etienne Congress in 1882. Their departure from the Second General Congress appeared to be in keeping with an old practice.[25]

After the exodus of the Guesdists, their traditional allies, the Blanquists, who had decided to remain at the congress in order to serve as a link between the departed delegation and the rest of the Socialist forces, assumed leadership of the opposition. During the succeeding session of the congress which was devoted to a general discussion of the broad issues raised in the four reports, Vaillant spearheaded the attack on *Ministérialisme*. It was in vain. Resolutions expressing opposition to *Ministérialisme* or calling for censure of the Ministerial Deputies were summarily rejected; and the discussion was brought to a close with the adoption of a resolution relative to the conduct of the Socialist parliamentary group which declared that, though the Deputies had pursued different tactics, all had "acted entirely in good faith and with the sole preoccupation of serving their party. . ."[26]

The adoption of this resolution was, of course, a victory for the Ministerialists. The stand taken by the Ministerial Deputies on the Chalon resolutions of June 15 had received the tacit approval of the congress, for did not the delegates agree that they had acted "entirely

[25] In this connection, see the articles by Viviani and Zévaès in the *Petit Sou*, October 2, 1900; Briand's article in the *Lanterne*, October 3, 1900; and Lavaud's article in the *Parti Ouvrier*, October 7, 1900.

[26] *Deuxième Congrès*, pp. 172–189, 206–221, 250–253.

in good faith and with the sole preoccupation of serving their party"
on June 15? Henceforth, these Deputies were free to believe that
they could pursue as a regular and legitimate tactic close collaboration with the republican groups in the Left Bloc in the Chamber
without fear of reproach by their party.

Having devoted most of the time scheduled for the congress to
the verification of mandates and the discussion of the reports of the
General Committee, its subcommittees, and the Socialist parliamentary group, the delegates were able to give the important matter of
Socialist unity only brief consideration. In the closing minutes of
the last session, Jaurès, who had not hitherto taken a prominent part
in the proceedings, broached the subject by taking the floor to present the report of the committee on party unification. This recommended that a new General Committee be set up without delay.
Its essential tasks would be to inquire, by means of direct consultation with all the political and economic groups comprising the
federated party, into the best method of unifying all the Socialist
forces, and to prepare a project of unification on the basis of its find-
ings. This project was to be submitted to the next party congress.
The report left the way open for the return of the Guesdists when
it anticipated that "in spite of transitory divisions" all the Socialist
factions would soon join forces to create "the final and complete
union of the Socialist party." [27] It was approved by an almost unanimous vote, and the congress was declared at an end.

The hope of some that the Guesdists would soon see the error
of their ways and return to the fold was proven to be without
foundation. The Guesdists did not construe their departure from the
Second General Congress as simply a gesture of indignation, a
temporary severance of ties with the federated party. On the contrary, they viewed their exist as marking the end of their relationship with the Ministerialists. They had been disappointed by the
failure of the International Congress at Paris to take a clear-cut
stand against *Ministérialisme*, and they had been outraged by the
conduct of the Ministerialists at the Second General Congress.
They were now determined to separate themselves entirely from

[27] *Deuxième Congrès*, p. 254. See also the *Petite République*, October 2, 5, 1900.

those Socialist elements that deviated fundamentally from what they, the Guesdists, conceived as the legitimate role of a Socialist party in a bourgeois society and the proper sphere and method of Socialist actions. (These related matters — the role of a Socialist party and its proper sphere and method of action — were the very heart of the question of *Ministérialisme*.) At a meeting which took place immediately following their departure from the Second General Congress, the Guesdists, after flaying their opponents as "pseudo-Socialists" and denouncing them for their "irregular and criminal" tactics, declared their intention of organizing a new Socialist party to be composed of those elements that were avowedly "revolutionary," that stood "resolutely on the terrain of the class struggle," repudiating without qualification "all compromise with the capitalist and governmental bourgeoisie." To realize this objective, the Guesdists set up (September 30) a committee charged with the task of drafting a project of party organization to be submitted to a national convention of all the revolutionary Socialist forces in the near future.[28]

The Guesdist decision to proceed with the creation of a new party placed the Blanquists in an ambiguous position. On the one hand, being themselves self-styled revolutionary Socialists as well as traditional allies of the Guesdists, they were naturally interested in the new party. On the other hand, they were not eager to break with the federated party (Parti socialiste français), which did, after all, bring together all the Socialist factions with the exception of the Guesdists. The Blanquist leadership still believed that if the federated party could be induced to modify its stand on *Ministérialisme* the Guesdists would rejoin their comrades. At any rate they were determined to make a final attempt to realize that objective — to wean the federated party from *Ministérialisme* — before casting their lot with the Guesdists.[29]

In keeping with this, the Blanquists, at the Third General Con-

---

[28] *Petit Sou*, October 2, 3, 1900; the *Socialiste*, October 7, 1900. See also Bracke, pp. 60–61.

[29] See Vaillant's articles in the *Petit Sou*, October 5, 19, 1900, March 22, April 12, May 3, 1901. See also the *Petite République*, November 27, 1900.

gress of the federated party, held in Lyons in May 1901, revived the Millerand Case. The arguments presented by both supporters and opponents of ministerial participation contained little that was new; the debate, therefore, does not merit detailed consideration.

Briefly, the conflict at the Lyons Congress centered around two opposing resolutions. One declared that Millerand, by his acceptance of a post in the Waldeck-Rousseau Ministry, had ruled himself *out* of the party. The second asserted that Millerand, in entering the ministry, had placed himself not outside of the party, but only *outside* the *control* of the party. Spokesmen for the Antiministerial faction rallied to the first resolution, contending that its adoption would pave the way for the unification of the Socialist forces. The expulsion of Millerand from the party, Vaillant told the delegates, was the one prerequisite for peace within the Socialist movement. "This peace will not exist," he affirmed, "until the turmoil and confusion of the present moment is removed and until this *Ministérialisme*, which has brought about the present difficulties, will have been dispelled." Ministerialist spokesmen supported the second resolution with equal vigor, arguing that it was in perfect harmony with the stand of the Socialist and Labor International on the question of ministerial participation. They insisted that the second resolution, disavowing as it did party responsibility for Millerand's conduct, provided a satisfactory basis for unity within the Socialist ranks. Many Ministerialists opposed the first resolution, not only because it involved the expulsion of Millerand, but also because they believed that it implied the excommunication of those party members who had supported Millerand during the past two years. This was perhaps what Viviani had in mind when he asserted that the adoption of the first resolution would not be the "preface to unity," but rather the "preface to even more profound discords." [30]

At the conclusion of debate on the Millerand Case, the first resolution was overwhelmingly defeated. Following the balloting, Lucien Landrin, a Blanquist militant, speaking on this occasion for the entire Antiministerial faction, declared that since the Antiminister-

---

[30] *Troisième Congrès général des organisations socialistes françaises, tenu à Lyon du 26 au 28 mai 1901* (Paris, 1901), pp. 65, 69–77, 277–281, 301–337, 340–366.

ialist resolution had been summarily rejected, the Antiministerialists no longer believed that it was possible for them to continue "for even a minute" to participate in the congress. Whereupon the Blanquist and Alliance communiste révolutionnaire delegations, together with the delegates of several autonomous federations and other independent groups, marched out of the hall and out of the party.[31]

The exodus from the Lyons Congress of the Blanquists and their allies completed the schism which had begun at the Second General Congress in Paris. The unity of the Socialist movement, so hopefully proclaimed in 1899, was now definitely destroyed. Henceforth, Ministerialists and Antiministerialists were to go their separate ways, the former taking up the standard of "Reformist Socialism," the latter that of "Revolutionary Socialism."

[31] *Troisième Congrès*, pp. 382–384.

Chapter 6

The Bifurcation of the Socialist Movement

During the months immediately following the Lyons Congress of 1901, representatives of the various Antiministerial elements, under the leadership of Guesde and Vaillant, held a series of meetings in Paris for the purpose of drafting a credo for unification. At the last of these meetings, on August 15, the representatives adopted a "Plan of Unity" which was to serve as the basis for the organization of a "revolutionary" Socialist party to be called the Parti socialiste de France (Socialist Party of France), with the subtitle Unité socialiste révolutionnaire.

The Plan was prefaced with a brief declaration of principles which included, in addition to a restatement of the three-point credo of the Saint-Mandé Program of 1896, an unqualified repudiation of *Ministérialisme*. "Party of revolution, and therefore of opposition to the bourgeois state, it is its duty to extort all the reforms that can improve the conditions of struggle of the working class, but it must not, under any circumstances, by participation in the central executive power, by voting for the budget, or by alliances with the bourgeois parties, provide any of the means that will prolong the domination of the enemy class."

According to the Plan, the new party was to be based on a federative form of organization. Groups and organizations affiliated with the party in the same commune were to form one section; and all the sections of the same department were in turn to constitute one federation. In the period between the annual congresses, which were to formulate doctrine and give general direction to the party, the party was to be administered by a Central Council. In accordance with Guesde's conception of the function of such an executive organ, the Central Council was to exercise rather extensive authority. It was to have complete supervision over the party press, party members holding political office (*élus*), as well as the party membership in general. To carry out its functions, it was empowered to take "all measures, however extraordinary they might be, that would be required by circumstances." [1]

On November 3, leaders of the Antiministerial forces gathered at a conference in Ivry-sur-Seine and formally ratified the Plan as the constitution of the new Parti socialiste de France. The conference decided, however, that, until such time as the unity of the revolutionary Socialist forces was realized in fact as well as on paper, that until the new party was actually functioning as a going concern, the existing nationally constituted organizations identified with it (the Guesdist and Blanquist parties) were to retain their constitutions and programs.[2] During the months that followed, the Central Council, which included the top men of the Antiministerial forces, devoted itself energetically — and with considerable success — to the tasks of coordinating the activities of the various organizations and groups affiliated with the new party and laying the foundation for an organic union.[3]

While this confluence of Antiministerial elements was taking place, the Ministerial Socialist party (Parti socialiste français) underwent yet another fission. The exit of the Blanquists and their allies from the Lyons Congress (May 1901) had by no means freed the party of all dissident elements. There had remained within the organization an outspoken left-wing minority which was composed essentially of two groups. One of these comprised a number of autonomous federations (such as the Federations of the Seine,

[1] For the text of the Plan, see the *Petite République*, August 13, 1901.

[2] *Petit Sou*, November 5, 1901; the *Socialiste*, November 10–17, 1901.

[3] *Socialiste*, January 13–20, May 18–25, 1902. For a list of the organizations that adhered to the new party, see the *Petit Sou*, November 5, 1901.

the Pas-de-Calais, and the Seine-et-Oise) which, though in sympathy with the Antiministerialists, had remained within the party in the hope of reconciling the reformist and revolutionary wings of the Socialist movement. The second group was made up of the Allemanist faction (which at this time was in the process of dissolution) and a number of autonomous federations (the Federations of the Ain, the Bretagne, and the Jura, among others) which together could be characterized as dissident Ministerialists or, as one observer waggishly labeled them, "Antiministerial Ministerialists." [4] These dissident Ministerialists, unlike the thoroughgoing Antiministerialists of the Parti socialiste de France, accepted class collaboration as long as coalitions between Socialists and progressive bourgeois parties were only momentary and provisional arrangements, formed for certain specific objectives. They were vigorously opposed to the idea of permanent collaboration. Both groups were dismayed by the party's failure to resolve the Millerand Case in a definitive manner, and they viewed with apprehension the gradual but steady drift of the party towards the Right following the Lyons Congress.[5]

It was a rather minor incident, however, which led a section of this left-wing faction to bolt the party early in 1902. In the summer of 1901 it was learned that Czar Nicholas II of Russia, hated by Socialists the world over for his repression of radical movements at home, had been invited to visit France. In anticipation of this event the General Committee of the Parti socialiste français issued a manifesto (August 21, 1901) which called upon Socialists to abstain from participating in demonstrations in honor of the royal visitor and which cautioned the Socialist Deputies against voting funds for the reception of the Czar "lest they compromise themselves in the eyes of the proletariat." [6] Completely disregarding the directive of

---

[4] E. Untermann, "Socialism Abroad," *International Socialist Review*, 2: 683–684 (1902). See also H. Lagardelle, "French Socialism and the Lyons Congress," *International Socialist Review*, 2: 101–102 (1901).

[5] *Parti Ouvrier*, January 5, 19, 26, 1902; J. Bourdeau, "Revue du mouvement socialiste," *Revue politique et parlementaire*, 32: 572–573 (1902); Francis de Pressensé, "La Question ministérielle," *Mouvement socialiste*, 7: 49–54 (1902).

[6] Quoted in Bourdeau, "Revue du mouvement socialiste," *Revue politique et parlementaire*, 30: 394 (1901).

his own party, Millerand took part in receptions for the Czar. This indiscipline aroused the ire of many of his comrades; and on October 9, at a special meeting of the General Committee, the representative of the autonomous Federation of the Loir-et-Cher, Amilcare Cipriani, introduced a resolution calling upon the General Committee to expel Millerand from the party for having "seriously compromised" it by his "shameful prostration at the feet of the Czar." [7] Several sessions of the General Committee were devoted to the discussion of this matter, and on December 26, the Cipriani resolution together with other motions censuring Millerand's conduct were voted upon and overwhelmingly defeated.[8] To many of the left-wing members of the Parti socialiste français, the refusal of the General Committee either to expel or to censure Millerand was the last straw. The Allemanists and the autonomous Federations of the Ain, Loir-et-Cher, Jura, and the Var severed relations with the General Committee and subsequently (January 1902) withdrew from the party.[9]

Two months after the departure of these dissident elements from its ranks, the Parti socialiste français held its Fourth National Congress in Tours. In sharp contrast to previous congresses, the sessions at Tours took place in an atmosphere of harmony and good will, with the debates singularly free of calculated insult and invective. Under these favorable conditions, the Tours Congress was able to accomplish a considerable amount of important work. For one thing, it formulated and adopted a "Declaration of Principles" for the party. This Declaration, which was largely the work of Jaurès, gave clear and elaborate expression to the moderate spirit, to the frankly reformist tendencies, of the party.

The Declaration first set forth the view that modern Socialism evolved simultaneously from the growth of democracy and from the capitalist mode of production. It stated that the objective of the Socialist movement was to realize in the economic sphere the rights

[7] *Petite République*, January 19, 1902.
[8] *Petite République*, January 22, 26, 29, 1902.
[9] *Petit Sou*, January 10, 1902; *Quatrième Congrès général du Parti socialiste français, tenu à Tours du 2 au 4 mars 1902* (Paris, 1902), pp. 406–417.

and liberties which had already been achieved in the political sphere; that is, to extend to all citizens the guarantees of the famous Declaration of the Rights of Man and the Citizen — the rights of freedom and security. In the political order, democracy was now a reality, with all citizens sharing equally, according to law, in sovereignty. There existed, in the words of the Declaration, "communism in political power." In the economic order, however, only a minority had sovereign power: "It is the oligarchy of capital which possesses, directs, administers, and exploits." It was, therefore, the pressing task of the proletariat to bring about in the economic order the democracy already realized in the political order: "Just as all citizens possess and utilize in common, democratically, political power, so they must possess and utilize in common, economic power, the means of production."

The Declaration affirmed that the proletariat could not expect its emancipation, which was dependent upon the total transformation of society, to be brought about by the good will and generosity of the capitalist class. Rather, it could expect emancipation only as a consequence of the "continual and methodical pressure" which it itself exerted on that class and on the government. It would be wrong for the proletariat to dismiss out of hand the real possibility of a revolution which might be brought about by the implacable resistence or the illegal aggression of the privileged classes of society. On the other hand, "it would be fatal, trusting in the one word revolution, to neglect the great forces which are at the disposal of the conscious, organized proletariat in a democracy." The most important of these means of action were free elections, trade-union organization, and the partial and general strike. But in any case, the Declaration made it clear, "no formula, no mechanism, can enable the working class to dispense with the constant effort of organization and education."

Turning from the question of how the transformation of society was to be accomplished, the Declaration spelled out the position of the party on such matters as republican institutions, civil liberties, and internationalism. The French Republic was characterized as the necessary means of liberation and education. Indeed, Socialism was declared to be essentially republican in spirit: "It could even be said to be the Republic itself, since it is the extension of the Republic to the regime of property and labor." As for civil liberties, the Declaration noted that the Socialist party required "free minds, emancipated from superstitions and prejudices," in order to organize the new social order. It therefore asked for and guaranteed every individual complete freedom of speech and press. Over against all religions and churches, the party posited "the unlimited right of free thought, the scientific conception of the universe, and a system of public education based exclusively on science and reason." Lastly, the realization of the international entente of the proletariat was necessary, the Declaration stated, "as well to curb the forces of aggression as to prepare by a concerted action the general triumph of Socialism." The Declaration concluded with a reaffirmation of the three principles of Socialism set forth in the Saint-Mandé Program.[10]

In addition to endowing the Parti socialiste français with a credo, the Tours Congress also established a definite plan of party organization. Henceforth, the party was to be organized on a federative basis. All the study and propaganda groups, permanent political

[10] The text of the Declaration is given in *Quatrième Congrès*, pp. 245–252. For an English translation, see Ensor, *Modern Socialism*, pp. 339–345. The task of drawing up the Declaration had been entrusted to a committee which included Jaurès, Briand, Deville, and Rouanet among its fourteen members. But that the statement produced by the committee was almost entirely the work of Jaurès — that it was an embodiment of his Socialist philosophy — is shown by a comparison of the Declaration with Jaurès's speech at the Tours Congress (*Quatrième Congrès*, pp. 135–149) and his articles in the *Petite République*, June 13, August 21, 24, 26, 29, September 1, 6, 7, 11, 13, 17, 1901, February 11, 15, 1902.

An extensive electoral program was affixed to the Declaration. Among the immediate political reforms called for were the following: direct universal suffrage without distinction as to sex; popular right of initiative and referendum; abolition of the Senate and the Presidency of the Republic; free education at all levels; separation of Church and State and the abolition of the religious budget; and the substitution of a militia for the standing army. Among the economic demands were the following: a progressive income tax; limitation of the length of the workday to eight hours and of the workweek to six days; prohibition of labor for children under fourteen years of age; a system of social security which would insure all industrial, commercial, and agricultural workers against sickness, accident, disability, old age, and unemployment; and the nationalization (among other things) of the railways, mines, big industrial establishments, and the bank of France. The full program is given in *Quatrième Congrès*, pp. 375–382; Ensor, pp. 345–350.

groups, labor unions, and cooperatives which were affiliated with the party and which were located in the same department or region were to form a single departmental or regional federation. Each federation would draw up its own statutes and largely determine its own affairs. A national congress of the party was to meet annually to determine general policy. The old General Committee was replaced by a new organ, the Interfederal Committee. This was to be composed of delegates from the party group in the Chamber of Deputies and from the departmental and regional federations. It was to have little real authority, being empowered only to direct the propaganda efforts of the party and to attend to the general administration of the organization. The task of seeing to it that the principles and program of the party were respected by the rank and file was entrusted to the federations.[11]

Finally, in the interest of party harmony, attempting to appease what remained of the left-wing faction, the Tours Congress unanimously adopted the following resolution dealing with the persistent issue of ministerial participation. "Executing the resolution adopted by the [International] Congress at Paris in 1900 with regard to the participation of one or several Socialists in bourgeois governments, the congress declares that beginning with the next legislature, no Socialist shall participate in any ministry until a congress of the party shall decide otherwise." [12] By adopting this resolution, the congress hoped to resolve the vexing question at last, without having to approve or censure Millerand himself. As subsequent events were to show, however, this action did little to end the matter.

Two months after the Tours Congress, legislative elections were

[11] For the plan of party organization, see *Troisième Congrès général des organisations socialistes françaises*, pp. 471–480; *Quatrième Congrès*, pp. 282–285.

[12] *Quatrième Congrès*, p. 386. To the Antiministerialists, the Tours Congress was added proof of the *embourgeoisement* of the Parti socialiste français. Charles Rappoport, a Guesdist spokesman, declared in the *Petit Sou* (March 18, 1902): "The congress has done nothing but deepen the chasm between Socialism and *Ministérialisme*. Ministerialists and *Arrivistes* on one side: Socialists and Revolutionaries on the other — that's the situation now!" See also Lafargue's article in the *Petit Sou*, March 17, 1902; Guesde's articles in the *Socialiste*, March 9–16, 23–30, 1902; and Lagardelle's articles in the *Mouvement socialiste*, 7: 433–435, 673–687, 774–781, 1009–1016 (1902).

held (April and May) throughout the country. The Socialists made a favorable showing. The total vote received by all the Socialist candidates was almost 900,000, and forty-eight Socialists won seats in the Chamber of Deputies, as compared with some 800,000 votes and forty-two seats in the last legislative elections (1898). Of the forty-eight *élus*, thirty-two were members of the Parti socialiste français, twelve were members of the Parti socialiste de France, while four were enrolled in the autonomous Federation of the Bouches-du-Rhône.[13]

Immediately following the elections, a series of political developments took place which exercised a strong influence on the course of French Socialism during 1902–1905. On June 3, Premier Waldeck-Rousseau, who had borne the heavy burdens of office for almost three years, tendered his resignation to President Loubet. Upon the dissolution of the ministry, Millerand, who as Minister of Commerce and Industry had initiated a more extensive program of social reforms benefiting the workers than any of his predecessors in that office,[14] rejoined the Ministerial Socialist group in the Chamber.

To prevent the disruption of the Left Bloc, which during the past three years had united the Moderate Republican, Radical, Radi-

---

[13] For detailed results of the elections as they concerned the Socialist parties and organizations, see the *Petit Sou*, April 29, 30, May 13, 14, 1902; the *Petite République*, April 29, 30, May 1, 2, 12, 13, 1902; the *Socialiste*, May 11–18, August 24–31, 1902; Jean Longuet, "Les Tendances du socialisme français et leurs forces électorales," *Mouvement socialiste*, 7: 1057–1068 (1902); and G. Rouanet, "Les Elections générales," *Revue socialiste*, 35: 513–518 (1902). The following Socialists were elected Deputies: Albert-Poulain, Félix Aldy, Allard, Henri Bagnol, Gabriel Baron, Basly, Bénézech, Jean Bouhey-Allex, Jean Bouveri, Boyer, Breton, Briand, Cadenat, Calvinhac, Etienne Camuzet, Alexandre Cardet, Carnaud, Charpentier, Chauvière, Colliard, Paul Constans, Coutant, Dejeante, Gustave Delory, Devèze, Dufour, Ferrero, François Fournier, Léon Gérault-Richard, Grousset, Hugues, Jaurès, Krauss, Labussière, Lamendin, Lassalle, Adrien Meslier, Millerand, Pastre, Jean Piger, Pressensé, Rouanet, Auguste Selle, Sembat, Léon Thivrier, Vaillant, Adrien Veber, and Walter. Calvinhac died in July 1902 and Krauss in October 1904. Four Socialists — Deville, François Isoard, Zévaès, and Victor Augagneur — were elected Deputies in special elections in Paris (March 1903), Forcalquier (June 1903), Grenoble (March 1904), and Lyons (November 1904) respectively.

[14] See A. Lavy, *L'Oeuvre de Millerand* (Paris, 1902); and Charles W. Pipkin, *Social Politics and Modern Democracies* (2 vols., New York, 1931), II, 54–73.

cal-Socialist, and Ministerial Socialist groups in the Chamber in support of the government's program of republican defense, and to see to it that a parliamentary leader sympathetic to the policies of Waldeck-Rousseau would be selected to form a new ministry, the leaders of the aforesaid groups set up a steering committee known as the Délégation des gauches to coordinate their parliamentary activities. The Délégation des gauches succeeded in having the nominee of the Left Bloc, Emile Combes, a Radical Senator who had been Minister of Education in the Bourgeois Cabinet of 1895–1896, designated by President Loubet to form a ministry. Shortly after the formation of his ministry, Combes and the Délégation des gauches entered into an agreement (July 2) by which the former promised to carry through the anticlerical program initiated by his predecessor — which meant a firm application of the Associations Law of 1901 that was aimed mainly against religious congregations — while the latter promised Combes the support of the Left Bloc.[15]

This steering committee, which for more than two years secured the Combes Ministry against assaults from the opposition and which gave unity and direction to the Left Bloc, included among its twenty-six members five Socialist Deputies — Jules Breton, Aristide Briand, Pierre Colliard, Jaurès, and Pressensé. These did not represent all the Socialists in the Chamber, however. They could speak only for the thirty-six members of the Socialist parliamentary group (Union socialiste) who were affiliated with the Ministerial Socialist party. The Revolutionary Socialist parliamentary group (Union socialiste révolutionnaire), composed of the twelve members of the Antiministerial party, refused to have anything to do with the steering committee.[16]

---

[15] *Petite République*, June 1, 3, 1902; Rudolph A. Winnacker, "The Délégation Des Gauches: a Successful Attempt at Managing a Parliamentary Coalition," *Journal of Modern History*, 9: 451–456 (1937). On the Associations Law, see Seignobos, *L'Evolution de la 3ᵉ République*, pp. 219–223.

[16] Winnacker, pp. 449–455. The following were members of the Union socialiste: Albert-Poulain, Aldy, Bagnol, Baron, Basly, Bénézech, Bouhey-Allex, Boyer, Breton, Briand, Cadenat, Calvinhac, Camuzet, Cardet, Carnaud, Charpentier, Colliard, Devèze, Ferrero, Fournier, Gérault-Richard, Grousset, Hugues, Jaurès, Krauss, Labussière, Lamendin, Lassalle, Meslier, Millerand, Pastre, Piger, Pressensé, Rouanet, Selle, and Veber. The Union socialiste révolutionnaire, which had been formed in May 1901

One of the dominant members of the Délégation des gauches was Jaurès, who had been instrumental in bringing about the participation of the Ministerial Socialists on that committee. Jaurès played a leading role in the formulation of its policy, and, as long as the committee continued to function, was constantly engaged in the dual task of maintaining the union between the various groups of the Left Bloc and of cementing relations between the Délégation des gauches and the ministry. On more than one occasion Jaurès's resourcefulness and energetic leadership alone prevented the disruption of the Délégation des gauches and the overthrow of the Combes Ministry itself.[17] In recognition of his services, in January 1903, by the votes of the Left Bloc, he was elected Fourth Vice-President of the Chamber of Deputies.

To Jaurès, the participation of the Socialists in the Left Bloc and on the Délégation des gauches was indispensable to the realization of the policies initiated by Waldeck-Rousseau. The latter had succeeded in the crucial task of republican defense: he had frustrated the attacks of the forces of reaction on republican institutions. It now remained, Jaurès believed, to push forward the program of "republican attack," to curb by legislative action, the political and social influence of the Church, which, in his opinion, had been the "principal inspirer and organizer of the whole anti-Republican campaign" during the past several years.[18] Since the Délégation des gauches and the Combes Ministry had agreed to pursue a thoroughgoing anticlerical policy, both merited the support of the Socialist Deputies. Moreover, Jaurès maintained that the collaboration of the Socialists with the progressive groups of the Left would enhance considerably the possibility of enacting such reforms as a progressive income tax, the extension of free education, and the establishment of a comprehensive system of workers' pensions.[19]

---

after the schism at the Lyons Congress, was composed of the following: Allard, Bouveri, Chauvière, Constans, Coutant, Dejeante, Delory, Dufour, Sembat, Thivrier, Vaillant, and Walter.

[17] Winnacker, pp. 466–468.

[18] Quoted in Weinstein, *Jean Jaurès*, p. 83.

[19] See Jaurès's speech in *Journal officiel*, session of June 12, 1902, pp. 1820–1824.

As was to be expected, the leaders of the Parti socialiste de France looked upon the participation of the Ministerial Socialists on the Délégation des gauches as another repudiation of the principle of the class struggle. Guesde charged that the formation of the Délégation des gauches was a preliminary step toward the merger of the Parti socialiste français with the Radical party, and he dubbed Jaurès "a leader of the bourgeois majority." [20] Another spokesman for the Antiministerial party, Pierre Bonnier, labeled the Ministerial Socialist Deputies as "lackeys" of the bourgeoisie and bitterly assailed them for selling out to the enemy class: "All those within the Socialist movement who could be bought by favours, by ambition, or by political office have joined the ministerial bloc." [21] While these spokesmen for the Antiministerial Socialist party denounced the Ministerial Socialists for allying themselves with the Combes Ministry, the conduct of their own Deputies in the Chamber during the tenure of this ministry did not differ significantly from that of the Ministerial Socialists. Although the former voted against the government when it presented its budgets (the latter supported the government), both joined in voting resolutions of confidence in the Combes Ministry whenever its life was menaced by a coalition of the groups of the Right-Center and the Right.[22]

The leadership of the Antiministerial Socialist party, however, was not alone in criticizing the tactics of the Ministerialists; within that party there was an undercurrent of opposition. A left-wing faction of the Parti socialiste français, as has been noted, did not approve

---

See also Jaurès's articles in the *Petite République*, April 12, May 18, 24, June 2, 14, 1902.

[20] *Socialiste*, June 22–29, 1902.

[21] *Socialiste*, July 13–20, 1902. See also the *Socialiste*, June 8–15, 1902.

[22] *Journal officiel*, sessions of October 17, 1902, p. 2399; November 24, 1902, pp. 2745–2746; January 15, 1903, pp. 21–22; May 28, 1903, pp. 1175–1176; October 22, 1903, pp. 2346–2347; February 5, 1904, pp. 284–285; March 17, 1904, pp. 793–800; July 12, 1904, pp. 2018–2019; October 22, 1904, pp. 2140–2141; October 28, 1904, pp. 2245–2247; November 4, 1904, pp. 2297–2300. In this connection, see also the report of the Socialist parliamentary group (Union socialiste) that was presented to the Saint-Etienne Congress (January 1904) of the Parti socialiste français in the *Revue socialiste*, 39: 129–161 (1904); the *Socialiste*, July 31–August 7, August 7–14, 1904; and Alexandre Zévaès, *Le Socialisme en 1912* (Paris, 1912), pp. 16–18.

of the policy of long-term collaboration between Deputies of their party and those of republican groups in the Chamber; this faction opposed the participation of the Deputies on the Délégation des gauches. When Jaurès accepted the post of Fourth Vice-President of the Chamber — a position which made him a sort of lieutenant of the Radical, Léon Bourgeois, who was President of the Chamber — this faction began to voice its opposition to the tactics of the party Deputies. But it was Millerand's conduct in the Chamber soon after Jaurès's assumption of office which brought this opposition into the open in an arresting manner.

On January 21, 1903, Millerand voted for the budget of secret funds of the Ministry of the Interior (a budget which Socialists believed was used among other things to pay police spies and *agents provocateurs*); all of his colleagues in the Socialist parliamentary group either voted against the budget or abstained. Two days later, of all the Socialists, only Millerand voted for a resolution approving the decision of the Minister of War to prosecute certain trade union leaders for issuing an antimilitarist pamphlet, the other Socialists had opposed the resolution. Three days later (January 26), Millerand voted against a resolution introduced by one of his colleagues, Jules Breton, calling for the abolition of the religious budget (funds provided for various religious organizations by the government), while the rest of the Socialist parliamentary group voted for it. On January 29, when a resolution to abolish the French ambassadorship at the Vatican, introduced by a member of Millerand's own parliamentary group, was put to a vote, he opposed it, while the other Socialist Deputies gave it their support.[23]

Millerand's votes occasioned widespread resentment within the Ministerial Socialist party. Pierre Renaudel, a leader of its left-wing faction, bluntly charged him with being a political opportunist.[24] Even Jaurès, who had allied himself with Millerand in the past, felt that the latter had been guilty of egregious tactical errors "with

[23] *Journal officiel*, sessions of January 21, 1903, pp. 135–136; January 23, 1903, pp. 171–189; January 26, 1903, pp. 233–238 (note the correction of the balloting on p. 264); January 29, 1903, pp. 298–299, 313.

[24] P. Renaudel, "Le 'Cas Millerand' et le congrès de Bordeaux," *Mouvement socialiste*, 9: 485–494 (1903).

which the Socialist party ought not associate itself." [25] The Federation of the Seine, of which Millerand was a member, held a special meeting at which a "severe censure" of the latter's conduct was voted; and several other groups affiliated with the party demanded that the next national congress take up the question of his expulsion.[26]

The Fifth National Congress of the Parti socialiste français, held at Bordeaux in April 1903, was almost completely occupied with that question. Renaudel and Gustave Hervé, a forceful left-wing militant, led the attack. After presenting an account of Millerand's "scandalous" votes, Renaudel declared that they were the expression of a tactic which was opposed "in a most absolute fashion" to the tactics of the party as defined at previous national congresses. While the party, Renaudel noted, approved the policy of collaboration when employed under certain conditions, for a limited period of time and for specific objectives, Millerand's conduct was based on a concept of tactics "which proposes an absolute, continuous, and uninterrupted alliance with the bourgeoisie." If the party were to accept this concept of parliamentary tactics, it would soon become a "purely reformist party," a party without a revolutionary ideal. It was necessary, he contended, to repudiate this "dangerous" concept by excluding Millerand from the ranks.[27]

Hervé, like Renaudel, did not oppose Millerand because he pursued the tactic of collaboration, but because he did it in too systematic, too unqualified a manner, and because he did not allow for the possibility of revolutionary action in the class struggle. Millerand, he believed, put too much faith in the reformist method, relied too much on the alliance of the Socialists and progressive bourgeois elements as the means of achieving social justice. What distinguished the left-wing faction of the party from Millerand and his right-wing supporters, Hervé told the congress, was that the former were "at the same time reformists and revolutionaries," while the latter were exclusively reformists. "We [the left-wing opposition] are reform-

[25] *Petite République*, March 14, 1904.
[26] Renaudel, pp. 486–487; the *Petite République*, March 29, 1903.
[27] See the report of Renaudel's speech in the *Revue socialiste*, 37: 570–581 (1903).

ists in the sense that we do not believe, with the old-time Marxists, that our societies are split sharply, with the proletariat on one side and great capitalists on the other, and the class war does not seem to us as rigid a dogma as it seemed to Karl Marx." Moreover, the left-wing was reformist in that it believed that the party "should seek, by moderation of form and language, to bring over to our side all the really democratic groups in the nation." On the other hand, Hervé and his colleagues were "at the same time revolutionaries" because they accepted the idea that the capitalist economic system really did create "hostile and antagonistic classes" in present-day society. Addressing his remarks directly to Millerand, who was making his first appearance at a national congress of the party, Hervé affirmed: "We are revolutionaries, because we know that the bourgeoisie possesses such powers, that the capital which it holds gives it such means of negating universal suffrage, that we are not at all sure, Citizen Millerand, of attaining the solution which we desire by the reformist method." The party should continue to work with the more progressive elements of the bourgeois class as long as these elements were determined to go forward and tended always to move toward the Left. Yet should they one day abandon this course and turn their backs on the Socialists, Hervé concluded, "I want us, after having been able to join hands, to be able on occasion to clench fists." [28]

In his speech to the delegates, Joseph Sarraute, a leading spokesman for the extreme right–wing of the party, undertook to explain and justify Millerand's conduct. He maintained that the conflict raging around Millerand was at bottom a clash between "democratic" and "revolutionary" Socialism, and held that the latter was based on a conception of the class struggle that was a "doctrinaire fancy," completely untenable and false. To the exponent of revolutionary Socialism, the class struggle was not merely the age-old clash between the haves and the have-nots — the clash which in modern society pitted capitalists against workers. The "dogma" of the class struggle was far more comprehensive: "It absorbs the whole life of society, and administrative, political, and judicial institutions

[28] See the report of Hervé's speech in the *Revue socialiste*, 37: 523–529 (1903).

are merely the instruments of combat and authority at the service of the possessing class. The state is a class-state." And because these institutions were class instruments, the revolutionary Socialist called for their destruction: "They are not to be conquered by the workers, but to be shattered; and the only issue open to the proletariat striving for emancipation is the revolutionary issue." Finally, the revolutionary Socialist contended that since society's whole life was absorbed in the class struggle, there could be no interests in common between the capitalist and proletarian classes, "and the supposed general interests of society — order, economic prosperity, and national independence — all these are only private interests in disguise, interests of the possessing class, which the proletariat, consequently, should not take into account." Sarraute hastened to add that all of this was, of course, abstract theory. As soon as the Socialist movement turned from speculation about the nature of society and the class conflict and began to participate in political action, as soon as it "clashed with the existing reality" which it endeavored to transform, "its practice at once ceased to be anything but a violation, perpetual and permanent, of the rules of action laid down by that intransigent revolutionary ideology."

He told the congress that the deviations and compromises for which certain party members, particularly Millerand, were reproached, did not date from the immediate past. Rather, they went back to that day when the Socialist movement first took shape in a political party and endeavored "to exert a serious influence on the course of events, the day when by its first and most crying contradiction, having laid down as a principle, as an axiom beyond any discussion, the class character of the state and the impossibility of reformist action, it elaborated the articles of a minimum program, a program of immediate demands, and applied to the public power, to the state itself, to realize it." Thus the explanation for this deviation from the abstract principle of the class struggle was not to be found in the "weakness of individuals" or in the "fascination or the corrupting effect of power." Rather, it was "entirely in the great fact which dominates our modern society — Democracy." In essence, democracy was the denial of the class-state. The class-state conception of revolutionary Socialism made sense when the property-owning class was by the very fact of possession the governing class as well, and when the "monopoly of property" was buttressed by the "monopoly of public power." But, as soon as the state was "democratized" (*où la démocratie pénêtre l'Etat*) and equal rights were granted to all, capitalists and proletarians alike, as soon as the class-oligarchy was replaced by the rule of majorities, it became contradictory and senseless to speak of a class-state. "Political and social institutions are no longer the work and the instrument of the possessing class; they become the work of the majority. They can be orientated and guided in the direction of the public interest." Since the class struggle was negated by the attainment of universal suffrage and equal rights, and since the concept of a class-state was invalidated by the establishment of democracy, it followed that democratic Socialism displaced revolutionary Socialism, and the traditional tactic of revolutionary action was replaced by the tactic of legal and reformist action. "The revolution does not have to take place," Sarraute declared, "because it has already taken place, because it is now in our institutions; and it suffices only to exercise normally and regularly our liberties — liberties of the press, organization, and assembly — in order to win over to our ideals the majority of people, and with them the state." Furthermore, as a second consequence of the democratization of the state, the Socialists could no longer disregard, as they had in the past, the general interests of society — order, economic prosperity, and national independence.

Millerand's conduct in the Chamber was the logical and inevitable consequence, Sarraute contended, of the tactic implicit in this broad conception of democratic Socialism. Hence, it was not only an individual, but a philosophy of Socialism, that the congress was to judge.[29] In a speech to the delegates, Millerand accepted substantially Sarraute's formulation as an explanation and justification for his behavior in the Chamber.[30]

[29] See the report of Sarraute's speech in the *Revue socialiste*, 37: 530–537 (1903).
[30] See the reports of Millerand's two speeches in the *Revue socialiste*, 37: 538–550, 601–608 (1903).

In his initial address to the congress, Jaurès took a middle-of-the-road position, endeavoring to reconcile the opposing factions. He criticized the exponents of revolutionary Socialism (and he included in this camp Guesde and his followers along with left-wing elements within the Parti socialiste français) as well as the exponents of democratic Socialism. He agreed with Sarraute that many Socialists in and out of the Ministerial Socialist party interpreted the class struggle notion in a way that was much too simplified. It was not enough simply to note the existence of a deep antagonism between the bourgeoisie and the proletariat. All Socialists must also recognize, as did Sarraute, that this class antagonism operated and developed within a democratic state, and that it was influenced and molded to a considerable degree by the nature of that state. The struggle between the two classes "cannot have either the same form, the same character, or the same means in a republican democracy and in a despotic or oligarchic state." This central fact, Jaurès insisted, must be admitted as "true and incontestable."

But Sarraute, Jaurès contended, was guilty of the same error of interpreting the class struggle in too simple a manner when he thought that it was enough "to lay down the principle of democracy in order to resolve, in a sort of automatic fashion, the antagonisms of society." He was not being realistic when he maintained that political democracy expressed itself above parties and classes "by the impartial and decisive law of majorities," and when he seemed to conceive of universal suffrage "as a sort of extraordinary supramundane God, living outside mankind and shaping the world." Sarraute failed to comprehend how universal suffrage was influenced and distorted by the economic power of the capitalist class and failed to realize that universal suffrage could only operate "freely" when the proletariat had achieved economic equality. Jaurès also held that, just as Sarraute "falsified" the relation of the proletariat to the state in one way, Guesde, his followers, and certain left-wing elements within the Ministerial Socialist party falsified it in another, believing that the state was exclusively a class-state, in no significant degree amenable to the will of the proletariat. In opposition, Jaurès asserted that in a democratic society, like France, where there was universal manhood suffrage, the state was not for the proletarian "a refractory, hard, absolutely impermeable and impenetrable block." Maintaining that the penetration of the state by the "Socialist and proletarian influence" had already begun, he expressed the hope, shared with Sarraute, that by means of organization and education that penetration would become "so full, deep, and decisive, that in time, by accumulated efforts, we shall find the proletarian and Socialist state to have replaced the oligarchic and bourgeois state." But though the state had been partially penetrated and while it was reasonable to expect that in time it would be entirely transformed, it nevertheless remained true that at present the state was overwhelmingly bourgeois in character. It was a state based on capitalist property relations, and, though at the present moment the state worked in part with the proletariat, tomorrow it might turn with violence and aggression against the proletariat. "And if we should never lose the chance of penetrating as fully as possible this democratic bourgeois state," he added, "we should never let the workers forget that it is still but partially won over, that it is still largely a hostile force." To him, it appeared that Sarraute omitted this consideration in his theory, while Millerand forgot it too frequently in practice.

Jaurès agreed with Sarraute that the party should concern itself with the general interests of the country. Socialism had legitimate interests in the preservation of the political freedom of all classes, in the maintenance of the nation's security as long as war or the menace of war continued to exist, and in the promotion of the economic well-being of the country. "It is our good fortune," he declared, "that the general interest of France and of civilization is tied up with the self-interest of a rising class, which is the proletariat." This concern for the general interests of the country, however, brought to the fore a difficult problem regarding political tactics. To what extent, if any, should the Socialist party work in concert with other democratic groups in promoting these general interests? And if it did collaborate with these groups, how was the party to pursue this tactic and still retain its identity, its particular ideal and ideas?

Guesde and those who agreed with him had no difficulty, Jaurès contended, in resolving the problem — if, indeed, it could be said that they conceived of it as existing at all. So far as Guesde was concerned there was nothing of interest to Socialists in present-day society but the working class. Against all other classes, Guesde fought "indiscriminately," making no distinction between those groups that were reactionary, clerical, or authoritarian, and the liberal and democratic groups of the bourgeoisie. "Guesde," Jaurès affirmed, "is shut up in an exclusive proletariat, as in a fortress surrounded by a deep moat, and fights impartially against every party encamped around it. Whether they come as friends or as foes, he turns his weapons against all sections of the horizon alike." This was an all-out class-struggle policy, a "supremely lazy policy that saves the trouble of acting, adapting, reflecting, and drawing distinctions." On the other hand, the solution to the problem of tactics offered by many reformist Socialists (like Millerand) was also "too easy," for they would simply abandon that part of the party program which exceeded the bounds of what was immediately realizable and would merge with the progressive groups of the bourgeoisie in order to pursue the common task of promoting the general interests of society.

To Jaurès, there was no easy solution. The party must concern itself with the direction of the general interests, but it must do so from the point of view of the proletariat, constantly keeping the Socialist ideal in mind. The policy pursued should be one "which consists in at once collaborating with all democrats, yet vigorously distinguishing one's self from them; penetrating partially into the state of today, yet dominating the state of today from the height of our ideal." He conceded that this was complicated, perhaps even "awkward," and would "create serious difficulties at every turn" for the party. But he believed that, during the period of transition from the capitalist to the Socialist order, such difficulties were unavoidable.

Jaurès criticized Millerand for his conduct in the Chamber of Deputies, declaring, in his desire to bring about the maximum degree of collaboration between Socialism and the rest of democracy, he had "attenuated in a dangerous fashion" the essential differences which separated the Socialist party from other democratic groups. Nevertheless, he strongly opposed the exclusion of Millerand from the party. Such action would be "not only brutal, but unjust and impolitic." It might have the effect of hampering "the free, fair, and needful criticism" of party policy. And it was just such criticism, he asserted, which was most effective in dealing with the tactic which had been "formulated here in theory by Sarraute and in practice by Millerand." Jaurès contended that there was room within the party for the widest variety of Socialist tendencies. He declared that an equilibrium would be established if the extreme revolutionaries, such as Guesde and his followers, were to join the ranks of the Parti socialiste français to counterbalance Millerand and his colleagues.[31]

At the end of the first phase of this long debate — the most significant debate on Socialist policy since the First General Congress of 1899 — the question of Millerand's exclusion was referred for further consideration to a committee composed of one representative of each of the party federations. After a lengthy discussion, the committee adopted (by a vote of nineteen to sixteen, with two abstentions) the following brief declaration: "The Congress decides that Citizen Millerand is excluded from the Socialist party on account of his anti-Socialist votes." Renaudel, chairman of the committee, submitted the declaration to the plenary session of the congress for final action. Millerand's fate appeared to be sealed.

Before a vote on the declaration was taken, however, Jaurès took the floor to wage a last-minute fight to save him. He presented a counterresolution which, while affirming that the party was a "party of free thought and perpetual scientific inquiry," censured by implication Millerand's disputed votes and engaged him not to vote in like manner again.[32] Jaurès stated that the resolution answered "every legitimate and reasonable anxiety of the congress." It lacked but one thing — "the exclusion, the excommunication" of Millerand. Indeed, this excommunication, Jaurès argued, would not only be a "crime" against Millerand, but also a "veritable crime"

[31] See the report of Jaurès's speech in the *Revue socialiste*, 37: 551–569 (1903).
[32] The text is given in the *Revue socialiste*, 37: 589 (1903).

against the entire party. It would be the expression of a sectarian spirit alien to the very nature of the party itself. The expulsion of Millerand might lead the party federations to set up their own inquisitions and to expel those members suspected of being sympathetic to Millerand. In the present circumstance it was necessary to reaffirm the freedom of conscience and thought of all members of the party, for, without this freedom, "we should be the most miserable of churches, claiming to set up an infallibility unsanctioned by divine intervention." Jaurès emphasized that his resolution reaffirmed this freedom, while asserting that in action, in voting, the party representatives must realize a "certain minimum of unity and discipline," and that each *élu* should bring his conduct into harmony with the collective decisions of the party.[33]

Jaurès achieved his purpose. The delegates were moved by his impassioned speech; a number of federations, hitherto undecided or determined to vote for the exclusion of Millerand, now declared their opposition to such action. When both resolutions were put to a vote, Jaurès's was carried by a slight margin.[34] Thus the Bordeaux Congress came to a close with Millerand still an accredited member of the party.

During the months that followed, the Ministerial Socialist party continued to be plagued by factional disputes, for the right-wing elements identified with Millerand grew steadily more and more reformist in their sympathies, while the left-wing revolt against this tendency grew apace. The unqualified support which a number of party Deputies gave the government again set the stage for open warfare and new party fissions. On two occasions the votes of these Deputies appeared to the opposition to be particularly inadmissible. On October 30, 1903, thirteen party *élus* joined the governmental majority in a vote which freed the ministry of responsibility in connection with a raid (October 29) on the Paris *Bourse du travail* by police agents. (This raid had resulted in the injuring of 140 workers.) Again, on November 4, twenty-three party *élus* supported the government by voting against a proposal made by Thivrier, a

[33] See the report of Jaurès's speech in the *Revue socialiste*, 37: 589–600 (1903).
[34] *Petite République*, April 6, 16, 1903.

member of the Revolutionary Socialist parliamentary group, which called for the suppression of that part of the budget of the Ministry of the Interior used to pay secret agents (*agents secrets de la sûreté générale*). On this occasion the other Socialist Deputies (with the exception of Veber, who abstained) had voted in favor of the proposal.[35]

As in the past, the votes of the Ministerial Socialist Deputies provoked a storm of protest within the Parti socialiste français. Hervé expressed the view of many members of the rank and file when he declared in the *Travailleur Socialiste*, the newspaper of the Federation of the Yonne, that the extreme "anti-revolutionary reformism" of these Deputies was making the militant proletariat adverse to "all parliamentary action, to all reformism." [36] The Interfederal Committee, the central administrative body of the Parti socialiste français, likewise reprimanded these Deputies; but it was unable to enforce discipline in the parliamentary group of the party since it had no direct authority over it.[37] However, the Federation of the Seine, with which Millerand was affiliated, was determined not to tolerate acts of indiscipline on the part of party Deputies; on January 4, 1904, it expelled Millerand from its ranks, and, consequently, from the Ministerial Socialist party, for having voted (November 23, 1903) against a resolution which called upon the government to take the initiative in making proposals to other countries regarding international disarmament.[38]

Millerand's expulsion sharpened the factional conflict within the Parti socialiste français, and the Sixth National Congress of the party, which took place in Saint-Etienne in February 1904, was occupied with this conflict almost to the exclusion of all other matters. At the congress, the battle between left- and right-wing

---

[35] *Journal officiel*, sessions of October 30, 1903, pp. 2414–2421, 2433; November 4, 1903, pp. 2475–2476, 2494–2495.

[36] Quoted in Louis Dubreuilh, "Action socialiste," *Mouvement socialiste*, 11: 559 (1903).

[37] Dubreuilh, p. 558. See also Dubreuilh, *De Japy à Bordeaux, unité interfédérale et unité révolutionnaire* (Lille, 1903), pp. 8–9.

[38] *Journal officiel*, session of November 23, 1903, pp. 2839–2843, 2845–2847; the *Petite République*, January 7, 1904.

factions was joined on a proposal to revise the party statutes so as
to bring the Socialist parliamentary group under the direct control
of the Interfederal Committee.[39] The left-wing faction, which was
well represented on the latter, vigorously supported this proposal
to curb the freedom of action of the party Deputies.[40]

Briand, a member of the party's parliamentary group, led the
attack on the proposal. He declared that to grant the Interfederal
Committee the power to direct the activities of the party Deputies
would result in the creation of a "dictatorial authority" harmful to
the interests of the party. "Under the pretext of correcting the incon-
sistency more apparent than real of our votes," he asserted, "it
appears that some wish to place all the Deputies under a rigid tute-
lage which would make of them a kind of automaton destitute of
all responsibility." [41]

At the close of the debate on the question — a debate which had
been relatively dull and sterile as compared with the high-level, in-
cisive debate on party policy at the Bordeaux Congress — a committee was set up to give the matter further study and to submit its
recommendations to the delegates for final action. Its report, which
the congress approved by a unanimous vote, was drafted by Jaurès,
who again filled the role of conciliator, mediating with considerable
success the conflicting views. The report called for certain modifications of the party statutes. A new central administrative organ, the
National Council, comprising both the old Interfederal Committee
and the Socialist parliamentary group, was created to direct the
political activities of the party. The National Council was to meet
at the opening of each ordinary and extraordinary session of the
Chamber of Deputies and in times of emergency to lay down the
general line of policy for the parliamentary group.[42] By placing the
responsibility for the direction of the political activities of the party
in this joint-committee of the members of the two existing groups,
the Saint-Etienne Congress had endeavored to satisfy the demands

[39] The text of the proposal is given in the *Petite République*, February 16, 1904.
[40] *Petite République*, February 17, 1904.
[41] See the report of Briand's speech in the *Revue socialiste*, 39: 328–335 (1904).
[42] For the text of the report, see the *Petite République*, February 18, 1904.

of the opposing factions for a voice in the formulation of policy.

However, like so many compromise arrangements that appear on paper to give due satisfaction to all parties concerned, the revision of the party statutes at Saint-Etienne failed to achieve the purposes for which it had been undertaken. The Ministerialists managed to gain a majority on the National Council and thus were able, as before, to impose their conception of political action on the party. And in the Chamber of Deputies, the Ministerial Socialist Deputies, confident of the support of the National Council, dissociated their votes from those of their colleagues in the parliamentary group just as they had in the past. Consequently, the old factional struggle within the Parti socialiste français went on unabated.[43]

This struggle had a most deleterious effect on the unity of the organization. It served as a powerful disintegrating force, encouraging the fragmentation of the party cadres. An ever increasing number of individual members and groups, having become disgusted with this internecine warfare, deserted the ranks. In the one year between the Bordeaux and Saint-Etienne Congresses, two of the strongest federations affiliated with the party — the Federation of the Yonne and the Federation of the Somme — severed connections with it. During the same year the total membership diminished from approximately 11,000 (April 1903) to approximately 8,500 (February 1904). Following the Saint-Etienne Congress, several departmental federations showed signs of disintegration, and it appeared to many Socialists that the complete dissolution of the once powerful Parti socialiste français was a real possibility.[44]

During the years 1902–1904, while the Ministerial Socialist party was being torn by internecine strife, the Antiministerial Socialist party, the Parti socialiste de France, was rapidly being unified and expanded. The pact of union which had been concluded between the diverse revolutionary Socialist forces at the Ivry Conference in

[43] See Ernest Lafont, "Le Congrès de Saint-Etienne," *Mouvement socialiste*, 12: 312–316 (1904); and the *Socialiste*, June 5–12, 1904.

[44] Dubreuilh, "Après le congrès de Reims," *Mouvement socialiste*, 11: 388 (1903); Lafont, p. 305.

November 1901 was ratified by the First National Congress of the new party which took place at Commentry in September 1902.[45] However, the complete amalgamation of all the revolutionary Socialist groups and organizations was far from being realized at the time of the Commentry Congress. It was not until the Second National Congress of the party at Rheims in September 1903 that the consolidation of these elements was achieved in fact as well as on paper. At the Rheims Congress, the Guesdist, Blanquist and Alliance communiste révolutionnaire organizations were abolished, and their constituent groups together with those of the affiliated autonomous federations were fused in a single party. At this time the party was composed of some 1,200 groups with a total membership of approximately 14,800, consolidated in thirty-eight departmental and regional federations. The party possessed fourteen journals (one daily and thirteen weeklies or biweeklies) in addition to its official organ, the *Socialiste*.[46]

The Rheims Congress set forth in bold relief the opposition of the new party to reformist Socialist tactics, to *Ministérialisme*, by adopting as its own statement of policy the resolution on Socialist tactics and method that had been approved by the National Congress of the German Social Democratic party which had taken place in Dresden earlier in September. For many years the question of tactics had occupied the attention of the German Socialists. Like their French comrades, they were sharply divided on this matter. One section of the Social Democratic party, led by Eduard Bernstein, took a position on the question analogous to that of the French Socialists of the Millerand and Sarraute variety. These German Socialists were called "Revisionists" because of their endeavor to revise the teachings of Karl Marx in the light of contemporary social and economic developments — "to bring Marx up to date." The Revisionists repudiated the Marxist conception of the class struggle

---

[45] *Socialiste*, October 19–26, 1902; André Morizet, "L'Organisation socialiste et le congrès de Commentry," *Mouvement socialiste*, 8: 1825–1834 (1902).

[46] *Deuxième Congrès national du Parti socialiste de France (Unité socialiste révolutionnaire), tenu à Reims les 27, 28 et 29 septembre 1903* (Bourges, 1903), pp. 32–35; the *Socialiste*, October 19–26, 1902, October 4–18, 1903; Dubreuilh, "Les Socialistes français et le congrès de Reims," *Mouvement socialiste*, 11: 168 (1903).

and argued that universal suffrage and the peaceful processes of democracy were the proper methods for attaining the aims of Socialism. The Revisionists were opposed within the Social Democratic party by a large section of the leadership, including such notables as August Bebel, Karl Kautsky, and Rosa Luxemburg, each of whom argued from what was taken to be the "orthodox" Marxist position.[47] This controversy reached its height at the Dresden Congress of the Social Democratic party. After a long drawn out debate, the congress, by an overwhelming majority, approved a resolution condemning the revisionist tendency and tactics. It was this resolution, in a slightly amended form, that the Rheims Congress adopted by a unanimous vote.

At the Third National Congress of the Parti socialiste de France, held at Lille the following year (August 1904), the Rheims-Dresden resolution was reaffirmed as party policy. At the same time, the congress, following the urgent request of Guesde, gave its approval to a proposal which called upon the Socialist and Labor International, at its next congress scheduled to take place shortly in Amsterdam, to adopt the Rheims-Dresden resolution as its official statement of the principles that should regulate the conduct of Socialist parties the world over.[48]

Guesde's purpose in wanting the Second International to accept the resolution was not difficult to discern. Approval of the resolution by what was recognized as the authoritative tribunal of the world Socialist movement would, of course, be a defeat for all revisionist and reformist tendencies. It would, in particular, constitute a major triumph for the Parti socialiste de France over its rival. Moreover, it was quite possible that, with the Parti socialiste français being fragmented as a consequence of the strife within its ranks, approval by the Second International of the resolution — and at the congress Guesde could count on the support and votes of the delegation from the most respected and influential party in the International, the German Social Democratic party — could well

[47] For a careful study of the Revisionist movement, see Peter Gay, *The Dilemma of Democratic Socialism* (New York, 1952).

[48] *Socialiste*, August 21–28, 1904.

put the quietus on it. In that event, Guesde, backed by a well-disciplined and rapidly growing party, would be in a position to unify the French Socialist movement on pretty much his own terms.

Hence, with so much at stake, with the future course of the Socialist movement in France in the balance, it was to be expected that the attention of all French Socialists would be riveted on the Concertgebouw in Amsterdam when the Socialist and Labor International Congress convened there in mid-August 1904.

THE RHEIMS-DRESDEN RESOLUTION

The Congress condemns most energetically the revisionist attempts in the direction of changing our tried and victorious tactics based on the class struggle, and of replacing the conquest of political power through the supreme struggle with the bourgeoisie by a policy of concession to the established order of society.

The consequence of such revisionist tactics would be to change us from a party seeking the swiftest possible transformation of bourgeois society into Socialist society — from a party therefore revolutionary in the best sense of the word — into a party satisfied with the reform of bourgeois society.

For this reason the Congress, convinced, contrary to the present revisionist tendencies, that class antagonisms, far from diminishing, are intensifying, declares:

1. That the party rejects any responsibility whatever for the political and economic conditions based on capitalist production, and consequently could not approve any methods tending to maintain the ruling class in power.

2. That the social democracy could accept no participation in the government within capitalist society, this decision being in accordance with the Kautsky resolution adopted by the International Congress of Paris in 1900.

The Congress further condemns any attempt to blur the evergrowing class antagonisms, for the purpose of facilitating an understanding with bourgeois parties.

The Congress relies upon the Socialist parliamentary groups to use their increased power — increased both by the greater number of its members and by the substantial growth of the body of electors behind them — to persevere in their propaganda toward the final goal of Socialism, and, in conformity with our program to defend most resolutely the interests of the working class, the extension and consolidation of its political liberties, to demand equality of rights for all; to continue more energetically than ever the struggle against militarism, against the colonial and imperialist policy, against all manner of injustice, oppression, and exploitation, and, finally, to exert itself energetically to perfect social legislation and to make it possible for the working class to accomplish its political and its civilizing mission.

The first paragraph of the Dresden resolution was deleted by the Rheims Congress since it dealt with a matter which specifically concerned the German Social Democratic party: the question of the candidacy of Socialists for certain posts in the Reichstag. The Rheims Congress also modified the Dresden resolution in one other respect, substituting in the first line of the fifth paragraph the word "accept" for the word "seek" which appeared in the original German version.

Sources: *Protokoll über die Verhandlungen des Parteitages der Sozialdemokratischen Partei Deutschlands, abgehalten zu Dresden vom 13 bis 20 September 1903* (Berlin, 1903), pp. 418–419; *Deuxième Congrès national du Parti socialiste de France*, pp. 44–46.

Chapter 7

The Realization of Unity

When the Sixth Congress of the Socialist and Labor International began its work in the beautifully appointed Concertgebouw in Amsterdam on August 14, 1904, the most important task before it was that of determining policy on the question of Socialist tactics and method. Realizing the significance of the task and the complexity of the many issues involved, the delegates devoted the major part of the time scheduled to the examination of this matter.

Shortly after the congress was convened, a committee was set up to study the question and to submit recommendations to the plenary session. This committee, made up of two delegates from each of the nationalities represented at the congress, included many of the leading figures in the Socialist world — Jaurès, Guesde, Kautsky, Bebel, Luxemburg, Vandervelde, Ferri, Victor Adler, Pablo Iglesias, J. Ramsay MacDonald, Daniel De Leon, and George Plekhanov. Guesde first posed the question of tactics and method before the committee by submitting to it the Rheims-Dresden resolution. A number of counter-proposals were then introduced, but only one, formulated jointly by Adler (Austria) and Vandervelde (Belgium) was accepted by the committee as a possible alternate motion. The first part of the Adler-Vandervelde motion called upon the congress to affirm the necessity of maintaining unyieldingly "our tried and glorious tactics based on the class struggle" and to assert its determination not to allow "that the conquest of political power through the supreme struggle against the bourgeois class be replaced by a policy of concessions to the established order." Such a policy would have the result of changing "a party which pursues the swiftest possible transformation of bourgeois society into a Socialist society — consequently a party that is revolutionary in the best sense of the word — into a party which contents itself with reforming bourgeois society." For this reason, the congress, aware of the fact that class antagonisms were constantly increasing rather than diminishing (as the Revisionists claimed), should: (a) decline "all responsibility whatsoever for the political and economic conditions based on capitalist production"; and (b) disapprove of any means which would tend to keep the dominant bourgeois class in power. With regard to the question of ministerial participation, the congress should re-affirm the Kautsky resolution passed at the International Congress of Paris in 1900. The second part of the motion was identical with the last two paragraphs of the Rheims-Dresden resolution.[1]

Vandervelde told the committee that this counter-proposal was simply a restatement of the Rheims-Dresden resolution in positive rather than negative terms, substituting for the condemnations set forth in the latter proposal a "series of affirmations of principle." [2] But in spite of Vandervelde's explanation, the objective of this motion appeared to be much less to define principles in positive terms than to strip the Rheims-Dresden resolution of its teeth; and Adler, at one point in the discussion, admitted as much.[3] The Adler-Vandervelde motion, however, did serve to draw attention to the somewhat defective construction of the Rheims-Dresden resolution. It pointed up the fact that this resolution, while condemning revisionist tactics and principles, did not spell out clearly "orthodox" revolutionary tactics and principles. Moreover, it brought into relief an ambiguity contained in the Rheims-Dresden resolution. On the one hand, the latter formally prohibited the participation of a Socialist in a bourgeois government, at the same time accepting the Kautsky

---

[1] *Sixième Congrès socialiste international, tenu à Amsterdam du 14 au 20 août 1904* (Brussels, 1904), pp. 141–142.

[2] *Sixième Congrès*, pp. 59–64, 139–140. See also Vandervelde's comments on this motion in his *Souvenirs d'un militant socialiste* (Paris, 1939), p. 155.

[3] *Sixième Congrès*, p. 95.

resolution which authorized such participation under certain circumstances. Nevertheless, its general character and tone made it out to be an antiministerial, anti-collaborationist statement of policy. Moreover, the discussion of the committee and the general debate of the plenary session of the congress centering around the Rheims-Dresden resolution gave it added point in this respect. Its essentially antiministerial character was accentuated by the firm support given it by such recognized anti-reformist Socialists as Guesde and Luxemburg as well as by the strenuous opposition voiced by outstanding reformists, notably, Jaurès. There could be little doubt, once the discussion got under way, that the adoption by the congress of the Rheims-Dresden resolution would sound the death knell for *Ministérialisme* in all its aspects.

The high point of the committee's consideration of the question of tactics was the arresting duel between Jaurès and Guesde. Jaurès endeavored first to justify the tactics pursued by his party, citing as evidence of their value and legitimacy, what he held to be the significant and "fecund" results they had achieved. First of all, the French reformist Socialists, in alliance with progressive bourgeois parties, had saved the Republic during the Dreyfus crisis: they had frustrated the efforts of the reactionary clerical and caesarian forces "to reawaken the religious and racial wars" and to deliver a death-blow to republican institutions. By so doing these Socialists had rendered a service of inestimable value to the cause of proletarian emancipation, for the Republic — "the logical and supreme form of democracy" — was the "necessary condition of social and economic progress."

In addition, the reformist Socialists had directly aided in promoting the secularization of the state and in advancing the cause of "intellectual emancipation," in achieving progressive labor legislation, and in maintaining international peace. The anticlerical policy pursued by the reformist Socialists in collaboration with liberal bourgeois elements was not, as the revolutionary Socialists charged, a policy which distracted the proletariat from its essential task of social emancipation. On the contrary, this policy made it easier for the proletariat to carry out its task. It was necessary to curb clerical power in France by bringing about the separation of Church and State and by secularizing public education, the latter assuring intellectual emancipation for all. "With the clerical power struck down and the terrain cleared of this problem which obstructed all the roads for us," Jaurès stated, "we would be able tomorrow to consecrate ourselves with a freer spirit to the task of achieving liberty." While pursuing this policy of anticlericalism, the reformist Socialists had not neglected the task of pressing for social reforms. Indeed, as a consequence of the constant efforts of these Socialists, working together with progressive bourgeois elements, the previous five years had witnessed the enactment of more social legislation directly beneficial to the workers than any comparable period since the formation of the Third Republic. He cited the enactment of a law limiting the length of the workday to ten hours in certain industries and the initial efforts of the government to institute a comprehensive system of workers' pensions. He also noted that the Chamber of Deputies had recently passed a bill establishing an eight-hour day for miners — a bill that was at the time before the French Senate. Lastly, Jaurès maintained that the reformist Socialists had rendered a great service to International Socialism in its struggle against militarism, in its efforts to preserve world peace, by waging a relentless battle against the "caesarian, chauvinistic, and bellicose" forces in France which on more than one occasion threatened to plunge Europe into war.

The reformist Socialists, he insisted, had accomplished all this without abandoning the class struggle or blurring class distinctions and without sacrificing their autonomy or freedom of decision. He contended that the French proletariat recognized the value of the work of the reformist Socialists, and he pointed to his party's increased vote in the 1902 general elections and its large group in the French parliament — a group three times the size of that of the antireformist Socialists — as substantiating his claim.

In addition to presenting this defense of the conduct of the reformist Socialists, this justification for their tactics, Jaurès challenged the competence of the international congress to regulate the tactics of each and every Socialist party. He declared that while it was both fitting and proper for the congress to formulate general principles that were to be accepted by all Socialist parties, it was beyond the province of the congress to prescribe the specific method of action, the line of tactics, for any particular party. He insisted that when the Socialist movement developed and gathered strength in a country and came to play an important role in its political life, that movement tended to assume the special characteristics of the country in which it existed: the movement was molded to a significant extent by the character of the country's institutions. Given this fact, it was impossible for the congress to formulate specific tactics applicable in equal measure and validity to Socialist parties of all countries. It was necessary for the congress to allow each party to determine the tactics best suited to the traditions and institutions of its own country.[4]

Guesde began his reply to Jaurès's speech by endeavoring to refute his claim to the support of the French workers for the tactics of the reformist Socialists. As evidence to the contrary, he noted that the membership of Jaurès's party had declined from 12,000 in April 1903 to 8,000 in February 1904, while his own party — which now had twice that membership — had added 3,000 names during the same period. And as for the large reformist Socialist group in the Chamber of Deputies, Guesde charged that its members had really been elected as "governmental candidates" rather than as Socialists. Jaurès and his colleagues had won their seats in the Chamber "as republicans battling against monarchists," not as Socialist candidates of one class — "as representatives of the proletariat against the bourgeoisie."

Guesde then examined in some detail the "enormous and fecund achievements" which Jaurès had credited to the reformist Socialists. He rejected the claim that these Socialists had helped to save the French Republic, denying point-blank that the Republic had been in real danger during the Dreyfus crisis. He asserted that the republican form of government was valued by Socialists only because it offered the most effective conditions, "the ideal terrain," for press-

---

[4] *Sixième Congrès*, pp. 174–198. The text of Jaurès's speech is given in the *Revue socialiste*, 40: 288–303 (1904).

ing the class war to a finish; for in a Republic there existed no feudal, dynastic encumbrances to conceal the direct antagonism between the proletariat and the bourgeoisie. Where republican institutions functioned, there were "no political barriers" to prevent the organized proletariat from coming to grips with the enemy class in the decisive struggle. But this superiority of republican institutions would disappear if the proletariat were to renounce the hope of achieving the Socialist Republic, if the proletariat were "to abandon its own proper struggle for emancipation," in order to "immobilize itself" in the defense of the "Republic of its masters." Were this to happen, "the Republic would become the worst form of government."

As for the anticlerical campaign waged by the reformist Socialists, Guesde stated that the victory of *la laïcité*, that the complete separation of Church and State, was yet to be realized; and that in any event the objective of the government's anticlerical policy was not so much to curb the power of the Church, to achieve the "intellectual emancipation" of the masses, as it was to "divert the workers from their struggle against capitalism." Concerning social reforms, the enactment of which Jaurès had attributed in large measure to the collaboration of the reformist Socialists with progressive elements of the bourgeoisie during the past five years, Guesde insisted that the greater part of the reforms either existed only on paper, or had been enacted before this collaboration had begun. He noted, for example, that the law limiting the length of the workday had been enacted in the early nineties, when "Socialism had not as yet abandoned its opposition to the state." The few reforms that had been enacted as a consequence of this alliance were "crumbs" and "pitiable alms." Lastly, he dismissed Jaurès's claim that the policy pursued by the reformist Socialists had served to curb the menace of militarism and promote international peace. He cited the fact that many reformist Socialist Deputies had voted for the army, navy, and colonial appropriations requested by the government. And it was just this colonial policy, he charged, "which, by unleashing the competitive lusts and contradictions of the capitalist classes of all countries," actually constituted the greatest danger for European peace. These Deputies, by helping to provide the government "with the ways and means of conducting this colonial policy," exposed Europe to "a permanent hazard of war."

Guesde attributed what he called the tactical "errors" of Jaurès and his colleagues to a "false" conception of modern Socialism. Jaurès viewed Socialism as "the prolongation or the consummation of the democratic movement which issued from the bourgeois revolution at the end of the eighteenth century" — from the great French Revolution of 1789. Hence, it was understandable that he should want to pursue a policy of "more or less permanent collaboration with the advanced elements, with the democratic and republican elements, of the bourgeoisie." For the revolutionary Socialists, however, modern Socialism had its origin in the economic phenomena identified with capitalism. Revolutionary Socialists were "the sons of mechanization, of the concentration of capital, and of the proletarization of labor." Wherever capitalism made its appearance, it engendered the same social conditions and provoked the same class struggle between the proletariat and the bourgeoisie. Therefore, contrary to Jaurès's contention that the tactics of each Socialist party must be determined in accordance with the traditions and institutions of the country in which it existed — and that in France this meant in keeping with the democratic traditions of the Great Revolution of 1789 — Guesde asserted that it was possible to formulate a single line of Socialist tactics for all capitalist countries, "whatever the diversity of governmental institutions." It was the responsibility and the duty of the international congress, as the central tribunal of the world Socialist movement to set forth in unmistakable terms this universal policy of Socialist tactics.[5]

At the end of the committee's discussion on tactics, a discussion which lasted three days, the Adler-Vandervelde motion and the Rheims-Dresden resolution were put to a vote. The committee rejected the former by a vote of twenty-four to sixteen, then adopted the latter by a vote of twenty-seven to three, with ten abstentions.[6]

[5] *Sixième Congrès*, pp. 198–206.
[6] *Sixième Congrès*, pp. 59–62.

Despite this action, Jaurès did not admit defeat; immediately after the report of the committee recommending the adoption of the Rheims-Dresden resolution was presented to the congress, Jaurès took the floor to wage a last-ditch fight. The central point of his speech was that the collaborationist tactics and method adopted by his party were dictated by the unique political circumstances in France. He explained that in France there existed powerful democratic forces "to the Right" of the Socialist movement proper — the mass of bourgeois liberals and progressives comprising the ranks of the Radical and Radical-Socialist party — which could and ought to be invoked by the Socialists to advance the interests of the proletariat. These non-Socialist elements, he granted, were certainly not proletarian; but neither were they exclusively capitalist, concerned only with the maintenance of the *status quo* and unalterably opposed to the Socialist ideal. It was necessary to distinguish these bourgeois democrats from the liberals of other European countries, for the former had goals in common with Socialism and were invaluable allies in the struggle against the forces of reaction. These bourgeois supported the laicization of the schools, accepted the notion of a progressive income tax, and worked for the progressive nationalization of, among other things, the banks, railways, and mines. "We do not identify ourselves with these bourgeois democrats," Jaurès told the congress, "because they are not communistic, collectivistic, and proletarian like ourselves." But when, with their aid and assistance, "we are able to stem the tide of reaction, to obtain reforms, and to enact labor legislation, we would be fools, we would be criminals, to reject this cooperation." He declared that his opposition to the Rheims-Dresden resolution was strengthened by his conviction that the definition of tactics contained in it was unsuitable and inapplicable to the French Socialist movement. This was so precisely because the resolution did not allow for the particular political milieu in which that movement had to operate. The Rheims-Dresden resolution, he reminded his audience, had been formulated in accordance with the political state of affairs existing in a single country, Germany, and that it had originally been intended to regulate the conduct of one party, the German Social

Democratic party. Jaurès called attention to the fact that the German Socialists, unlike their French comrades, could not exercise real governmental power in the state. This was due to the fact that the German Reichstag was but a "demi-Parlement," unable to control the executive branch of the government since, in contrast to France and England, there existed no ministerial responsibility to the legislature. Thus, even if the Social Democratic party were to gain the majority of the seats in the Reichstag, it would still find the executive power of the state beyond its reach. It was in keeping with this state of affairs that the Dresden resolution had been formulated. Why, therefore, should this resolution, national in character, applicable only to the German Social Democratic party rendered impotent by the structuring of its country's political institutions, be imposed upon the Socialist parties of other countries, upon his own party, functioning in an altogether different political milieu? The adoption of the Rheims-Dresden resolution by the congress, would render all Socialist parties as politically impotent as the German Social Democratic party and thwart "the development of International Socialism." [7]

Jaurès's speech was well received and almost carried the day for the reformist cause. In the balloting at the end of the debate, the Adler-Vandervelde motion, which was presented as an amendment to the Rheims-Dresden resolution and as such took precedence over it, received a tie vote (with each national delegation casting two votes which it could split), twenty-one to twenty-one.

The Adler-Vandervelde motion was thereupon set aside, for under the rules of procedure of the congress, a tie vote defeated a motion. Before the Rheims-Dresden resolution was acted upon, it was amended slightly: upon the request of the German delegation, the word "rejects" was substituted for the word "condemns" in the first line of the first paragraph and in the first line of the sixth paragraph. This was done for the ostensible purpose of freeing the resolution of what some delegates felt was its unfraternal condemnatory tone. In addition, "seek" was substituted for "accept" in the

[7] *Sixième Congrès*, pp. 67–82. The text of Jaurès's speech is given in the *Revue socialiste*, 40: 303–312 (1904).

first line of the fifth paragraph, in order to rectify the translation in keeping with the original German text (*erstreben*). In this amended form the resolution was adopted by the congress by a vote of twenty-five to five, with twelve abstentions.[8] Thus, the Second International had finally decided the question of tactics and method in favor of the anti-moderate, anti-reformist Socialists.

Just prior to the balloting on the two resolutions, a group of German, Italian, Austrian, Belgian, and Dutch delegates had introduced a joint resolution aimed specifically at the division in the French Socialist movement. This resolution declared that "in order that the working class may develop its full strength in the struggle against capitalism," it was necessary that there be but one Socialist party in each country to stand in opposition to the bourgeois parties, "just as there is but one proletariat in each country." It was, therefore, the "imperative duty" of all Socialists "to strive to the utmost of their power to bring about this party unity on the basis of the principles established by the International Congresses. . ." To assist in the attainment of this objective, the International Socialist Bureau, as well as all Socialist parties within the countries where this unity already existed, would, the resolution concluded, "gladly offer their services and cooperation."[9] Both sections of the French delegation joined with the rest of the congress in unanimously approving this unity resolution. On this note of harmony the congress ended.

Immediately upon their return to France, the leaders of the revolutionary Socialist party took the first step to execute the unity resolution approved by the Amsterdam Congress. On August 30, 1904, the Central Council of the Parti socialiste de France, in a note to

[8] *Sixième Congrès*, pp. 114–116. The votes were distributed as follows: The Argentine, Australian, Austrian, Belgian, British, Danish, Dutch, Swedish, and Swiss delegations voted for the Adler-Vandervelde amendment; the American, Bohemian, Bulgarian, German, Hungarian, Italian, Japanese, Russian, and Spanish delegations voted against it; while the French, Norwegian, and Polish delegations split their votes. The American, Austrian, Bohemian, Bulgarian, German, Hungarian, Italian, Japanese, Polish, Russian, and Spanish delegations voted for the Rheims-Dresden resolution; the Australian delegation voted against it; the British, French, and Norwegian delegations split their votes; while the Argentine, Belgian, Danish, Dutch, Swedish, and Swiss delegations abstained.

[9] *Sixième Congrès*, pp. 65, 113.

the Parti socialiste français expressed its willingness to enter into negotiations with the latter with the objective of unifying the Socialist movement on the basis of the principles laid down by the Amsterdam Congress. For several weeks following this *démarche*, the leadership of the reformist Socialist party, somewhat chagrined as a consequence of the defeat of its cause at the International Congress, maintained a guarded silence. Then, late in September, Jaurès, on behalf of the party leadership, proffered the suggestion that a Comité d'entente be constituted, charged, not with the task of bringing about the unification of the Socialist movement, but simply to establish a closer *rapprochement* among the separate Socialist organizations. The Central Council of the revolutionary Socialist party rejected this suggestion, asserting, in a second note (October 4) that it was not in harmony with the Amsterdam resolution which envisioned the complete fusion of the organizations. The Central Council then renewed its offer to enter into negotiations with the Parti socialiste français to this end. The response of the latter to this second *démarche* was not long delayed. On October 23 its National Council issued a statement expressing its readiness to open discussions on the question of unity.[10] On November 15, a delegation led by Guesde, Lafargue, Sembat, and Vaillant from the Parti socialiste de France met with a delegation headed by Jaurès, Briand, Renaudel, and Viviani representing the Parti socialiste français to consider the matter. The delegates immediately set up a Commission for Unification to study ways and means of unification. At its first meeting (November 29), the Commission approved a proposal that each party and autonomous federation draw up a memorandum specifying the conditions it considered necessary as the basis for unification; at its second meeting (December 12), these were presented to the Commission for examination.[11]

In its memorandum, the Parti socialiste de France set forth as the *conditio sine qua non* for unity the withdrawal of the Ministerial

---

[10] *Socialiste*, August 28 – September 4, October 2–9, 1904; the *Petite République*, October 8, 1904.

[11] *Petite République*, November 18, 1904; the *Socialiste*, November 27 – December 4, 1904. The membership of the Commission is given in the *Socialiste*.

Socialist Deputies from the Délégation des gauches and the Left Bloc in the Chamber and the reconstitution of the Socialist parliamentary group as a single bloc, separate from and opposed to all other parliamentary groups.[12] It did not come as a surprise to anyone that the Antiministerial Socialists should have set this requirement as the prerequisite for unity, for to the Parti socialiste de France, the identification of the Ministerial Socialists with the Left Bloc and its steering committee was the embodiment of *Ministérialisme*. Regarding this, it is significant that in spite of the fact that the parliamentary group of the Parti socialiste français was officially enrolled in the Left Bloc, while the parliamentary group of the Parti socialiste de France was not, the conduct of the two groups in the Chamber was quite similar. For, as the government, against the stubborn opposition of the Right-Center and Rightist parties, pressed for the final enactment of its anticlerical program, both Socialist groups had joined to support the Combes Ministry. Notable instances of this conduct were the votes of confidence given the ministry by all the Socialist Deputies on October 28 and November 4 (1904), following interpellations from the opposition concerning the system of espionage being carried on within the army by the Minister of War, General André, with the assistance of members of Masonic lodges. On both occasions, the ministry had been saved by Socialist votes.[13] That there was a wide discrepancy between the antiministerial assertions of the leaders of the Parti socialiste de France and the actual conduct of that party's parliamentary representatives was conceded by Sembat, himself a party Deputy. "We of the Revolutionary Socialist group have always been careful to emphasize our determination," he declared in an interview published in the *Petite République*, on November 2, 1904, "not to give our vote to a govern-

[12] For the text, see the *Petite République*, December 14, 1904.

[13] *Journal officiel*, sessions of October 28, 1904, pp. 2221–2247; November 4, 1904, pp. 2273–2300. As a part of his policy of "republicanizing" the army, General André ordered secret investigations of officers suspected of clerical or antirepublican sentiments, with Freemasons serving as spies. In October 1904, this espionage system was disclosed in the press. See D. W. Brogan, *France Under the Republic* (New York, 1940), pp. 379–387; and Seignobos, *L'Evolution de la 3ᵉ République*, pp. 238–240.

ment except when it had merited it. But, as a matter of fact, since the Russo-Japanese War, it is undeniable that we have systematically supported the Ministry. . ." [14] Sembat's candid statement did not draw denial from Guesde, Vaillant, or any other leader of the Parti socialiste de France.

In the memorandum which its representatives submitted to the Commission, the Parti socialiste français declared that the principles formulated by the International Congresses of Paris (1900) and Amsterdam should serve as the basis for a union of the French Socialist forces. It asserted that the new party should be a "class party" and that alliances between it and bourgeois parties should be prohibited except in certain "special circumstances." The reformist Socialist party also held that the parliamentary group of the projected party should form a separate bloc, "distinct from all the groups of the bourgeois parties." However, it left the way open to the formation of parliamentary alliances with the provision that if the "interests of the proletariat" were endangered by a political crisis, the unified party should not prohibit a "momentary coalition against reaction." The Allemanist party and the autonomous Federations of the Somme, Hérault, and Yonne also submitted memoranda which declared, in brief, that the unification of the Socialist movement should be achieved on the basis of the principles laid down by the International Congresses of Paris and Amsterdam. Only the Federation of the Hérault specifically set forth as a prerequisite for unity the withdrawal of the Ministerial Socialist Deputies from the Left Bloc.[15]

The Commission turned over these memoranda to a subcommittee, composed of two delegates from each of the major Socialist parties and two delegates representing all seven autonomous federations, directing it to utilize them in formulating a single text to serve as the charter for the unified party. This subcommittee, which included Allemane, Briand, Hervé, and Renaudel among its mem-

[14] Quoted in Edgard Milhaud, *La Tactique socialiste et les décisions des congrès internationaux* (2 vols., Paris, 1905), II, 142. See also Jaurès's article in *Humanité*, August 10, 1904.

[15] For the texts, see the *Petite République*, December 14, 1904; the *Socialiste*, December 11–18, 1904; and the *Vie socialiste*, 1: 294–296, 302–303 (1905).

bers, held a series of meetings during the following two weeks, at the last of which (December 30), it completed its assignment. The following day the drafted text was handed to the Commission, which in turn submitted it to the Socialist parties and autonomous federations for their approval. These acted with dispatch; and on January 13, 1905, the Commission announced that the central administrative organ of each of the contracting organizations, with the single exception of the Federation of the Nord (which gave its approval on January 29), had accepted the subcommittee's text, henceforth called the "Pact of Union," as the bases upon which the Socialist forces would merge.[16]

The Pact defined the projected party as a distinctly revolutionary organization. It stated that, while the party would utilize "to the profit of the workers the secondary conflicts of the property-owning classes," or might even "combine accidentally" its own action with that of some bourgeois party "in order to defend the rights and interests of the proletariat," it would remain "always a party of fundamental and irreducible opposition to the whole of the bourgeois class and to the state which is its instrument." The party was to pursue the immediate attainment of reforms demanded by the proletariat, but it would not be a party of reforms; rather it was to be by "its goal, its ideal, and by the means" which it made use of, a party "of class struggle and revolution." Its goal would be the socialization of the means of production and exchange — "that is, the transformation of our capitalist society into a collectivist or communist society." In the Chamber of Deputies, party members were to form a single bloc, separate from all bourgeois political groups. They were to "refuse to the government all the means that assure the domination of the bourgeoisie and its maintenance in power." Consequently, the party Deputies were to refuse to vote "military credits, credits for colonial conquest, secret funds, and the budget as a whole." These stipulations constituted a positive repudiation of the class collaboration: they definitely prohibited the participation

[16] *Socialiste*, January 22–29, 1905; the *Petite République*, December 14, 1904, January 1, 12, 31, 1905.

of Socialist Deputies in the Left Bloc. The only comfort that the Ministerial Socialists could draw on this score was the stipulation in the Pact which stated that "in case of exceptional circumstances" the party might undertake to reconsider this prohibition.[17] Thus, the approval of the Pact by the National Council of the Parti socialiste français was a striking victory for the Antiministerial Socialists.

With the administrative organs of all the Socialist factions now in agreement on the bases for unity, it only remained for the Pact to be implemented by the actual formation of the new party. The Commission for Unification undertook this task by transforming itself (January 13) into a "Committee of Organization" to prepare the ground for a congress of all the Socialist forces and to formulate a constitution for the projected party.

It had hardly begun its work, however, when a crisis occurred within the Parti socialiste français which threatened momentarily to prevent the realization of unity. The approval of the Pact of Union by the Ministerial Socialist party had been given official expression by its central administrative organ — the National Council — which, since the Amsterdam Congress, had come under the control of the left-wing faction of the party. This faction, as has been indicated, had long been opposed to the collaborationist policy pursued by the party group in the Chamber of Deputies. When the Antiministerial Socialists made the withdrawal of the Socialist parliamentary group from the Left Bloc the prerequisite for unity, the National Council was prepared to assent. By so doing, the National Council had given expression to the deeply felt desire of the mass of the rank and file of the party which considered the unification of the Socialist movement to be of much greater importance than the continued participation of their party Deputies in the Left Bloc.[18] However, the decision of the National Council, rendered manifest by its acceptance of the Pact (January 10), did not meet with the approval of many Ministerial Socialist Deputies. Victor Augagneur, Jules Breton, Léon Gérault-Richard, and other members of the parliamentary group believed that the tactics it pursued were both legitimate and fruitful,

[17] The text of the Pact is given in the *Petite République*, January 1, 1905.
[18] Albert Thomas, "Le Congrès de Rouen," *Revue socialiste*, 41: 392 (1905).

indispensable for the realization of progressive social legislation; they therefore viewed the decision of the National Council as ill-advised and unacceptable.[19]

These Deputies soon had an opportunity to make known their opposition to the action of the National Council. On January 30, just about two weeks after the Pact had been ratified by the Commission for Unification, the parliamentary group of the Parti socialiste français met at the Palais Bourbon. This meeting had been occasioned by a recent political development: on January 19 the Combes Ministry had resigned and had been succeeded shortly after by the more moderate ministry of Maurice Rouvier. The meeting had been called to define the course of action of the Socialist parliamentary group in the light of this event. The immediate issue was to decide whether the group should continue its collaboration with the parties of the Left in support of the Rouvier Ministry; the group resolved the question by adopting a resolution declaring its intention to continue participation in the Left Bloc.[20]

On February 7 the National Council of the Parti socialiste français met to consider the action of the party Deputies. Following a stormy discussion, in the course of which Breton defended the action, while Jaurès sharply criticized the right-wing majority of the parliamentary group for compromising the unity negotiations, citing the fact that the National Council had already formally put the party on record as opposing class collaboration by its approval of the Pact, two resolutions were brought before the National Council. The first, formulated by Jaurès, simply called upon the parliamentary group to accept the Pact. The second, drafted by Breton, approved the stand of the party Deputies, declaring that "the resolution voted by the parliamentary group is in no way contrary to the engagements taken by the party to realize Socialist unity." When the resolutions were put to the vote, that of Jaurès was carried by a wide majority.[21]

[19] See the statements of these and other Ministerial Socialists in the *Petite République*, August 21, 23, October 17, 18, 1904, February 10, 11, 1905. See also E. Fournière, "L'Action socialiste," *Revue socialiste*, 41: 332–337 (1905).

[20] *Petite République*, February 1, 1905.

[21] *Petite République*, February 9, 1905. See also P. Renaudel, "La Délégation des

This action did not settle the matter. On February 9, the parliamentary group met again and repudiated the decision of the National Council. By a vote of nineteen to four it adopted a resolution reaffirming its intention to remain in the Left Bloc. The Deputies also approved by unanimous vote a resolution which demanded that a national congress of the party be convoked "to resolve the deadlock" between the parliamentary group and the National Council.[22] Faced with this challenge to its authority — this "rebellion of the Deputies against the party" as Guesde called it (*Socialiste*, February 12–19, 1905) — the National Council had no alternative but to acquiesce in the demand of the parliamentary group: it summoned a national congress of the Parti socialiste français to meet at Rouen the following month.

At the Rouen Congress (March 26–28, 1905) Gérault-Richard and Breton vigorously defended the stand of the parliamentary group. Gérault-Richard justified the group's refusal to abandon the Left Bloc on the grounds that this collaboration was indispensable if the work of disestablishing the Church in France were to be completed. He also voiced opposition to the stipulation in the Pact of Union which imposed upon the parliamentary group the duty of voting against the budget. "I believe that Socialism is indissolubly bound to the Republic," he declared, "and the day when, by refusing to vote the budget, we prevent the Republic from accomplishing its mission, all the reforms which comprise the better part of our proletarian program will be impossible."[23] Breton insisted that the continued collaboration of Socialists and progressive bourgeois factions in the Chamber was rendered imperative by the need to press the Rouvier Ministry, which was more moderate than its predecessor, into orientating its policy more toward the Left. "If the Socialist group abandons the Délégation des gauches," he cautioned, "its place will be

gauches et l'unité socialiste," *Vie socialiste*, I: 492–494 (1905). For the membership of the National Council, see the *Petite République*, February 9, 1905.

[22] *Petite République*, February 10, 1905. The membership of the Socialist parliamentary group (Union socialiste) is given here.

[23] See the résumé of Gérault-Richard's speech in the *Petite République*, March 28, 1905.

taken by the *Progressistes* and there will be a retreat in policy toward the Right." [24]

Jaurès led the attack on the right-wing Ministerial Socialists. He insisted that the real issue at hand did not involve the principle of participation in a ministerial bloc, but that it was simply a tactical question, a matter of political expediency. He maintained, contrary to the assertions of these Socialists, that collaboration with the bourgeois groups of the Left no longer made sense. The minimum program upon which the Left Bloc and the Délégation des gauches had been constituted was all but realized; and since there had been a considerable shift to the Right in the Chamber of Deputies under the Rouvier Ministry, the time had come for the Socialist parliamentary group to end its "temporary close alliance" with the Radicals and "to inaugurate a more extensive program of social action" than that undertaken by the Left Bloc. Yet Jaurès by no means ruled out the possibility of a reconstitution of that Bloc at some future date. He asserted that the Socialists should continue to distinguish between the Right and the Left among bourgeois parties, adding that in "exceptional circumstances" the projected unified party would undoubtedly collaborate with the advanced bourgeois elements of the Left "with more authority than ever." As for the Pact's stipulation which obliged the Socialist Deputies to vote against the budget, Jaurès, while maintaining that the directive was a proper one, conceded that this act had primarily "a symbolic value" and would give way to realistic political considerations as the situation required. "I do not see why we should not make this manifestation even though it be but symbolic against a social state that we wish to overthrow. But the day when it would endanger a reformist government and a reform supported by the Socialist proletariat, such a manifestation would be a veritable suicide." In any event the unification of the Socialist movement was the immediate, paramount consideration, and he concluded his speech with the recommendation that the congress repudiate the stand of the intransigent Deputies

---

[24] See the résumés of Breton's speech in the *Petite République*, March 28, 1905, and Thomas, p. 392. See also Winnacker, "The Délégation des Gauches," p. 468; Thomas, pp. 387–388.

by reaffirming the Pact, already accepted on behalf of the party by the National Council.[25]

By the stand which he took in support of unification, Jaurès, whose authority and influence within the Parti socialiste français were decisive, assured the defeat of the right-wing party Deputies. At the close of the discussion of the conflict between the National Council and these Deputies, the congress, voting by federations, unanimously approved the Pact and instructed the Socialist parliamentary group to withdraw from the Left Bloc.[26]

It now remained to be seen whether the parliamentary group would accept this verdict as final. On April 4, the party Deputies met to review the action of the Rouen Congress. Two die-hard Ministerialists, Breton and Augagneur, pleaded with their colleagues to repudiate the action. But Jaurès again argued the case, and the group by an overwhelming vote adopted a resolution approving the decisions of the Rouen Congress.[27]

Shortly after this meeting, some of the right-wing Ministerial Socialist Deputies, including Augagneur, Colliard, Deville, Boyer, and Zévaès, withdrew from the parliamentary group (Union socialiste) of the Parti socialiste français. The principal reason for their departure was patent: they desired to continue their collaborationist tactics at all costs. As Augagneur and Colliard expressed it in their joint resignation: "We continue to believe that the policy of the Bloc, which has been pursued during the past six years with such fecund results, is still as useful today as it was yesterday to Socialism and the Republic."[28] During 1906, these Deputies and a number of

[25] See the résumés of Jaurès's speech in the *Petite République*, March 29, 1905, and Thomas, pp. 392, 396. See also Jaurès's articles in the *Dépêche de Toulouse*, September 23, 1904, and *Humanité*, August 22, 1904.

[26] *Petite République*, March 28, 1905. Breton, in his book, *L'Unité socialiste*, p. 51, declares that Jaurès held the balance of power at the Rouen Congress, and that it was Jaurès's desire to realize unity "at any cost" which led him to "abandon his friends" and oppose participation in the Left Bloc. This descision, Breton adds, doomed the cause of the right-wing party Deputies: "Rien ne pouvait résister au courant impétueux, à l'impulsion irraisonnée qui entraînait à ce moment les socialistes vers l'unité. Le pacte fut donc approuvé, la déclaration adoptée et la tactique réformiste sacrifiée sur l'autel de l'unité."

[27] *Petite République*, April 5, 1905.

[28] *Petite République*, May 17, 1905. See also the *Petite République*, April 1, 14,

local groups of the Parti socialiste français that had refused to adhere to the unified party when their own party was officially dissolved united to revive the reformist organization, retaining the same party label. The right-wing Socialist Deputy Viviani, who had resigned from the unified party shortly after its formation, and the ex-minister Millerand identified themselves with this party. Avowedly reformist and collaborationist in doctrine and tactics, the revived Parti socialiste français held three annual national congresses, but by 1910 it was in a full state of dissolution. In July 1911, it was reorganized under the name of the Parti républicain socialiste. By this date, however, the party had moved so far to the Right ideologically, that it was Socialist only in name.[29]

The departure of the dissident right-wing elements from the Parti socialiste français following its Rouen Congress removed the last obstacle to the unification of the great mass of the French Socialist forces. At an historic "Unity Congress" which took place in the Globe Hall in Paris from April 23 to 25, this union, so long awaited by the rank and file of the Socialist movement, was at last effected. After the Unity Congress had reaffirmed the Pact of Union, the merger of the contracting organizations — the Parti socialiste français, the Parti socialiste de France, the Parti ouvrier socialiste révolutionnaire, and the autonomous Federations of the Bouches-du-Rhône, Bretagne, Hérault, Somme, Nord, Var, and Yonne — in a single party, called the Parti socialiste, section française de l'internationale ouvrière (Socialist party, French Section of the Workers' International) was proclaimed.

The Unity Congress formulated a charter for the new party. According to it, the action of the Socialist party was to be based on the following fundamental principles: (1) the international entente of all workers; (2) the political and economic organization of

May 18, 1905. In addition to those named above, the following resigned from the Socialist parliamentary group after the Rouen Congress: Gérault-Richard, Grousset, Charpentier, Baron, Isoard, and Krauss.

[29] See the *Petite République*, April 26, 27, 28, May 20, 1905; Zévaès, *Le Socialisme en 1912*, pp. 47–56; and Orry, *Les Socialistes indépendants*, pp. 76–81. See also A. Zévaès and J. Prolo, *Une Campagne politique, le Parti républicain socialiste, 1910–1917* (Paris, 1918).

the proletariat for the purpose of capturing governmental power; and (3) the socialization of the means of production and exchange, that is, the transformation of the existing capitalist society into a collectivist or communist society. Membership in the unified party was contingent upon the acceptance of these guiding principles. The charter provided that the basic units of the party were to be the permanent local groups, those devoted to "social studies" as well as those concerned with "political action." All groups located in the same commune were to form one section; [30] and all sections located in the same department were in turn to constitute a single federation, to be administered by a federal committee. The federations were charged with the task of seeing to it that the "principles and program as well as the decisions of the national and international congresses" were respected by their memberships. They were to make certain that their electoral candidates pledged themselves in writing to observe the programs, principles, and decisions of these congresses.

The party's general affairs were to be regulated by the national congress, convened annually. Delegates to the congress were to be chosen by the departmental federations, with each federation being represented in proportion to the number of its dues-paying members. In the interval between national congresses, the party was to be directed by a central executive authority — a National Council — composed of (1) delegates from the federations; (2) the party group in the Chamber of Deputies; and (3) the Permanent Administrative Committee, whose twenty-two members were to be elected annually by the national congress. The National Council was to execute decisions of the congress, to organize the general propaganda activity, and to supervise the party workers, the party *élus*, and the party press. The party press was to be permitted freedom of discussion on all questions of doctrine and method. But, with regard to party action, all the newspapers and reviews were to conform to the decisions of the national and international congresses as interpreted

[30] In the department of the Seine, all the groups located in the same *arrondissement* of Paris or in the same canton of the suburbs were to form one section of the party. This special provision also applied to the city of Lyons.

by the National Council. The National Council was empowered by the charter to take all the measures, "even exceptional ones," that might be required to carry out its functions.

The charter provided that the party group in the Chamber of Deputies was to form a separate bloc, "distinct from all the political factions of the bourgeoisie." It was to regulate its conduct in accordance with the Pact of Union, to conform strictly to the tactics determined by the national congresses of the party. The group was to make an annual report of its activities to these congresses. Individual members of the parliamentary group were subject to the supervision of their respective federations, while the group as a whole was subject to the authority of the National Council. As regards other party *élus*, the charter provided that in communes and departments, municipal, *arrondissement*, and general councilors were to collaborate closely with the party groups located in the communes and with the federal committee of their departmental federation in order to facilitate the work of propaganda and political organization.[31]

The brief declaration of principles set forth in the charter requires little comment, for it was simply a restatement of the credo contained in Millerand's Saint-Mandé Program of 1896. The now defunct Parti socialiste de France and the Parti socialiste français had both included these principles in their constitutions. It was a credo which had become part of the traditions of the Socialist movement. It was sufficiently vague to win the approval of reformist and revolutionary Socialists alike. The plan of organization of the unified Socialist party can be described as being on the whole a compromise between a strongly centralized party structure, such as that of the Parti socialiste de France, and an extremely decentralized one, like that of the Parti socialiste français. Supreme power within the unified party was vested in the annual national congress, which was so constituted as to be a reflection of the opinion of the party membership as a whole. The administrative authority of the new party was shared by the central organ, the National Council, and the depart-

---

[31] The text of the charter is given in *Parti socialiste, section française de l'internationale ouvrière, 1er Congrès national (Congrès d'unité), tenu à Paris les 23, 24 et 25 avril* (Paris, n.d.), pp. 23-32.

mental federations. The departmental federations were directly responsible for the conduct of their members, and they possessed broad power of decision in matters concerning electoral action. On the other hand, the National Council supervised the party membership as a whole. It is noteworthy that the provisions for the recruitment of the former as set forth in the charter were such as to make certain that the National Council would not become subject to the control of any minority faction within the party. The fact that the departmental federations and the national congress were to designate the majority of the National Council would seem to indicate that this was the intention of the Unity Congress.[32] With but slight modification, the charter approved by the Unity Congress in April 1905 remained in force until after the First World War.

Some six months after the Unity Congress a census of the new Socialist party disclosed that it had 46,380 members in good standing (as compared with the approximately 28,000 members claimed by the defunct organizations), enrolled in some two thousand study and action groups. These groups in turn were consolidated in sixty-five departmental federations. The party held thirty-six seats in the Chamber of Deputies and included among its members one hundred departmental councilors and more than fifteen hundred municipal councilors. The census also disclosed that the party possessed forty newspapers and reviews in addition to the official organ, the *Socialiste*, which had formerly been the official journal of the Parti socialiste de France.[33] It was a strong, aggressive Socialist party that now made its entrance into the arena of national politics to struggle for political power and the realization of a new vision of society.

The formation of the Socialist party checked the tendency toward the multiplication of groups and the dispersion of forces which had on the whole characterized the French Socialist movement since its

---

[32] The delegates from the parliamentary group were to constitute, in terms of voting power, only a small fraction of the National Council.

[33] *Parti socialiste, section française de l'internationale ouvrière, 2ᵉ Congrès national, tenu à Chalon-sur-Saône les 29, 30, 31 octobre et 1ᵉʳ novembre 1905* (Paris, n.d.), pp. 53–68.

revival after the Paris Commune. The creation of the new organization, however, did not mean that complete harmony and unanimity within the ranks on all major issues was attained. Given the history of the French Socialist movement since the 1870's, a history replete with bitter feuds, ugly recriminations, and numerous schisms, it would have been a remarkable achievement indeed had the contending factions, in 1905, broken entirely with the past and created a monolithic party whose membership adhered unwaveringly to a single program, method, and goal. Unity on the organizational level did not eliminate serious differences of opinion on questions of program and tactics. On all the issues of paramount importance to the party from 1905 to 1914 — for example, the relation of the party to the syndicalist movement, its attitude toward patriotism and militarism, and the question of political tactics — both old and new factional tendencies and groupings appeared. Although a detailed consideration of these matters lies beyond the province of this study, they should be examined at least summarily as they were of the utmost importance in determining the political orientation and the character of the Socialist party from its formation to the outbreak of the First World War.

Before taking up the first of these matters — the relation of the Socialist party to the syndicalist movement — it is appropriate, for the sake of clarifying some of the issues involved, to present a brief survey of that movement and its ideology since 1902. In a congress at Montpellier in September 1902, the two national labor organizations, the Fédération des Bourses du travail (Federation of Labor Exchanges), and the Confédération générale du travail (General Confederation of Labor, often referred to as the C.G.T.), were unified. The new organization, retaining the name of the latter, claimed a membership of some 200,000.[34] The dominant ideology of the C.G.T. was an eclectic combination of Anarchist and Socialist conceptions, drawn largely but not exclusively from Marxist, Proudhonist, and Bakuninist sources. The principal tenets of this ideology, known as "Revolutionary Syndicalism," were the following: the class struggle and "direct action"; the *syndicat* as the basis for the

[34] Louis Levine, *Syndicalism in France* (New York, 1914), p. 179.

future collectivist society; antipatriotism and antimilitarism; and the superiority of economic over political action.

For the Revolutionary Syndicalist, as for the Marxist, the conflict between the bourgeoisie, which owned the means of production, and the "exploited" proletariat was the fundamental fact of life under capitalism. He believed that only resolution of that conflict in favor of the proletariat could bring about the latter's emancipation and the achievement of social justice. To the Revolutionary Syndicalist, the state was bourgeois in essence and function, serving only to defend the interests of the ruling class. The triumph of the proletariat could only be realized, therefore, through the destruction of the existing state machinery.

The Revolutionary Syndicalist held that the proletariat must work out its own emancipation through the instrument of its own creation, the labor union. The union was to exercise direct action (the direct face-to-face struggle on the economic level against the enemy class in contrast to the indirect, impersonal struggle on the political level) against the capitalist class and the state. The chief forms of direct action were the partial strike, the general strike, the boycott, and sabotage. By these methods, the Revolutionary Syndicalist hoped to force employers to make concessions and to impose the will of the proletariat on the government. The general strike was to him the most powerful weapon possessed by the workers. He believed that at the proper time, when the class struggle will have become most acute, the proletariat would make its supreme bid for power through its employment. At that time the workers of one industry would go on strike; soon the strike would spread until it enveloped all essential industries of the country. As a consequence, economic life would become completely disorganized, the capitalist ruling class would find itself helpless, and the instrument of its domination, the state, would collapse. Then the workers, united in their *syndicats*, would take over the paralyzed economy. They would reorganize the country's economic life in accordance with democratic collectivist ideals and on the basis of their own *syndicats*, federated in a national body similar to the C.G.T. itself. Such was the Revolutionary Syndicalist pattern of revolution.

His antipatriotic and antimilitaristic notions, were the logical con-comitants of the Revolutionary Syndicalist's conception of the state. Patriotism was an ideological conception employed by the bourgeois state to deceive the proletariat, to blind the workers to the real social injustices and class distinctions existing in capitalist society. It could have no meaning to the mass of underprivileged workers who pos-sessed no property and were not bound to the nation by ties of in-tellectual and moral traditions. Similarly, the antimilitarist ideology of the Revolutionary Syndicalist stemmed from his conception of the bourgeois state. The army was the instrument by which the ruling class, operating through the instrumentality of the state, dominated the proletariat. The state employed the army to defeat the efforts of the workers to improve their status by mass action, as in the case of strikes. Hence, to gain its emancipation, the pro-letariat must undermine the army by carrying on an incessant anti-militarist campaign within the army ranks as well as in the nation at large. The Revolutionary Syndicalist also believed that militarism was a constant menace to the welfare of the proletariat because it promoted colonial and international wars, which always resulted in the killing of the workers of one country by those of another. In case of a declaration of war a general strike should be called, to paralyze the military efforts of the bourgeois state. Thus the Revolu-tionary Syndicalist held that the existence of the French nation and its defense in time of war were affairs of the bourgeoisie which in no way concerned the proletariat.

Lastly, the attitude of the Revolutionary Syndicalist toward party politics was dictated by his conceptions of the class struggle and the state as well as by his evaluation of the political action of the various Socialist factions since 1893. On the economic level, the Revolution-ary Syndicalist maintained, the class struggle was direct and naked: the workers clashed head-on with the bourgeoisie. There was no confusion of interests, no compromise, no mistaking the real class enemy. On the other hand, he believed that the political level was a poor terrain for waging the class struggle. The parliamentary sys-tem, instituted by the bourgeoisie to serve its own class interests, involved the political representatives of the working class in all sorts of intrigues and maneuvers which ultimately compromised and then corrupted them. He held that as the inevitable consequence of the collaboration of the working class representatives with the representatives of the bourgeois class in parliament, the former were always led to jettison their initial revolutionary ideology and policies. The Revolutionary Syndicalist believed that the conduct of the Socialist Deputies since their entry en masse into the Chamber in 1893 constituted conclusive proof of the "pernicious influence" of the parliamentary system. He contended that as soon as the Socialist Deputies — even the most revolutionary of them, the Guesdists — became involved in the system, they began to retreat from their early revolutionary views and gradually appeared more and more moderate in aspiration and behavior. They ceased to talk about revolution and social transformation and instead spoke of working for social peace. Caught up in the "snares" of parliamentary activity, the Socialist parties were being converted into orthodox political parties, distinguished from bourgeois parties only by their somewhat more radical orientations. The distaste of the Revolutionary Syndicalist for party politics was also based on the belief that Socialist political action had failed to improve substantially the condition of the working classes. The belief of the Revolutionary Syndicalist that Millerand, as Minister of Commerce and Industry, had failed to achieve more than partial reforms likewise strengthened this antipolitical tendency.[35]

The opposition of the Revolutionary Syndicalists to party politics and political action and their determination to keep the syndicalist movement, specifically the C.G.T., aloof from such activity and independent of all political parties, Socialist or otherwise, were clearly indicated at the Amiens Congress of the C.G.T. in September 1906. The formation of the unified Socialist party had taken

[35] On Revolutionary Syndicalism, see A. Zévaès, *Le Syndicalisme contemporain* (Paris, 1911), pp. 140–153; Levine, *Syndicalism in France*, 118, 126–136; Robert Goetz-Girey, *La Pensée syndicale française, militants et théoriciens* (Paris, 1948), pp. 44–45, 50–52; and Val R. Lorwin, *The French Labor Movement* (Cambridge, Mass., 1954), pp. 29–46. See also Weinstein, *Jean Jaurès*, pp. 89, 96–97, 99–104; H. Largadelle, "Antimilitarisme et syndicalisme," *Mouvement socialiste*, 18: 121–126 (1906).

place the year before, and in recognition of this, a minority of the C.G.T. membership, known as "Political Syndicalists," proposed that some sort of working agreement be established between the C.G.T. and the Socialist party. Victor Renard, secretary of the important Federation of Textile Workers and a Guesdist, argued the case for the Political Syndicalists, declaring that in the struggle for the emancipation of the proletariat, various methods of action, political as well as syndicalist, must be utilized. The union alone could not achieve that goal. Collaboration between the *syndicats* and the Socialist party, which, he asserted, had always supported legislation to improve the condition of the workers, was both useful and necessary. The Revolutionary Syndicalists, who were in the majority and who occupied most of the important posts in the C.G.T., vigorously opposed this view; and by an overwhelming vote the congress adopted a resolution affirming the antipolitical stand of Revolutionary Syndicalism. This resolution, which came to be known as the "Charter of French Syndicalism," read in part as follows: "In so far as syndicalist organizations are concerned, the Congress decides that, in order that syndicalism may attain its maximum effectiveness, economic action should be exercised directly against the class of employers, and the Confederal organizations must not, as syndical groups, pay any attention to parties and sects which, outside and by their side, may pursue in full liberty the transformation of sosciety." [36]

Shortly after the Amiens Congress, the Third National Congress of the Socialist party was held at Limoges (November 1906). For the first time at a national congress, the question of the relation of the party to the syndicalist movement was on the agenda. There was no common agreement concerning this matter; and in the course of the debate which took place, three major factional tendencies or groupings became manifest.

One of these tendencies was represented by Hervé, who had fallen under the influence of the Revolutionary Syndicalists in 1904

[36] See the report of the debate and the text of the resolution in Zévaès, *Le Syndicalisme contemporain*, pp. 177–179.

and had become the chief exponent of some of the tenets of their ideology within the Socialist party. He staunchly defended the decision of the Amiens Congress to keep the C.G.T. independent of all political parties and called upon the Socialists to respect that decision by recognizing the autonomy of the syndicalist organization. Jaurès represented the second major factional tendency. He likewise maintained that the decision of the Amiens Congress should be respected. The C.G.T. and the Socialist party each had its own legitimate sphere of action even though both drew their support from the same class and had the same objective — the emancipation of the proletariat. Unlike Hervé, however, Jaurès believed that though the two working-class organizations should be independent, they should not remain entirely aloof from one another. He contended that the two organizations should seek to establish close and harmonious relations, cooperating "freely" with one another. The third major factional tendency found its spokesman in Guesde. In contrast to both Hervé and Jaurès, he argued that the C.G.T. should not remain autonomous, but that there should be "unity of action" between it and the Socialist party. He attacked the stand of political neutrality taken by the Amiens Congress, reiterating the familiar Marxist argument that the essential function of the labor union was to serve as a focal point for organizing the working class in preparation for its struggle for complete emancipation. The *syndicat* was obliged not only to safeguard the immediate day-to-day economic interests of the workers, but also to prepare the workers for the more important political contest whose final resolution was the conquest of governmental power by the proletariat. It fulfilled this task by spreading Socialist propaganda and by recruiting members for the Socialist party. Guesde sharply attacked the notion of the Revolutionary Syndicalists that direct action by the workers on the economic level was in itself sufficient to achieve proletarian emancipation, insisting, on the contrary, that political action was indispensable in the struggle for this objective. The interests of the workers could best be served by a consolidation of proletarian political and syndicalist organizations under the leadership of the Socialist party. At the close of the debate, the congress adopted a resolution which embodied the views of Jaurès.[37]

Similarly, on the important issues of patriotism and militarism, the ranks of the Socialist party were sharply divided. These related issues were given detailed consideration by the party at its Limoges and Nancy (1907) Congresses. Again three major factional tendencies were clearly discernible. One of these tendencies was again represented by Hervé, who spoke for the extreme antipatriotic and antimilitaristic elements within the party. Hervé, labeled by some Socialists as the "Déroulède of Antipatriotism" because of his uncompromising, vitriolic denunciation of any manifestation of patriotic sentiment, maintained that it was impossible to reconcile the conceptions of the class struggle and the international entente of the proletariat — two of the fundamental ideas of revolutionary Socialism — with notions of patriotism and militarism. The workers, he contended, had no fatherland and therefore could have no interest in the destiny of any particular country. For them, all nations were of "equal value" in the sense that in all the proletariat occupied the same lowly status; in every nation they were exploited by the bourgeois class that controlled the government. To Hervé, as to the Revolutionary Syndicalists, patriotism was a "false religion" inculcated in the working classes by their rulers so as to separate the workers of one country from those of another and to inveigle them into serving the interests of the bourgeois ruling class: "They [the bourgeoisie] have succeeded in creating in each country a sort of religion of patriotism which has its sacred symbols and ceremonies of a religious character — a religion which stimulates hatred toward the infidels on the other side of the frontiers and which renders the people susceptible to international slaughter when that happens to serve the interests of the rulers." To this "invidious patriotism" of the ruling class, Hervé opposed "Socialist patriotism," which was not an attachment to any single region or country or to any "national or governmental ceremonial system," but rather "an attachment to all the workers of the entire world."

[37] *Parti socialiste, section française de l'internationale ouvrière, 3ᵉ Congrès national, tenu à Limoges les 1ᵉʳ, 2, 3 et 4 novembre 1906* (Paris, n.d.), pp. 157-164, 165-180, 184-194.

The "true patriotism" of Socialists was "patriotism of class." Since the workers had no fatherland, it was senseless for them to concern themselves with matters of national defense. Indeed, rather than defend the nation, the workers should, upon a declaration of war, instigate a general strike and a military insurrection at home. This should be done whether the war be offensive or defensive in character; for Hervé maintained that in modern warfare, citing the Franco-Prussian, the Boer, and the Russo-Japanese wars as cases in point, it was almost impossible to know who was the "true aggressor" when the conflict broke out.[38]

The second major factional tendency within the Socialist party on the allied issues of patriotism and militarism was represented by Jaurès and Vaillant. Vaillant attacked Hervé's contention that patriotism was a false belief evolved by the bourgeois ruling classes to serve their interests. The identification of the worker with his country, he asserted, was a natural "fact" of life. The nation was the environment in which the working class of a country evolved. It was the *milieu* in which the workers became "class conscious," and began to feel that they were bound to the workers of other countries, "with the international working class, in the defense and struggle against internal and external rulers." Although Vaillant did not believe that Socialists must be antipatriotic, he did maintain that they must certainly be antimilitaristic. Opposition to the bourgeois state meant opposition to the armed forces of the state which served as its instrument of oppression. It was impossible for the proletariat to be indifferent either to the armed forces which held it "in check under the yoke of capitalism" or to the bellicose tendencies of the government which threatened the proletariat with "slaughter" in wars. It was the duty of the Socialists to wage an incessant antimilitaristic campaign. Vaillant, however, did not go along with Hervé when the latter suggested that the general strike and military insurrection be employed at the outbreak of war. He contended that it would be the duty of the Socialists to defend the nation if she were the

[38] *Parti socialiste . . . 3ᵉ Congrès national*, pp. 214–220; *Parti socialiste, section française de l'internationale ouvrière, 4ᵉ Congrès national, tenu à Nancy les 11, 12, 13 et 14 août 1907* (Paris, n.d.), pp. 210–225, 294–304.

victim of unprovoked aggression.[39] Jaurès also attacked Hervé's antipatriotism, arguing that nations were the necessary "cadres" of the future Socialist order. To bring about the triumph of international Socialism and the institution of the future international society, it was first necessary for the proletariat to take over governmental power in each separate country. The nation was the necessary terrain of proletarian action, for it was on the national level that the workers were obliged to achieve "their emancipation and their organization." To Jaurès, therefore, there was no conflict between patriotism and internationalism. Like Vaillant, Jaurès believed that it was imperative for the Socialist party to fight the menace of militarism. But again like Vaillant, he declared his opposition to the employment of the general strike and military insurrection whenever war threatened or actually broke out. He drew a distinction between offensive and defensive wars, asserting that if France were attacked, it would be the duty of the Socialists to rally to her defense. In defending the nation, the Socialists would be serving their own interests, for they would be safeguarding for future generations and for the future Socialist society all that was precious in the existing social order. Jaurès conceded that it would be difficult to determine the aggressor at the outbreak of war, but he believed that the willingness of the opposing countries to arbitrate their dispute might serve as a means of determining which country was guilty of aggression and which was not.[40]

The third major factional tendency on the allied questions of patriotism and militarism was represented by Guesde. Like Vaillant, he vigorously attacked Hervé's contention that the workers had no fatherland, were *sans-patrie* and therefore could have no interest in the nation. Guesde conceded that at the time Marx and Engels wrote the *Communist Manifesto*, it was correct for them to declare that the workers had no country. But since that time, since universal suffrage had been put into his hands as a weapon for struggle, the

[39] *Parti socialiste . . . 3ᵉ Congrès national*, pp. 221–228, 259; *Parti socialiste . . . 4ᵉ Congrès national*, pp. 182–195.
[40] *Parti socialiste . . . 3ᵉ Congrès national*, pp. 251–256; *Parti socialiste . . . 4ᵉ Congrès national*, pp. 257–286.

worker did have a fatherland; and if the worker "did not act with his *patrie*" it was his own fault. "The factories, mines, railways all belong to the worker, but he has not as yet made the necessary effort to take possession of it all. To say to the worker that he has no *patrie* is most certainly to lie to him; he does have one. It is only that the worker, deceived by the maneuvers of the bourgeoisie, misled by anarchist abstention, has refused until now to take power and to take control of this property." He also agreed with Jaurès that the nation was the necessary terrain of proletarian action, that the "national duty" of Socialists and workers was to bring about the social revolution within their own country. The proletariat, he stated, had the assigned task of dispossessing its own capitalist class: this was the fundamental obligation that it owed to the proletariat of other countries. Guesde likewise agreed with Hervé, Vaillant, and Jaurès that the Socialist party must fight incessantly against militarism and war. However, he rejected Hervé's proposal that a general strike and a military insurrection be instigated at the outbreak of war. The general strike, proposed by Hervé in case of any war whatsoever and by Jaurès in the event of an offensive war, would not, he contended, achieve its objective, that is, paralyze the war effort and bring about an end to hostilities. For, at the first sign of such a strike the government would employ its full force to smash it, arresting the leaders of the movement as traitors to the fatherland. Indeed, Guesde held that the general strike proposal was a "counter-revolutionary" rather than a "revolutionary" conception of Socialist tactics, for if it were employed at the outbreak of war, the defense of the country which had the stronger, more disciplined, Socialist movement would be the more weakened and disorganized; and as a consequence, it would probably be defeated by an opposing nation whose Socialist movement was weaker, less organized. In that event the stronger Socialist movement would be crushed by the victorious nation and the international Socialist movement would receive a setback. Finally, Guesde opposed the adoption by the party of Hervé's proposal on rather opportunistic grounds, insisting that such action would constitute "an insurmountable obstacle" to the extension of the Socialist movement — that it would, by giving the country the impression that the Socialists were indifferent to the fate of their country, alienate sections of the public and frustrate the propaganda and recruitment efforts of the party.

Rejecting outright the notion of a general strike and military insurrection even in a case of a war of aggression by France, Guesde maintained that the party could best carry on the struggle against militarism and war by concentrating its efforts on the fight against capitalism itself. It was of little value to rail against militarism and war as long as the capitalist system existed. "War and militarism," he stated, "are the fruits of contemporary society and will disappear only with that society." Guesde did propose, however, that the party include in its general program certain measures aimed specifically at curbing the menace of militarism and war. He held that the party should call for the reduction of the length of military service in all nations; refuse to vote credits for the army, navy, and colonies; and demand the substitution of the general arming of the people for professional armies.[41] It is interesting that Guesde's stand on the question of Socialist tactics in a war crisis was quite different from what it had been in the days when he was an intransigent revolutionary. In the early nineties, he had advocated that in the event of war the workers should take advantage of the opportunity for mass action offered by the crisis to press the class struggle to its conclusion — to overthrow the rule of the bourgeois class at home.[42]

At the close of the debate on patriotism and militarism at the Limoges Congress (1906), three separate resolutions — embodying the views of Hervé, Vaillant and Jaurès, and Guesde respectively — were presented to the delegates. When they were put to a vote, the Vaillant-Jaurès resolution was adopted by a wide majority.[43] This decision was reaffirmed the following year at the Nancy Congress. Thus the Socialist party went on record as being in favor of a general strike and military insurrection in the event of aggressive action

[41] *Parti socialiste . . . 3ᵉ Congrès national*, pp. 239–244, 246–247; *Parti socialiste . . . 4ᵉ Congrès national*, pp. 178–181, 231–232, 304–313. See also Weinstein, *Jean Jaurès*, pp. 163–165.

[42] See the *Socialiste*, September 2, 1891.

[43] For the text of the resolutions, see *Parti socialiste . . . 3ᵉ Congrès national*, pp. 260–262.

by the French government, while at the same time it took the position that the Socialists and workers were obliged to defend their country in case of an unprovoked attack.

On the allied issues of patriotism and militarism Hervé represented the extreme left-wing factional tendency, Jaurès and Vaillant the centrist tendency, and Guesde the right-wing tendency. By repudiating Hervé's antipatriotic stance, Guesde and his followers, who constituted one of the most powerful blocs in the party, greatly strengthened the position of the patriotic Socialist elements and did much to assure the triumph of patriotism within the Socialist party at the outbreak of the First World War.[44]

On the question of tactics — the third and last of the party matters examined here that were of paramount importance to French Socialists during the period 1905–1914 — two major factional tendencies appeared within the organization. One of these, as on the other major issues, was represented by Hervé, who again took an extreme left-wing position. His stand was dictated by his notion of how the future Socialist order was to be instituted. Positing the conquest of state power as the prerequisite for the establishment of that order, he argued that this must be achieved through violent revolution rather than by peaceful, legal means. Participation in electoral contests was useful only because it presented the Socialists with excellent opportunities for propagandizing their doctrines and for gaining recruits for the party. In his view, the aim of electoral action was to spread Socialism, not to win political offices; and he was uncompromisingly opposed to having the Socialists enter into electoral alliances or coalitions with any other political party.[45]

The major opposing factional tendency on this question was represented by Jaurès and Vaillant. While Hervé's approach was that of a revolutionary Socialist, that of Jaurès and Vaillant was strictly reformist. Although both maintained, as did Hervé, that the conquest of state power was the prerequisite for the realization of

[44] See Weinstein, *Jean Jaurès*, p. 163. For a detailed study of the question of patriotism and the French Socialist party, see Weinstein, pp. 89–187.

[45] *Parti socialiste, section française de l'internationale ouvrière, 6ᵉ Congrès national, tenu à Saint-Etienne les 11, 12, 13 et 14 avril 1909* (Paris, n.d.), pp. 496–504.

Socialism, they differed from him in their belief that this could be achieved without revolution. They contended that the utilization of universal suffrage and legal political action by the organized proletariat would permit the peaceful conquest of state power and the gradual introduction of Socialism. Both Jaurès and Vaillant argued that in its electoral campaigns the Socialist party should aim directly at the conquest of political office. "Like all struggle," Vaillant told the Saint-Etienne Congress (1909), "electoral action has real value only when victory is sought." And to enhance the possibility of electoral victories, both leaders, in contrast to Hervé, favored collaboration between the Socialist party and other political organizations on the second balloting (the run-off election) in legislative and municipal elections.[46]

Although Guesde's approach to the question differed from that of Jaurès and Vaillant on the one hand and Hervé on the other, his attitude toward electoral alliances and coalitions was identical with that of the Jaurès. Guesde contended that it was impossible to foretell, as Jaurès, Vaillant, and Hervé endeavored to do, whether the assumption of state power by the proletariat would be achieved through violent revolution or legal political action. Therefore, Socialists could not definitely rule out either method. "We must be prepared to seize political power, the essential instrument of our emancipation," he declared at the Nancy Congress (1907), "by all methods, from the ballot to the general strike and insurrection." But while he did not rule out the possibility of revolution, Guesde's own predilection was definitely for democratic procedures. At the Nancy Congress, he asserted that the workers who "have spilled and still spill their blood" in order to possess the ballot would not believe that it was a weapon of merely "secondary importance."

---

[46] For Jaurès's stand, see *Parti socialiste . . . 2ᵉ Congrès national*, pp. 100–102; *Parti socialiste . . . 3ᵉ Congrès national*, pp. 174–175; *Parti socialiste . . . 6ᵉ Congrès national*, pp. 473–481; and *Parti socialiste, section française de l'internationale ouvrière, 9ᵉ Congrès national, tenu à Lyon les 18, 19, 20 et 21 février 1912* (Paris, n.d.), p. 188. For Vaillant's stand, see *Parti socialiste . . . 2ᵉ Congrès national*, pp. 89–90; *Parti socialiste, section française de l'internationale ouvrière, 5ᵉ Congrès national, tenu à Toulouse les 15, 16, 17 et 18 octobre 1908* (Paris, n.d.), pp. 154–168; and *Parti socialiste . . . 6ᵉ Congrès national*, pp. 449–455.

Political democracy constituted, he stressed, "a considerable advance in the evolution of the working class toward its Social Revolution. It is not universal suffrage, it is not the ballot which can be held responsible for its sterility; it is the working class which must be accused — the working class, which, having in its hands such a weapon, has not known how to use it." It was this high estimation of the value of the democratic method in the struggle for power which in large measure determined Guesde's stand on the question of electoral tactics. Believing along with Jaurès and Vaillant that the Socialists should seek to win public offices as well as to spread their doctrines and recruit new members for the party in waging their political campaigns, Guesde sided with them against Hervé on the question of tactics, maintaining that the party should collaborate with advanced bourgeois parties whenever such arrangements served to promote the interests of Socialism.[47]

The great majority of the Socialist party went along with Guesde, Jaurès, and Vaillant on this issue. Lafargue was the only leader who sided with Hervé.[48] The views of the majority were embodied in the decisions on tactics taken by national congresses of the party. In preparation for the general legislative elections of 1906, the Chalon-sur-Saône Congress (1905) adopted a resolution which provided that the party should place its own candidates in as many electoral districts as possible on the first balloting (which was in conformity with the traditional policy of the Guesdists), but that the departmental federations, keeping in mind "the best interests of the proletariat and the Social Republic," should use their own judgment concerning the tactics they were to employ on the second balloting. By implication, this allowed electoral pacts with other political parties. Subsequent party congresses were more explicit on this point. The Saint-Etienne Congress (1909) approved a resolution

[47] *Parti socialiste . . . 2ᵉ Congrès national*, pp. 102–104; *Parti socialiste . . . 4ᵉ Congrès national*, pp. 180, 311; *Parti socialiste . . . 6ᵉ Congrès national*, p. 500.

[48] As he had in the 1880's, Lafargue believed in the revolutionary method of social transformation. See, for example, his articles in the *Petit Sou*, November 19, 1900, February 10, March 24, 1902; and his speech at the Toulouse Congress in *Parti socialiste . . . 5ᵉ Congrès national*, pp. 133–140. See also Eduard Bernstein, "Paul Lafargue," *Sozialistische Monatshefte*, XVI, 1:24 (1912).

which provided that in an electoral district where the Socialist candidate could not be expected to win on the second balloting, the party should support the leading republican candidate against any and all candidates of reactionary parties. The Saint-Quentin Congress (1911) voted to grant the departmental federations authority to enter into alliances with bourgeois parties whenever the local political situation rendered such a tactic "necessary and useful" in promoting the interests of the Socialist party. Lastly, the Amiens Congress (1914) approved a resolution which stated that, on the second balloting, the departmental federations, in instances where the party candidates had little chance of victory, should support those candidates of republican parties who were pledged to fight against the three-year military service law, "against war, against chauvinism, and against the clerical and military coalition." [49]

In accordance with its decision to participate in electoral contests with the aim of conquering political positions, the Socialist party formulated electoral programs designed to facilitate the garnering of votes. In preparation for the legislative elections of May 1906, for example, its National Council issued a manifesto setting forth the party program. Affirming that the party was uncompromisingly republican, pacifistic, and anticlerical, it presented a legislative platform which included demands for the legal limitation of the workday to eight hours in all industries; a progressive income tax; the inauguration of an extensive system of social insurance; the nationalization of monopolies; and the adoption of proportional representation. Although the manifesto spoke more of reform than it did of revolution, it, nevertheless, affirmed that social legislation could only be of value to the workers as a means of "increasing the

[49] For the text of the resolutions, see *Parti socialiste . . . 2ᵉ Congrès national*, pp. 122–123; *Parti socialiste . . . 6ᵉ Congrès national*, pp. 592–596; *Parti socialiste, section française de l'internationale ouvrière, 8ᵉ Congrès national, tenu à Saint-Quentin les 16, 17, 18 et 19 avril 1911* (Paris, n.d.), pp. 444–446, 453–456; and *Parti socialiste, section française de l'internationale ouvrière, 11ᵉ Congrès national, tenu à Amiens les 25, 26, 27 et 28 janvier 1914* (Paris, n.d.), pp. 424–427. See also the resolution of the Nîmes Congress in *Parti socialiste, section française de l'internationale ouvrière, 7ᵉ Congrès national, tenu à Nîmes les 6, 7, 8 et 9 février 1910* (Paris, n.d.), pp. 490, 500–506.

strength" of their "whole demands" and of preparing the way for
the eventual elimination of the "capitalist edifice of exploitation." [50]
This program was similar in many important respects to the political program of the Radicals; [51] and Eugène Fournière, one of the
spokesmen for the more reformist wing of the Socialist party, declared publicly that the legislative demands contained in the manifesto were "so clearly republican and reformist that the moderate
newspapers have mocked us because of the modest character of our
ambitions, and the Radical press has approached us for having pur-
loined their program." [52]

Interestingly enough, in its electoral campaigns, the Socialist party
made a special effort to win the support of broad sections of the
peasantry. The votes of at least a part of this important segment
of the population were indispensable if an effective Socialist majority in the Chamber of Deputies was to be realized. The peasantry
as a class, however, had traditionally been hostile to any movement
which raised the question of the legitimacy of the right of private
property, and the party, therefore, took pains to reassure it on this
score. Thus, in a propaganda tract issued shortly before the legislative elections of 1914, the party pledged itself to respect the rights
of peasant proprietors and to aid them in defending their landholdings against capitalist "exploitation." "Not only does Socialism not
intend to expel the peasants from their lands," the tract stated, "but
on the contrary it intends . . . to free them from iniquitous taxa-
tion; to procure cattle, fertilizer, and machines for them; to aid them
in improving their soil by drainage and irrigation works. . ." The
appeal ended with the following sentence: "And since the social
transformation pursued by the Socialist party will not be made
against the peasants any more than it will be made without their
aid, let all small peasant proprietors, tenant farmers, *métayers*, and
agricultural laborers support the Socialist candidates at the polls;

---

[50] The text is given in the *Revue socialiste*, 43: 210–212 (1906). For other electoral manifestoes, see *Parti socialiste . . . 7ᵉ Congrès national*, pp. 487–489; and
the *Mouvement socialiste*, 35: 215–217 (1914).

[51] See the program in Léon Jacques, *Les Partis politiques sous la Troisième République* (Paris, 1912), pp. 493–498.

[52] "L'Action politique et sociale," *Revue socialiste*, 43: 619 (1906).

and Socialism, finally victorious with you, by your aid, and for you, will at last assure you of the full ownership of the wealth which you will have caused to burst forth from the venerable soil of France." [53]

It should also be noted that the Socialist party, in its 1914 electoral manifestoes, appealed for the support not only of the urban proletariat and the peasantry, but of shopkeepers and craftsmen as well — indeed, for the votes of "all men of sincere conscience" who were dismayed by "the moral disorder and the economic anarchy of present-day society." [54]

Thus, armed with attractive reform programs and strengthened by alliances with Radicals and Radical-Socialists, the Socialist party registered ever increasing successes in legislative and municipal elections during the years 1906–1914. In the legislative elections of May 1906, the party polled 877,999 votes, approximately the same number received by all the Socialist factions in 1902; while it elected fifty-four Deputies in 1906 as compared with forty-eight in 1902. In the municipal elections of May 1908, the party won a majority of the seats on 197 municipal councils, electing 2,000 municipal councilors, approximately 500 more than the total number elected by all the Socialist factions in 1904. In the legislative elections of April 1910, the party polled a total of 1,106,047 votes, 228,048 more than in 1906. This was an increase of 20 percent. Moreover, the party won seventy-six seats in the Chamber of Deputies, twenty-two over the 1906 figure. In the municipal elections of May 1912, it registered new victories, winning a majority of the seats on 294 municipal councils, ninety-seven more than in 1908; while electing 3,000 municipal councilors, 1,000 more than in 1908. Finally, the party won even more striking victories in the legislative elections of April and May 1914, receiving 1,398,771 votes, an increase of 292,724 votes (20 percent) over 1910. It secured 101 seats in the Chamber of Deputies, an increase of twenty-five over the 1910 figure. The party obtained one-sixth of the total popular vote (8,328,876) and won one-

---

[53] The text of the tract is given in the *Mouvement socialiste*, 35: 219–221 (1914).
[54] *Mouvement socialiste*, 35: 215–217 (1914).

sixth of the total number of seats in the Chamber.[55] The Socialist party now held more seats in the Chamber than any other political party, and it appeared to some that the creation of a Socialist majority in the Chamber was only a matter of time.

Having abandoned for all practical purposes any intention of seizing political power through revolutionary action and having come to exercise a rather strong influence in the Chamber of Deputies as a consequence of its electoral triumphs, the Socialist party, in the years immediately preceding the First World War, devoted itself largely to the task of obtaining the enactment of social legislation on the local and national level. In the Chamber, its representatives pressed for the adoption of such measures as old-age pensions, minimum wage and hour laws, the nationalization of mines, and a progressive income tax. In local governments, its representatives sought the extension of existing public services and the introduction of new ones.[56] The Socialist group in the Chamber did not hesitate to collaborate with bourgeois factions in working for social reforms. Alexandre Varenne, a party Deputy, in his report to the Nancy Congress (1907) on the activities of the party's parliamentary group, characterized its line of conduct in these words: "With the republicans who still have confidence in democracy and social progress, we shall defend the guarantees of republican liberty and the protective labor laws. With those democrats who retain the hope of a successful evolution of democracy toward new forms of freed labor, we shall oppose to all cunning or cynical policies of repression or re-

---

[55] *Revue socialiste*, 43: 732–748 (1906); *Parti socialiste . . . 8ᵉ Congrès national*, pp. 25–26, 29; *Parti socialiste, section française de l'internationale ouvrière, 10ᵉ Congrès national, tenu à Brest les 23, 24 et 25 mars 1913* (Paris, n.d.), pp. 25–30; J.-B. Séverac, "Les Elections législatives et le Parti socialiste," *Mouvement socialiste*, 35: 324–328 (1914).

[56] *Parti socialiste . . . 4ᵉ Congrès national*, pp. 45–51, *Parti socialiste . . . 5ᵉ Congrès national*, pp. 57–62; *Parti socialiste . . . 7ᵉ Congrès national*, pp. 435–438; *Parti socialiste . . . 8ᵉ Congrès national*, pp. 61–85, 442–443, 461; *Parti socialiste . . . 9ᵉ Congrès national*, pp. 41–48; *Parti socialiste . . . 10ᵉ Congrès national*, pp. 48–58; *Parti socialiste . . . 11ᵉ Congrès national*, pp. 55–64. See also Hubert Rouger, *La France socialiste* (Paris, 1912), pp. 314–325; and A. Zévaès, *Le Parti socialiste de 1904 à 1923* (Paris, 1923), pp. 33–41.

action the policy of incessant realization of bold reforms." [57] And it is significant that when a ministry did show a sincere interest in one of these reforms, the Socialist Deputies gave that ministry their support. Thus the Socialist Deputies rallied to the Poincaré Ministry (January 1912–January 1913) when it sought to enact an electoral reform embodying the principle of proportional representation.[58] From 1905–1914, the Socialist Deputies, it is true, did not join with republican groups in the Chamber in reviving the old Left Bloc. But, as a matter of fact, they were never formally invited to join a governmental coalition during that period.

On the basis of the brief account presented in the preceding section of this chapter, it is now possible to delineate the character and political orientation of the unified Socialist party as it existed on the eve of the First World War. Suffice it to say, it was not the revolutionary organization, "the class struggle party, a party of fundamental and irreducible opposition to the whole of the bourgeois class," envisioned in the Pact of Union of 1905. It was a party committed in actual practice to the peaceful, legal transformation of the existing capitalist society. It was not a proletarian party, as conceived of in the Pact; it was rather a mass party which sought the support and endeavored to represent the interests of certain broad non-proletarian segments of the population — the petite bourgeoisie and the peasantry, including the peasant proprietors — as well as the working class. The stand taken by the Socialist party on the question of the nationalization of the landholdings of the small peasant proprietors constituted a departure from revolutionary Socialist principles. The same could be said for its position on the question of electoral tactics — its acceptance of class collaboration — and for its stand on the question of the relation of the party to the syndicalist movement. On these and other questions, the Socialist party had, by 1914, deviated from the principles upon which it had ostensibly been organized. Only on the allied questions of ministerial participation

[57] *Parti socialiste . . . 4ᵉ Congrès national*, p. 51.
[58] *Parti socialiste . . . 10ᵉ Congrès national*, pp. 51–52; Georges Weill, *Histoire du mouvement social en France, 1852–1924* (Paris, 1924), p. 382.

and membership in the Left Bloc — the only two issues upon which the reformist Socialists had yielded to the revolutionary Socialists in 1905, thus opening the way to the formation of the unified party — did the party adhere obediently to the stipulations in the Pact. On almost every major question which the Socialist party considered and resolved during 1905–1914, the left-wing Socialists yielded to the reformists. At the outbreak of the First World War, therefore, the French Socialist party was to all intents and purposes a "radical" or "progressive" party of social reforms. It was a political organization that had come to accept — as the Guesdist party had in the early 1890's for much the same reasons — democratic institutions as the environment within which it was to operate. It functioned in accordance with the democratic rules of the game of politics, while still proclaiming from time to time that it was prepared to employ extra-constitutional, extralegal means of action to achieve its ends. But, as a matter of fact, the Socialist party at no time had recourse to such means. The party made no discernible effort to educate its members in an all-out class-war policy, nor did it train them for extralegal action — tasks that one would have thought were incumbent upon a self-styled revolutionary party. At the outbreak of the First World War, the Socialist party was a constitutional party serving as the avant-garde of democracy. And it was this conception of its function in the political life of France which determined in large measure the attitude of the Socialist party toward the crisis which overtook Europe in the summer of 1914.

Bibliography

In the preparation of this study, the author made use of the Jules Guesde Archives located at the Internationaal Instituut voor Sociale Geschiedenis in Amsterdam. The Guesde Archives contain both published and unpublished materials. The former, which bulk the larger, consist mainly of press clippings of articles written by Guesde, or about him, or articles dealing with some aspect of the French Socialist and labor movements; pamphlets written by Guesde and other Socialists; campaign literature, such as manifestoes, handbills, and stickers; and reports of national, regional, and departmental Socialist and labor congresses. The unpublished materials include *pneumatiques* and letters to and from Guesde (there are relatively few letters by Guesde); correspondence of other French Socialists, such as Raymond Lavigne's letters to Edouard Fortin; manuscripts of articles and notes for speeches by Guesde; and a variety of materials related to the administration of the Guesdist party and the Parti socialiste (S.F.I.O.) and to the work of Socialist congresses, both national and international.

This study is based in large part on the following published materials: Socialist newspapers and periodicals; reports of Socialist party congresses; and books and pamphlets written by French Socialists. The Socialist press is, of course, an indispensable source for the reconstruction of the day-to-day developments in the Socialist movement. It is also the primary source for the writings of the Socialist leaders. Jean Jaurès, for example, contributed thousands of articles to Socialist (and Republican) journals. According to his English biographer (Jackson), Jaurès wrote 800 articles for the *Petite République* (1893–1904) and 2,000 for *Humanité* (1904–1914). Jules Guesde, Paul Lafargue, Gustave Rouanet, and Edouard Vaillant also contributed regularly to the Socialist press. There are no important lacunae in the collections of French Socialist newspapers and periodicals for the period 1893–1905. Complete runs of the latter are to be found in several American libraries — the Widener Library of

Harvard University and the New York Public Library, to name only two. Rather complete files of the newspapers are available in the Bibliothèque Nationale and the Bibliothèque du Musée Social in Paris.

There are, however, rather serious shortcomings and gaps in the reports of the Socialist party congresses. Stenographic reports of the following were published: the Marseilles Congress (1879); the four General Congresses of French Socialist Organizations (1899–1902); and the National Congresses of the Parti socialiste (S.F.I.O.), 1907–1914. Published analytic (abridged) reports of the National Congresses of the Parti socialiste held in 1905 and 1906 are quite satisfactory. But of the reports that were published of the thirty-odd national congresses of the Guesdist, Possibilist, and Allemanist parties held during the period 1880–1902, only two (Saint-Etienne, 1882, and Châtellerault, 1890) were analytic reports, while the rest are condensed reports, containing in many instances little more than a list of the delegates and the groups they represented and the text of the resolutions adopted by the congress. The report of the Rheims Congress (1903) of the Parti socialiste de France is typical. Each of these must be supplemented by accounts of the congress published in the Socialist press. The author was unable to find a stenographic, analytic, or condensed report of any of the following congresses: the Lille (1904) and Paris (1905) Congresses of the Parti socialiste de France, the Bordeaux (1903), Saint-Etienne (1904), and Rouen (1905) Congresses of the Parti socialiste français.

All of the books and pamphlets written by French Socialists are available in the French libraries named above.

The materials used in the preparation of this study are grouped under the following headings:

    I. Bibliographical Guides
    II. Publications of the French Government
    III. Reports of Labor and Socialist Congresses
    IV. Books, Pamphlets, and Articles
    V. Newspapers and Periodicals

I. BIBLIOGRAPHICAL GUIDES

Dolléans, Edouard, and Michel Crozier. *Mouvements ouvrier et socialiste: chronologie et bibliographie: Angleterre, France, Allemagne, Etats-Unis, 1750–1918.* Paris, 1950.

Grandin, A. *Bibliographie générale des sciences juridiques, politiques, économiques et sociales de 1800 à 1925–26.* 3 vols. Paris, 1926. Nineteen supplementary volumes have been published covering the period 1926–1950.

Socialist International. *International Socialist Bibliography.* Published semimonthly in London since January, 1954 as a supplement to the *Socialist International Information.*

Stammhammer, Josef. *Bibliographie des Socialismus und Communismus.* 3 vols. Jena, 1893–1909.

Zimand, Savel. *Modern Social Movements.* New York, 1921.

II. PUBLICATIONS OF THE FRENCH GOVERNMENT

Ministère du commerce. *Annuaire statistique de la France, 1882.* Paris, 1882. Contains figures on the 1881 legislative elections.

Ministère du commerce, de l'industrie, des postes et des télégraphes. Office du travail. *Les Associations professionnelles ouvrières.* 4 vols. Paris, 1899–1904. A valuable source for information on the post-Commune labor movement.

Journal officiel. Chambre des Députés. Débats parlementaires. Compte rendu in extenso. The verbatim report of the proceedings of the Chamber of Deputies.

III. REPORTS OF LABOR AND SOCIALIST CONGRESSES

Séances du congrès ouvrier socialiste de France, tenu à Marseille du 20 au 31 octobre 1879. Marseilles, 1880.

Cinquième Congrès national du Parti ouvrier socialiste français, tenu à Reims du 30 octobre au 6 novembre 1881. Paris, 1882.

Sixième Congrès national du Parti ouvrier socialiste révolutionnaire français, tenu à St. Etienne du 25 au 30 septembre 1882. Paris, 1882.

Fédération des travailleurs socialistes de France. *Compte rendu du Septième Congrès national, tenu à Paris du 30 septembre au 7 octobre 1883.* Paris, 1883.

Septième Congrès national du Parti ouvrier, tenu à Roubaix du samedi 29 mars au lundi 7 avril 1884. Paris, n.d.

Fédération des travailleurs socialistes de France. *Compte rendu du Huitième Congrès national, tenu à Rennes du 12 au 19 octobre 1884.* Paris, 1885.

Fédération des travailleurs socialistes de France. *Compte rendu du Neuvième Congrès national, tenu à Charleville du 2 au 8 octobre 1887.* Paris, 1888.

Huitième Congrès national du Parti ouvrier, tenu à Lille 1890. Lille, 1890.

Fédération des travailleurs socialistes de France. *Compte rendu du Dixième Congrès régional de l'Union fédérative du Centre, tenu à Paris les 1ᵉʳ, 2, 3 et 5 octobre 1890 et les 12, 13, 14, 15, 16 et 17 mars 1891.* Paris, 1891. A condensed report.

Fédération des travailleurs socialistes de France. *Parti ouvrier socialiste révolutionnaire. Compte rendu du Dixième Congrès national, tenu à Châtellerault du 9 au 15 octobre 1890.* Poitiers, 1891.

Parti ouvrier socialiste révolutionnaire. *Compte rendu du Dixième Congrès national, tenu à Paris du 21 au 29 juin 1891.* Paris, 1892.

Neuvième Congrès national du Parti ouvrier, tenu à Lyon du 26 au 28 novembre 1891. Lille, n.d.

Dixième Congrès national du Parti ouvrier, tenu à Marseille du 24 au 28 septembre 1892. Lille, n.d.

Parti ouvrier socialiste révolutionnaire. *Compte rendu du Onzième Congrès national, tenu à Saint-Quentin du 2 au 9 octobre 1892.* Paris, 1893.

Onzième Congrès national du Parti ouvrier, tenu à Paris du 7 au 9 octobre 1893. Lille, 1893.

Douzième Congrès national du Parti ouvrier français, tenu à Nantes du 14 au 16 septembre 1894. Lille, 1894.

Parti ouvrier socialiste révolutionnaire. *Compte rendu de la Conférence nationale de 1895, tenu à Paris les 29 et 30 septembre 1895.* Paris, 1896. A condensed report.

Parti ouvrier socialiste révolutionnaire. *Compte rendu du Quatorzième Congrès national, tenu à Paris 24–25 septembre 1896.* Paris, 1897.

Quinzième Congrès national du Parti ouvrier, tenu à Paris du 10 au 13 juillet 1897. Lille, 1897.

Parti ouvrier socialiste révolutionnaire. *Union fédérative du Centre. Compte rendu du XVᵉ Congrès régional, tenu à Paris en avril-mai 1899.* Paris, 1899. An analytic report.

Congrès général des organisations socialistes françaises, tenu à Paris du 3 au 8 décembre 1899. Paris, 1900.

Cinquième Congrès socialiste international, tenu à Paris du 23 au 27 septembre 1900. Paris, 1901. An analytic report.

Deuxième Congrès général des organisations socialistes françaises, tenu à Paris du 28 au 30 septembre 1900. Paris, 1901.

Troisième Congrès général des organisations socialistes françaises, tenu à Lyon du 26 au 28 mai 1901. Paris, 1901.

Dix-Neuvième Congrès national du Parti ouvrier, tenu à Roubaix du 15 au 18 septembre 1901. Paris, 1901.

Quatrième Congrès général du Parti socialiste français, tenu à Tours du 2 au 4 mars 1902. Paris, 1902.

Protokoll über die Verhandlungen des Parteitages der Sozialdemokratischen Partei Deutschlands, abgehalten zu Dresden vom 13 bis 20 September 1903. Berlin, 1903. A stenographic report.

Deuxième Congrès national du Parti socialiste de France (Unité socialiste révolutionnaire), tenu à Reims les 27, 28 et 29 septembre 1903. Bourges, 1903.

Sixième Congrès socialiste international, tenu à Amsterdam du 14 au 20 août 1904. Brussels, 1904. An analytic report.

Parti socialiste de France. Unité socialiste révolutionnaire. Compte rendu du XXXIVᵉ Congrès régional, tenu à Houplines le 26 février 1905. Lille, 1905. A condensed report of a Regional Congress of the *Fédération du Nord.*

Parti socialiste, section française de l'internationale ouvrière, 1ᵉʳ Congrès national (Congrès d'unité), tenu à Paris les 23, 24 et 25 avril. Paris, n.d.

Parti socialiste . . . 2ᵉ Congrès national, tenu à Chalon-sur-Saône les 29, 30, 31 octobre et 1ᵉʳ novembre 1905. Paris, n.d.

Parti socialiste . . . 3ᵉ Congrès national, tenu à Limoges les 1ᵉʳ, 2, 3 et 4 novembre 1906. Paris, n.d.

Parti socialiste . . . 4ᵉ Congrès national, tenu à Nancy les 11, 12, 13 et 14 août 1907. Paris, n.d.

Parti socialiste . . . 5ᵉ Congrès national, tenu à Toulouse les 15, 16, 17 et 18 octobre 1908. Paris, n.d.

Parti socialiste . . . 6ᵉ Congrès national, tenu à Saint-Etienne les 11, 12, 13 et 14 avril 1909. Paris, n.d.

Parti socialiste . . . 7ᵉ Congrès national, tenu à Nîmes les 6, 7, 8 et 9 février 1910. Paris, n.d.

Parti socialiste . . . 8ᵉ Congrès national, tenu à Saint-Quentin les 16, 17, 18 et 19 avril 1911. Paris, n.d.

Parti socialiste . . . 9ᵉ Congrès national, tenu à Lyon les 18, 19, 20 et 21 février 1912. Paris, n.d.

Parti socialiste . . . 10ᵉ Congrès national, tenu à Brest les 23, 24 et 25 mars 1913. Paris, n.d.

Parti socialiste . . . 11ᵉ Congrès national, tenu à Amiens les 25, 26, 27 et 28 janvier 1914. Paris, n.d.

IV. BOOKS, PAMPHLETS, AND ARTICLES *

Allemane, Jean. *Nôtre Programme.* Paris, 1895. Comments on the Allemanist party program by its leader.

—— *Le Socialisme en France.* Paris, 1900. A brief survey.

Almanach du Parti ouvrier pour 1896. Lille, 1895. Contains an important article by Jules Guesde.

Auclair, Marcelle. *La Vie de Jean Jaurès, ou la France d'avant 1914.* Paris, 1954. The best biography.

Badie, Vincent. *Les Principaux Aspects du socialisme réformiste en France.* Montpellier, 1931. A short account of the development of reformist Socialism.

Balabanoff, Angelica. *My Life as a Rebel.* New York, 1938. The memoirs of one of the prominent figures in the Italian Socialist party.

Benjamin, Gilbert Giddings. "German and French Socialists and the Agrarian Question," *Journal of Political Economy,* 34: 349–376 (1926).

Bernstein, Eduard. "Paul Lafargue," *Sozialistische Monatshefte,* XVI, 1: 20–24 (1912). An appreciation by the noted German Revisionist.

Bernstein, Samuel. *The Beginnings of Marxian Socialism in France.* New York, 1933. A scholarly account.

—— "Jules Guesde, Pioneer of Marxism in France," *Science and Society,* 4: 29–56 (1940). A sympathetic but not uncritical evaluation of the man and his work.

Blanqui, Auguste. *Critique sociale.* 2 vols. Paris, 1885. The ideology of this colorful figure is set forth in a rather disorganized manner.

Blum, Léon. *Les Congrès ouvriers et socialistes français.* 2 vols. Paris, 1901. Extremely useful survey of the Socialist and labor congresses during 1876–1900.

—— *Souvenirs sur l'Affaire.* Paris, 1935.

Bourdeau, Jean. "La Crise du socialisme et la fin d'une doctrine," *Revue des deux mondes,* 155: 241–264 (1899). A penetrating examination of the Millerand Case.

Bourgin, Georges. "Jules Guesde." *Archiv für die Geschichte des Sozialismus und der Arbeiterbewegung,* 14: 88–101 (1929).

---

* This section includes only articles published in journals not listed in section V of this bibliography.

Bourgin, Hubert. *De Jaurès à Léon Blum, l'Ecole Normale et la politique*. Paris, 1938. The Ecole Normale viewed as the "seminary" of French politicians.

Bracke [Alexandre-Marie Desrousseaux]. *Leur Congrès à la Salle Wagram*. Paris, 1901. A partisan account (pamphlet) of the General Congress of 1900 by a leading Guesdist.

Breton, J.-L. *L'Unité socialiste*. Paris, 1912. Vol. VII of *Histoire des Partis socialistes en France*, edited by Alexandre Zévaès, 12 vols. Paris, 1911–23. A sketch of the unity movement (1898–1905) by one of the prominent reformist Socialists.

Brogan, D. W. *France Under the Republic: The Development of Modern France, 1870–1939*. New York, 1940. The best history of the period in English.

Brousse, Paul. *La Propriété collective et les services publics*. Paris, 1883. Sets forth the public services doctrine of the leader of the Possibilist party.

Cachin, Marcel. "Le Centenaire de Guesde," *Pensée*, 5: 19–28 (1945). An appreciation by the editor of the French Communist journal, *Humanité*.

Challaye, Félicien. *Jaurès*. Paris, 1936. A fair account of the man and his thought.

Chapman, Guy. *The Dreyfus Case: A Reassessment*. New York, 1955. A detailed, judicious study.

Charnay, Maurice. *Les Allemanistes*. Paris, 1912. Vol. V of Zévaès, *Histoire des Partis socialistes en France*. A sketch.

Charpentier, Armand. *The Dreyfus Case*. Trans. by J. Lewis May. London, 1935. A brief, reliable account.

Cole, G. D. H. *Socialism in Evolution*. Harmondsworth, England, 1938. A collection of essays and articles by one of the leading historians of modern Socialism.

Compère-Morel, Adéodat. *Grand Dictionnaire socialiste du mouvement politique et économique national et international*. Paris, 1924. Contains brief biographies of many of the leading Socialists.

——— *Jules Guesde*. Paris, 1937. An adequate biography of this important figure remains to be written.

Conseil national du Parti ouvrier français. *Aux Travailleurs de France*. Paris, 1901. A collection of the manifestoes issued (1889–1900) by the Guesdist party.

Coulet, Jean. *Histoire du socialisme à Marseille depuis le ∪ongres ae 1879 jusqu'au 1ᵉʳ mai 1890.* Marseilles, 1891. A sketch.

Da Costa, Charles. *Les Blanquistes.* Paris, 1912. Vol. VI of Zévaès, *Histoire des Partis socialistes en France.* Most of this little book is devoted to the period before 1871.

Daniel, André. *L'Année politique.* Paris, 1875–1906. These annual volumes, covering the period 1874–1905, are useful surveys of political developments in France.

De Leon, Daniel. *Flashlights of the Amsterdam International Socialist Congress, 1904.* New York, n.d. A collection of the articles which this American Socialist leader wrote in 1904 on the Amsterdam Congress.

Delevsky, J. *Les Antimonies socialistes et l'évolution du socialisme français.* Paris, 1930. Contains a good section on Jaurès.

Delory, Gustave. *Aperçu historique sur la Fédération du Nord du Parti socialiste.* Lille, 1921. A brief history of this important Guesdist organization.

Detot, P. *Le Socialisme devant les Chambres françaises.* Paris, 1903. A brief account of the parliamentary activity of the Socialist Deputies, 1893–1898.

Deville, Gabriel. *Principes socialistes.* Paris, 1896. A collection of lectures and articles dating from the period 1893–1895. Deville was one of the pioneers of Marxism in France. This collection discloses the extent to which he (like other Guesdists) had modified his early revolutionary views. Shortly after this book was published, Deville abandoned the Guesdist party and identified himself with the Independent Socialists.

—— *Socialism, Revolution, and Internationalism.* Trans. by Robert R. La Monte. New York, 1900. The text of a lecture delivered in Paris in November 1893. (Included in *Principes socialistes.*)

—— "L'Affaire Dreyfus et le Parti socialiste," *Devenir social,* 4: 785–803 (1898).

Dreyfus, Alfred and Pierre. *The Dreyfus Case.* Trans. and ed. by Donald C. McKay. New Haven, 1937. A standard work.

Dubreuilh, Louis. *De Japy à Bordeaux, unité interfédérale et unité révolutionnaire.* Lille, 1903. A pamphlet comparing the organization of the Parti socialiste français with the Parti socialiste de France by a member of the latter.

Engels, Friedrich. "Die Bauernfrage in Frankreich und Deutschland,"

Neue Zeit, XIII, 1: 292–306 (1894). The famous critique of the Guesdist agrarian program.

Engels, Friedrich, and Karl Marx. *The Communist Manifesto.* New York, 1932.

Ensor, R. C. K., ed. *Modern Socialism, as Set Forth by Socialists in Their Speeches, Writings, and Programmes.* Second edition, New York, 1908. Contains, among other things, a translation (abridged) of Millerand's Saint-Mandé Program, the Declaration of Principles and the Program of Reforms of the Parti socialiste français (Tours, 1902), and excerpts from the proceedings of the Bordeaux Congress (1903).

Fesch, Paul., ed. *L'Année sociale en France et à l'étranger 1898.* Paris, 1899. A useful survey.

Fournière, Eugène. *La Crise socialiste.* Paris, 1908. A collection of articles expounding reformist Socialism that appeared (1905–1907) in French and German journals. Fournière was editor (1905–1913) of the *Revue socialiste.*

François, G. "Socialism in France," *Journal of Political Economy,* 7: 25–41 (1898). A survey of the contemporary Socialist movement.

Gay, Peter. *The Dilemma of Democratic Socialism: Eduard Bernstein's Challenge to Marx.* New York, 1952. Widely acknowledged as being the best account of Revisionism in English.

Goetz-Girey, Robert. *La Pensée syndicale française, militants et théoriciens.* Paris, 1948. A competent examination of French Syndicalist theory.

Guérard, Albert Léon. *French Civilization in the Nineteenth Century.* New York, 1914. An interesting book containing an informative section on the Dreyfus Affair.

Guesde, Jules. *La République et les grèves.* Paris, 1878. Some of Guesde's early Socialist views.

────── *Services publics et socialisme.* Paris, 1901. A critique of Brousse's doctrine of public services.

────── *Cà et là.* Paris, 1914. A collection of articles published in various Socialist journals, 1876–1895.

────── *Etat, politique et morale de classe.* Paris, 1901. Articles published in various Socialist journals, 1881–1886.

────── *Le Socialisme au jour le jour.* Paris, 1899. Articles published in the *Cri du Peuple,* 1884–1886.

────── *Quatre Ans de lutte de classe à la Chambre, 1893–1898.* 2 vols.

Paris, 1901. A collection of speeches delivered in the Chamber of Deputies.

Guesde, Jules, and Paul Lafargue. *Le Programme du Parti ouvrier, son histoire, ses considérants, ses articles.* Paris, 1883. The program of the Parti ouvrier français with a commentary.

Humbert, Sylvain. *Les Possibilistes.* Paris, 1911. Vol. IV of Zévaès, *Histoire des Partis socialistes en France.* A brief account.

Huret, Jules. *Enquête sur la question social en Europe.* Paris, 1897. Contains an informative interview with Guesde.

Hyndman, Henry M. *The Record of an Adventurous Life.* New York, 1911. Memoirs of the British Socialist leader.

—— *Further Reminiscences.* London, 1912. More of the same.

Jackson, J. Hampden. *Jean Jaurès, His Life and Work.* London, 1943. The best biography of Jaurès in English.

Jacques, Léon. *Les Partis politiques sous la Troisième République.* Paris, 1912. An excellent source for information concerning the programs and policies of French political parties in the period dealt with in this study.

Jaurès, Jean. *Les Preuves.* Paris, 1898. A collection of the articles on the Dreyfus Affair that Jaurès wrote for the *Petite République* in the summer of 1898.

—— *La Constituante, 1789–1791.* Paris 1901(?). Vol. I of *Histoire socialiste, 1789–1900,* edited by J. Jaurès, 12 vols. Paris, 1901–8(?).

—— *La Convention, 1792.* Paris, 1904(?). Vol. III of Jaurès, *Histoire socialiste.*

—— *Discours parlementaires.* Collected and annotated by Edmond Claris. Paris, 1904. Speeches delivered in the Chamber of Deputies, 1886–1894.

—— *Oeuvres de Jean Jaurès.* Ed. Max Bonnafous. 9 vols. Paris, 1931–1939. Several volumes remain to be published.

Joll, James. *The Second International, 1889–1914.* London, 1955. A good account. However the definitive work on the subject remains to be written.

Josephson, Matthew. *Zola and His Time.* New York, 1928. Contains a graphic account of the Dreyfus Affair and the text of Zola's famous "J'accuse."

Kohler, Max J. "Some New Light on the Dreyfus Case," *Studies in Jewish Bibliography and Related Subjects in Memory of Abraham Solomon Freidus,* pp. 293–318. New York, 1929.

Lafargue, Paul. *Programme agricole du Parti ouvrier français.* Lille, 1894. The agrarian program of the Guesdist party with a commentary.

—— *Le Socialisme et la conquête des pouvoirs publics.* Lille, 1899. A sharp attack on ministerial participation.

—— "Die Sozialistische Bewegung in Frankreich von 1876–1890," *Neue Zeit,* 8: 337–353 (1890).

Lafargue, Paul, and Jules Guesde. *Le Programme du Parti ouvrier, son histoire, ses considérants, ses articles.* Paris, 1883.

Lavy, A. *L'Oeuvre de Millerand.* Paris, 1902. A study of Millerand's achievements as Minister of Commerce and Industry, 1899–1902. The text of Millerand's Saint-Mandé Program is included in the book.

Levine, Louis. *Syndicalism in France.* Second revised edition, New York, 1914. One of the first works in English on the subject, and still useful.

Liesse, André. "Les Travaux parlementaires de la Chambre des Députés, 1893–1894," *Journal des économistes,* 20: 3–18 (1894).

Lorwin, Val R. *The French Labor Movement.* Cambridge, Mass., 1954. Contains a perceptive, succinct account of Revolutionary Syndicalism.

Louis, Paul. *Le Parti socialiste en France.* Paris, 1912. Vol. II of *Encyclopédie socialiste, syndicale et coopérative de l'internationale ouvrière,* 8 vols. edited by Adéodat Compère-Morel. Paris, 1912–13. Contains useful documentary material.

—— *Histoire du socialisme en France, 1789–1945.* Fourth edition, Paris, 1946. A general account.

Maitron, Jean. *Histoire du mouvement anarchiste en France, 1880–1914.* Paris, 1951. The best work on the subject.

Malon, Benoît. *Le Nouveau Parti.* 2 vols. Paris, 1882. Observations on the contemporary Socialist movement by the influential editor (1885–94) of the *Revue socialiste.*

Marx, Karl. *The Civil War in France.* New York, 1940.

Marx, Karl, and Friedrich Engels. *The Communist Manifesto.* New York, 1932.

Mason, Edward S. "Blanqui and Communism," *Political Science Quarterly,* 44: 498–527 (1929).

Michels, Robert. *Political Parties: A Sociological Study of the Oligar-*

chical Tendencies of Modern Democracy. Trans. by Eden and Cedar Paul. Glencoe, Ill., 1949. A classic.

Milhaud, Edgard. *La Tactique socialiste et les décisions des congrès internationaux*. 2 vols. Paris, 1905. An examination of the problem of Socialist tactics by a Ministerialist.

Millerand, Alexandre. *Le Socialisme réformiste français*. Paris, 1903. A collection of Millerand's speeches.

Orry, Albert. *Les Socialistes indépendants*. Paris, 1911. Vol. VIII of Zévaès, *Histoire des Partis socialistes en France*. A useful account.

Parti ouvrier socialiste révolutionnaire. Secrétariat Général. *La Vérité sur l'Union socialiste*. Paris, 1897. A critical evaluation of the character and conduct of the Socialist parliamentary group, 1893–1897.

Pignatel, Fernand, ed. *Jaurès, par ses contemporains*. Paris, 1925. Appreciative essays by L. Jouhaux, L. Lévy-Bruhl, G. Renard, and others.

Pipkin, Charles W. *Social Politics and Modern Democracies*. 2 vols. New York, 1931. Volume two was useful for its sections on Millerand's reforms and Revolutionary Syndicalism.

Posse, Ernst. *Der Marxismus in Frankreich, 1871–1905*. Berlin, 1930. A competent study of the Guesdist party in terms of its doctrinal development.

Prélot, Marcel. *L'Evolution politique du socialisme français, 1789–1934*. Paris, 1939. A general account.

Le Procès Zola devant la Cour d'Assises de la Seine et la Cour de Cassation, 7 février–23 février — 31 mars–2 avril 1898. 2 vols. Paris, 1898. Zola's "J'accuse" is reprinted in volume one.

Prolo, J., and A. Zévaès. *Une Campagne politique, le Parti républicain socialiste, 1910–1917*. Paris, 1918. A short history of the party by two of its leading figures.

Rappoport, Charles. *Socialisme de gouvernement et socialisme révolutionnaire*. Paris, n.d. A collection of articles on the Millerand Case that were published in the *Socialiste* in 1899. Rappoport was a sharp critic of *Ministérialisme*.

—— *Jean Jaurès, l'homme, le penseur, le socialiste*. Paris, 1915. Composed largely of excerpts from Jaurès's writings and speeches.

Reinach, Joseph. *Histoire de l'Affaire Dreyfus*. 7 vols. Paris, 1901–1911. A standard work.

Rouger, Hubert. *La France socialiste*. Paris, 1912. Vol. III of Compère-

Morel, *Encyclopédie socialiste, syndicale et coopérative de l'internationale ouvrière.* Contains brief biographies of leading French Socialists and other useful information.

Seignobos, Charles. *L'Evolution de la 3ᵉ République, 1875–1914.* Paris, 1921. Vol. VIII of *Histoire de France contemporaine depuis la révolution jusqu'à la paix de 1919,* edited by Ernest Lavisse. Paris, 1920–1922. 10 vols. A standard history.

Seilhac, Léon de. *Les Congrès ouvriers en France de 1876 à 1897.* Paris, 1899. Contains useful excerpts from the proceedings of Socialist and labor congresses. Must be used with caution for the author was prejudiced against Socialism.

—— *Le Monde socialiste.* Paris, 1904. Useful for the period 1899–1903.

—— "L'Organisation socialiste," *Revue politique et littéraire (Revue bleue),* 4: 301–315, 365–369, 434–438, 556–559 (1895); 5: 108–111, 237–240 (1896).

Séverac, J.-B. "Der Fall Dreyfus und die französischen Sozialisten," *Sozialistische Monatshefte,* 3: 349–353 (1899). Informed comments on the Socialists and the Dreyfus Affair and the opening phase of the Millerand Case.

Soulé, Louis. *La Vie de Jaurès.* Paris, 1921. A short biography.

Vandervelde, Emile. *Jaurès.* Paris, 1921. A short biography by one of the leading figures in the modern Belgian Socialist movement.

—— *Souvenirs d'un militant socialiste.* Paris, 1939.

Varlet, J. *Paul Lafargue, théoricien du marxisme.* Paris, 1933. A brief biography of Lafargue together with selections from his writings.

Veber, Adrien. *Le Socialisme municipal.* Paris, 1908. A brief account.

Vérecque, Charles. *Trois Années de participation socialiste à un gouvernement bourgeois.* Lille, 1903. An antiministerial pamphlet by a leading Guesdist.

—— *Dictionnaire du socialisme.* Paris, 1911. Among other things, the book has brief biographies of French Socialists and some documentary material for the period 1899–1905.

Vogüé, Eugène-Melchior de. "Explorations parlementaires," *Revue des deux mondes,* 125: 201–216 (1894).

Weill, Georges. "Die Sozialistische Bewegung in Frankreich, 1893–1910," *Archiv für die Geschichte des Sozialismus und der Arbeiterbewegung,* 1: 134–175 (1911).

———— *Histoire du mouvement social en France, 1852–1924.* Third revised edition, Paris, 1924. A standard work.

Weinstein, Harold. *Jean Jaurès, A Study of Patriotism in the French Socialist Movement.* New York, 1936. An excellent study.

Winnacker, Rudolph A. "The Influence of the Dreyfus Affair on the Political Development of France," *Papers of the Michigan Academy of Science, Arts and Letters,* 21: 465–478 (1935).

———— "The Délégation Des Gauches: a Successful Attempt at Managing a Parliamentary Coalition." *Journal of Modern History,* 9: 449–470 (1937).

Zévaès, Alexandre. *Aperçu historique sur le Parti ouvrier français.* Lille, 1899. A brief history of the Guesdist party by one of its young adherents. Zévaès was active in the Socialist movement from the 1890's until after the First World War, and has written more on the history of that movement than anyone else.

———— *Le Socialisme en France depuis 1871.* Paris, 1908. An uncritical account, with a useful appendix of documents.

———— *De la Semaine sanglante au congrès de Marseille, 1871–1879.* Paris, 1911. Vol. II of Zévaès, *Histoire des Partis socialistes en France.* Contains useful documentary material.

———— *Les Guesdistes.* Paris, 1911. Vol. III of Zévaès, *Histoire des Partis socialistes en France.* A brief account.

———— *Le Syndicalisme contemporain.* Paris, 1911. A good survey of the contemporary labor movement.

———— *Le Socialisme en 1912.* Paris, 1912. Vol. XI of Zévaès, *Histoire des Partis socialistes en France.* Has useful appendices.

———— *Notes et souvenirs d'un militant.* Paris, 1913.

———— *Auguste Blanqui.* Paris, 1920. A short biography.

———— *Le Parti socialiste de 1904 à 1923.* Paris, 1923. Vol. XII of Zévaès, *Histoire des Partis socialistes en France.* A brief account.

———— *Jules Guesde.* Paris, 1929. An uncritical biography.

———— *Sur l'Ecran politique, ombres et silhouettes, notes, mémoires et souvenirs.* Paris, 1928.

———— *L'Affaire Dreyfus.* Paris, 1931. A short history.

———— *De l'Introduction du marxisme en France.* Paris, 1947. A summary treatment.

———— "L'Introduction du marxisme en France," *Nouvelle Revue,* 138: 81–94, 221–226 (1935).

———— "L'Affaire Dreyfus: quelques souvenirs personnels," *Nouvelle*

Revue, 141: 15–23, 96–110, 197–208, 287–296 (1936); 142: 45–53, 96–104 (1936).

—— "Jules Guesde et Jean Jaurès," *Revue de Paris*, 4: 79–111 (1936).

—— "Jean Allemane et l'allemanisme," *Nouvelle Revue*, 145: 23–36 (1936).

Zévaès, A. and J. Prolo. *Une Campagne politique, le Parti républicain socialiste, 1910–1917.* Paris, 1918.

V. NEWSPAPERS AND PERIODICALS *

Aurore, L'. Daily, October 1897–August 1914. Republican. Useful for the years 1898–99.

Citoyen, Le. Daily, October 1881–October 1882. Guesde was one of the editors of this unaffiliated Socialist journal.

Cri du Peuple, Le. Daily, October 1883–January 1889. Socialists of all nuances as well as Anarchists wrote for this self-styled "Revolutionary" journal.

Dépêche de Toulouse, La (La Dépêche). Daily, since April 1875 (with interruptions). Jaurès published some 1,500 articles in this Republican newspaper.

Egalité, L'. Weekly, November 1877–November 1882 (with interruptions), February 1889–October 1891. Appeared as a daily, February 1883. Published at Meaux (1877–78) and St. Cloud (1880). Socialists of all persuasions wrote for this journal. For a time it served as the official organ of the Guesdist party.

Homme Libre, L'. Daily, June–August 1888. A Blanquist organ.

Humanité, L'. Daily, since April 1904 (with interruptions). Founded by Jaurès, this journal became the official newspaper of the French Communist party in 1921.

International Socialist Review, The. Monthly, Chicago, July 1900–February 1918. Published articles by prominent French Socialists.

Lanterne, La. Daily, April 1877–March 1928. Millerand, Jaurès, Viviani, and other Socialists contributed articles (1898–1900) to this Republican newspaper.

Mouvement socialist, Le. Weekly, biweekly, monthly, and bimonthly, January 1899–June 1914. Edited by Hubert Lagardelle, the pages of this review were open to Socialists of all schools until about 1902.

* Unless indicated otherwise, all of the newspapers and periodicals listed in this section were published in Paris.

It then became an Antiministerial organ. In 1904, Lagardelle became an active Revolutionary Syndicalist, and thereafter the review gave less attention to the Socialist movement.

Ni Dieu Ni Maître. Daily and weekly, November 1880–November 1881. A Blanquist organ.

Parti Ouvrier, Le. Daily (to November 1890), then biweekly and weekly (irregularly), April 1888–April 1914. Up to 1890 it was a Possibilist organ. Then it came under the control of the Allemanists.

Parti Socialist, Le. Weekly, May 1892–March 1895 (with interruptions). A Blanquist organ.

Petit Sou, Le. Daily, September 1900–July 1914. Up to May 1902, the pages of this newspaper were open to Socialists of all nuances. Ceased to be a Socialist journal after that date.

Petite République, La. Daily, July 1893–July 1914. Although the pages of this newspaper (formerly called the *Petite République Française*), under the editorship of Millerand (1893–1896), were open to Socialists of all schools, it came increasingly to be identified with the Independent Socialists. It subsequently became one of the leading organs of the Ministerial Socialists. An indispensable source for the period 1893–1905.

Prolétaire, Le. Biweekly and weekly, November 1878–April 1894 (with interruptions). Up to 1882, it was not affiliated with any Socialist party. Then it became the official organ of the Possibilists.

Revue politique et parlementaire. Monthly, since July 1894. This independent, widely-respected political review published excellent articles on Socialism from time to time as well as regular quarterly surveys of developments in the French Socialist movement written by Jean Bourdeau, an informed and perceptive observer.

Revue socialiste, La. Monthly, January 1885–June 1914. In January 1910, the name of this review, founded by Benoît Malon, was changed to: *Revue socialiste, syndicaliste et coopérative*. During the period covered in this study, it was the leading organ of the reformist Socialists.

Socialiste, Le. Weekly, August 1885–August 1913 (with interruptions). During the years 1885–1903, it was the official journal of the Guesdist party. In 1904 it served as the official journal of the Parti socialiste de France. The following year it became the central organ of the Parti socialiste (S.F.I.O.).

Vie socialiste, La. Bimonthly, November 1904–August 1905. This short-lived review, whose pages were open to Socialists of all persuasions, was dedicated to the task of bringing about the unification of the French Socialist forces.

Index

HARVARD HISTORICAL MONOGRAPHS

* Out of print.